A JOURNEY THROUGH LAKELAND:
the history, customs and beauty of the English Lake District

Kenneth Fields

Oh, to be in England
Now that April's there,
And whoever wakes in England
Sees, some morning, unaware,
That the lowest boughs and the brushwood sheaf
Round the elm-tree bole are in tiny leaf,
While the chaffinch sings on the orchard bough
In England – now!

(Robert Browning, 1812-89)

Published by Sigma Leisure – an imprint of
Sigma Press, 1 South Oak Lane, Wilmslow, Cheshire SK9 6AR, England.

British Library Cataloguing in Publication Data
A CIP record for this book is available from the British Library.

ISBN: 1-85058-445-1

Cover: Castlerigg Stone Circle, Keswick; Bowness-on-Windermere; St Michael's Church, Hawkshead *(photographs by the author)*.

Typesetting and Design by: Sigma Press, Wilmslow, Cheshire.

Printed by: MFP Design and Print

Preface

When I wrote the companion to this volume, *A Journey Through Lancashire*, I reached the northern limit of my travels at Arnside. The blue Lakeland mountains lay tantalisingly close across the waters of the Kent, but I had to reserve them for another day. Thankfully, that day came the following March when the cold winds of winter had at last begun to lessen. With the flowers of early springtime making a welcome appearance it was a perfect time to begin another journey. In these pages you will find the record of what I discovered as I drove, walked and sometimes just stared in wonder, at this magical corner of Britain we call Lakeland.

As I drove northwards, passing the sign which announces 'Cumbria', I became acutely aware that I was following in the steps of so many highly gifted writers of the past. But any doubts that I may have had that all of Lakeland's secrets had already been revealed, were quickly dismissed. For happily, I soon discovered that Lakeland remains an ever changing mixture of romance and reality. In this landscape of mountains and lakes, a curious traveller could explore for a lifetime and still at times be surprised.

Much of the excitement of travel lies in thoughts of the unknown, the anticipation of new horizons. But although a flexible, unplanned journey may in theory seem attractive, without some form of overall aim it may be doomed to disaster, for many places of interest can so easily be missed. So, with the intention of visiting as much of Lakeland as possible, I laid out a route which is shown on the enclosed map. It begins at Cumbria's southern gateway of Milnthorpe, follows a twisting, northern path towards Keswick, then takes a series of wide loops from east to west, finally ending to the south of Shap. It embraces bustling market towns and peaceful villages, it passes fast-flowing rivers and placid lakes, and it leads from the rugged splendour of England's highest mountains to the green flatness of the silver coast; such is the astonishing change of landscape to be found in such a small area.

Of course, as well as being renowned for its unique natural beauty, the English Lakes have been the inspiration for so many talented people. Poets and artists, writers and walkers, climbers and adventurers, some known worldwide and others now half-forgotten, have over the centuries lived and worked and died here. I have visited some of the sites where memories of them linger on, looked at the scenes which they cherished, and remembered both their successes and their failures. For I feel much of the pleasure derived from visiting new places, lies in knowing something of their history and of the people who once lived there

Finally, I hope that having read this account of my journey, you too may be filled with the desire to discover, or perhaps rediscover, both the romance and the splendour of Lakeland.

Acknowledgements

To enjoy to the full the splendid diversity of landscape which lies in Lakeland an essential requirement for every visitor is a good map. During my journey I found that my faithful, if ancient, One Inch Ordnance Survey Tourist Map continued to serve me well. So I recommend to those who wish to explore Lakeland's hidden corners that they first purchase one of the latest range of similar maps.

Although many excellent guide books of the area are available, it was from the local Tourist Information Centres that I gained most up-to-the-minute information. So I thank the staff of these centres, for their cheerful guidance and help, and for supplying me with a host of free leaflets.

The illustrations found in this book are from a number of different sources. Most of the sketches are the work of Mike Ince from Croston in Lancashire, to whom I am particularly grateful. I would like to thank Alan Hinkes for his fine photograph of Chris Bonington from the Chris Bonington Picture Library, and to Melvyn Bragg and W.R. Mitchell for their kindness in allowing me to use photographs of themselves. Also my thanks to John Lannaghan, the editor of the *Westmorland Gazette*, for supplying the photograph of Donald Campbell from his newspaper's archives. All the other photographs, the route map, and the sketches of Katherine Parr and Steeple Jackson, are by the author.

The scores of books about Lakeland, many very old, which I have consulted are too numerous to list in detail. However, when taking to the mountains it has always been Alfred Wainwright's classic *Pictorial Guides* which have successfully led me to the summits.

Finally, the finished manuscript of this book owes much to my wife Wynne, who read, re-read, criticised and suggested improvements. For her patience, help and support during my journey I offer my special thanks.

This book is dedicated to the memory of my mother, Mary Elizabeth Sewards.

Kenneth Fields

Contents

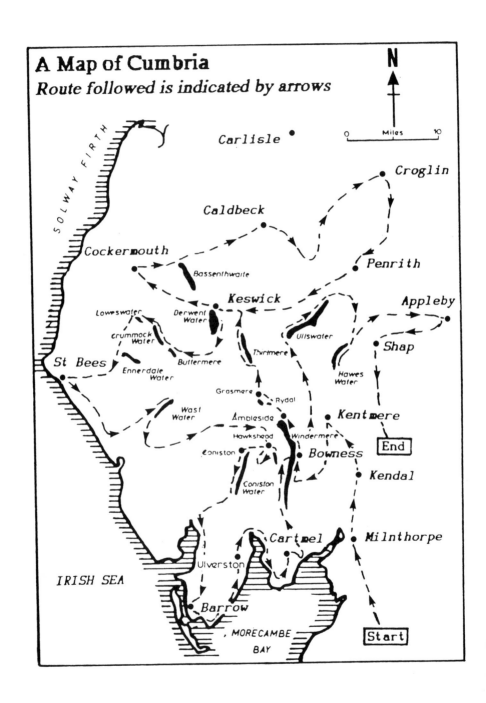

A Map of Cumbria
Route followed is indicated by arrows

N

Carlisle

0   Miles   10

Croglin

Caldbeck

Cockermouth

Penrith

Bassenthwaite

Keswick

Appleby

Lowswater

Derwent Water

Ullswater

Shap

crummock Water

Thirlmere

St Bees

Buttermere

Hawes Water

Ennerdale Water

Grasmere

Rydal

Wast Water

Kentmere

Ambleside

End

Hawkshead

Windermere

Coniston

Bowness

Coniston Water

Kendal

Cartmel

Milnthorpe

Ulverston

IRISH SEA

Barrow

MORECAMBE BAY

Start

SOLWAY FIRTH

1

Milnthorpe to Bowness-on-Windermere

I leave Lancashire in early springtime to begin my Lakeland journey. I stop at Milnthorpe, remembering novelist Constance Holme, I storm Sizergh Castle then reach Lakeland's southern gateway. In Kendal I eat mint cake, read the *Westmorland Gazette* and hear about the local girl who became Queen. I find tranquillity in hidden Kentmere, then cross the lovely Lyth Valley to discover England's longest Lake.

1

I opened the curtains of my bedroom window wide apart and gazed out on to a bright March morning that was full of promise. The Lancashire hills, which had endured the longest and most dreary winter for twenty years, seemed at last to be smiling. The mist of morning was lifting fast from their brown flanks and from a patch of blue which suddenly appeared in the sky came a diffused sunbeam. My feeling of optimism was confirmed when a blackbird which lay hidden on the rooftop began to sing out loudly, to be answered by the raucous call of a magpie which was perched on the high branches of an ash tree. With this proclamation of springtime in England now firmly in my thoughts it seemed to be the perfect time to begin my journey.

As I drove slowly northwards, filled with excited anticipation, there were further signs of the death of winter. Wind tossed daffodils in suburban gardens had began to spread their yellow heads among the purple of the crocuses and the fragile white of the snowdrops. On the moorland edges peewits, flying like pieces of black and white paper in the stiff breeze, were busily surveying possible nesting grounds. Curlews too had returned from their coastal retreat, gliding in demure silence over a stark landscape that would soon be buzzing with activity. But even more promising than all of these was the thin veil of greenery that was slowly returning to the hawthorns which lined the lanes as I approached Lancaster.

I crossed the Lune in a line of heavy commuter traffic, casting a sideways glance at John of Gaunt's grey castle and the adjacent Priory Church which dominates the skyline. Soon I had left the office workers to their word processors and the craftsmen to their machine tools, I was alone on my way to the Lakes. Beyond the limestone walls of Yealand Redmayne I passed a sign that told me I was about to leave Lancashire and enter Cumbria; my Lakeland journey had now really begun.

The meandering river Bela, which skirts the east of Milnthorpe, was running fast with white water but the deer which sometimes feed on its banks were not to be seen. As I turned into the centre of the little town I was surprised to find that it was bustling for I had I arrived on Friday which is market day. Finding a single parking place outside Birketts' bakers shop, which advertised *Simnel Cake Now Available*, I began to stroll among the stalls. Light rain which had suddenly swept down from the limestone crags of Hutton Roof had not dispersed the local shoppers who were busily purchasing twelve buns for £1, fruit tea-cakes for 65p and potted primula to brighten up their cottages. A grey haired man was trying on a pair of sturdy black shoes while his wife looked on, offering her frustrated advice: "They look fine to me. You know you always buy this type anyway."

It is strange to think that this little market town, now a popular 'watering place' for Lakeland bound travellers, was once the only port in Westmorland. I suppose the Vikings were the first settlers to bring their longboats up the Kent then into the shallows of the Bela, for 'thorpe' is said to be Scandinavian in origin. The 'Miln' part of the town's name refers to a water-mill which is known to have been in existence here in the 15th century. The river became a useful means of transporting corn and flour in an area which had notoriously bad roads until the railway finally pushed its way northwards during the middle of the last century.

As I strolled away from the market, admiring the sturdy tower of St Thomas's church with its blue-dialled clock which overlooks the busy square, I remembered that it was here in 1955 that the funeral of novelist Constance Holme took place. This fine writer, who is now sadly almost forgotten, had been born here in Milnthorpe in 1880. She was the youngest of a huge family of fourteen children, but they were not poor for her father had a well paid position as the agent for nearby Dallam Tower estate. It is said that she showed literary talent even as a child, creating stories which she told to her school friends. In 1909 the Kendal Mercury and Times published her first novel, *Hugh of Hughdale*, as a serial. Another of her writings failed to find a publisher but her breakthrough came when *Crump Folk Going Home* was published in 1913. But it is her next book, *The Lonely Plough*, which is regarded by many as being her best work. It was inspired by a great storm which swept over this southern corner of Lakeland in 1907 causing the famous Arnside tidal bore to sweep inland bringing terrible floods.

In 1916, at the age of 36, she was married to Frederick Punchard who, like her father was the agent for a large country estate. She moved with her new husband to Underlay Hall near Kirkby Lonsdale, which was the home of Lord Henry Bentinck. Her third book, *The Old Road from Spain* which was published in the same year, is based on a local legend concerning one of the ships from the Spanish Armada which was wrecked on the treacherous sands of Morecambe Bay. She believed that her mother was a descendant of a member of the Spanish crew who settled in the area.

When her fourth work, *The Splendid Fairing*, won a prestigious French literary award in 1920 she became recognised as an important regional writer in the great rural tradition. She went on to complete a total of eight successful novels, each being published in the World Classic series by Oxford University Press, together with a collection of one act plays and a book of short stories. After the retirement of her husband the couple returned once more to her childhood home in Milnthorpe where Frederick died in 1946. Grief stricken, she lived in the town until 1954 when she moved just four miles to Arnside where she died the following year.

Just a few months ago I had a piece of luck while browsing through the 'Books for Sale' in a Clitheroe charity shop, for among the dog-eared paperbacks I spotted one of Sir Hugh Walpole's works. It was a first edition of *Jeremy*, which was published in 1919, but more importantly it had the signature of Constance Holme inside. So for just two pounds I was able to buy a volume I now treasure, for it is a link between two fine Lakeland writers.

After leaving Milnthorpe I was filled with uncertainty for two great houses lie on the town's doorstep and I had only time to visit one. Would it be Levens Hall which is celebrating three centuries of its world famous topiary garden or Sizergh Castle, home of one of England's oldest families? I tossed a coin then I headed for Sizergh.

2

"Were all the Stricklands really as handsome as this?" asked a bemused young woman as she stared up at one of Romney's fine portraits in Sizergh Castle.

The National Trust attendant, a jolly faced man dressed in a thick tweed suit, smiled and walked over.

"I suspect not. The artist knew it was in his best interest to flatter the customer, then more commissions would follow."

I had come to Sizergh Castle (pronounced Sizer) on a bright afternoon expecting to find a sombre turreted, half deserted structure, but I was pleasantly surprised. Even so early in the tourist season the car park was almost full

Ancient Sizergh Castle has been the home of the Strickland family for over 700 years.

and the castle was not really a castle at all but a warm and beautiful stately home. True, it had begun as a stout pele tower built in the mid 14th century, but to this has been added a magnificent Tudor great hall, two Elizabethan wings and a host of other outbuildings, courtyards and gardens which have transformed it into a splendid architectural kaleidoscope. Like Milnthorpe it was Viking settlers who first gave this elevated pastureland its name, then after the Conquest the Deincourt family were given the land by King Henry II about 1170. Seventy years later a Deincourt sole heiress, Elizabeth, married Sir Thomas Strickland and since that time, for an incredible 755 years, it has been the family residence. In 1950 both the house and estate were given to the National Trust but the present generation of the family still continue to live here.

As I wandered through the immaculate rooms of the house, looking at oak furniture, fine pottery, carved panels and portraits of long departed Stricklands which line every wall, my thoughts began to dwell on the beginnings of this unique building. Prior to 1603, when England and Scotland were finally united, Cumbria had suffered centuries of border warfare. Bands of marauding Scots would descend like ghosts from the mist, for the land taken by the

Normans was regarded as fair game. Cattle, horses and anything of value was taken, men were put to the sword and women were heartlessly raped. It was a period of grotesque savagery in which the Stricklands, living at the sharp end of the conflict, became inevitably involved. As a means of providing a safe haven from these raids a series of massive yet simple towers were constructed in the north. The Sizergh Pele, which was built in 1350 and stands sixty feet high with huge limestone walls that are almost ten feet thick, hides many forgotten secrets of this bloodthirsty period.

To look back at the events which have shaped this ancient family is like turning over the pages of an English history book. In 1306 Sir Walter Strickland was created a Knight of the Bath for his courage in fighting in the Border Wars and his only sister, Joan, was married to Robert de Wessington from whom the first President of the USA, George Washington, became a descendant. It was a Strickland who carried the premier banner of St George at the Battle of Agincourt, then the next generation forged a marriage link with the Parr family from which was born Queen Katherine Parr, the last wife of King Henry VIII. During the 17th century the family were deeply involved in the court of the Stuarts, Sir Thomas Strickland became Keeper of the Privy Purse to the wife of King Charles II, Katherine of Braganza. His second wife, Winifred, was a member of the household of Mary of Modena who was married to the ill-fated King James II. Lady Winifred Strickland was present at the birth of James, Prince of Wales, who was to become the Old Pretender and she later became his governess when the Royal Family were forced into exile. Many of the fascinating Stuart relics which I saw dotted around the house were acquired at this time.

The 18th century saw the family in a financial crisis but the marriage of Charles Strickland to wealthy Lancashire heiress, Cecilia Towneley, saved the day. In her portrait by Romney which was painted in 1762 she looks like an elegant personification of the nursery rhyme character Bo-peep. In recent times it is probably Sir Gerald Strickland who gained the most prominence following his marriage to Lady Edeline Sackville, who was the daughter of Earl De La Warr. He had a distinguished career in the colonial service becoming the Prime Minister of Malta, an English MP, then he entered the House of Lords as the 1st Baron Strickland of Sizergh. Following his death in 1940 the line continued through his eldest daughter and her descendants, the Hornyold-Stricklands.

My stroll through the house ended in the pele tower for the most delicious aroma of coffee had permeated upwards; I could resist it no longer. I stole down the narrow stone spiral staircase, as men have been doing for seven centuries, but happily the only fighting I needed to do was in the queue for scones and cream in the small café.

Kendal was busy as always, cars were jam-packed up Stricklandgate, visitors were gazing with admiration at the fine Carnegie Library or heading for the Abbot Hall Museum, while the women of Oxenholme, Staveley and Underbarrow were seriously shopping. There was a time not long ago when much of the Lakeland tourist traffic crawled through this splendid market town, then a new by-pass was finally built. Peace temporarily returned to its streets, but such is progress that the ever increasing volume of local traffic has once more created a pedestrian's nightmare.

It was the meandering River Kent which first attracted settlers to this green valley and the river still lies at the very heart of the town, bounded by lovely waterside pathways. The Romans had a camp here, the Saxons worshipped Christ here and the Normans built an impressive castle here, but it was the humble sheep that really created the town. 'Wool is my Bread' is still the town's motto.

As early as the 13th century the monks of the rich Furness Abbey were involved in exporting wool from their farms which were scattered around Lakeland. Kendal's cloth trade, which by the 14th century was well established, attracted a number of Flemish weavers who came here to escape persecution. Although Kendal Cloth was coarse, being regarded as low quality and suitable only for the poor, the local expertise in dyeing became famous throughout England. The distinctive *Kendal Green* was a term which entered into literature, being mentioned by Shakespeare in Henry IV and later by Sir Walter Scott. The town continued to prosper during the 17th century for much of its cloth was exported to the colonies where it was used to clothe slaves. The flexibility of the people of Kendal became apparent when this export trade began to decline for a new industry then took its place, the hand-knitting of stockings. Perhaps the most famous product mow associated with Kendal is footwear, for it is the home of the world-famous K Shoes.

Strangers who are of a curious nature will soon discover that Kendal is a fascinating town to explore, for it is full of inviting alleyways known as Yards and tempting old coaching inns. These narrow passageways of limestone which often lead down to the river, were first created as a means of defence from the raiding Scots, with the added protection of sturdy gates. Today they allow a marvellous glimpse back in time to what was known as the 'Auld Grey Town', where craftsmen once worked in tiny cottages dyeing wool, making ropes or blending snuff. As I continued past the Town Hall I was reminded of a more recent craftsman who came here from Blackburn and left his permanent mark on the whole area. Alfred Wainwright, whose pictorial guide books to the Lakeland mountains are the bible of all who walk, worked here as the Borough Treasurer.

Glancing up at a plaque which fronts Stricklandgate I read that both Bonnie

Stramongate Bridge, Kendal

Prince Charlie and his greatest enemy, the Duke of Cumberland, slept in the same bed in this building, but of course not at the same time! A nearby bakers shop had Westmorland Parkin, Borrowdale Tea Bread and Windermere Banana Cake on display in the window but I resisted the temptation. I was determined to do the two things all visitors to Kendal should do, so I went in to a newsagent's shop and bought a slab of Kendal Mint Cake and a copy of the *Westmorland Gazette*.

Sitting beside the river I began munching the delicious mint flavoured sweet which the label told me had been taken on the first successful ascent of Everest by Sir Edmund Hillary and Sirdar Tensing in 1953.

"We sat on the snow and looked at the country far below us... we nibbled Kendal Mint Cake," recorded a member of the famous climbing team, who went on to say "it was easily the most popular item on our high altitude ration."

What better recommendation could there be? This mixture of sugar, glucose syrup, water, peppermint oil and propylene glycol would surely give me enough energy for an ascent of Skiddaw or even Scafell Pike.

I have found that one of the best ways to quickly get to the heart of a new area is to read a local newspaper, but few can live up to the reputation of the Westmorland Gazette. It was founded here in Kendal in 1818 by the two Lowther brothers who were the sons of the Earl of Lonsdale. William

Wordsworth is said to have encouraged its foundation and it can boast Thomas de Quincey as its second editor. It has grown over the last century and a half to become one of Lakeland's great institutions, being recently voted the UK weekly newspaper of the year. Not surprisingly it was to the paper's printing department that the modest Alfred Wainwright turned to produce his first guide book in 1955, which resulted in a one-man industry. By doing this he was continuing a Kendal tradition, for Wordsworth's famous guide book to the Lake District had also been published here by Hudson & Nicholson in 1835

The *Westmorland Gazette*, as one would expect, remains a traditional broad-sheet happily leaving the sordid world news to the here-today-gone-to-morrow tabloids. It concentrates on those news stories that are small by national standards, but reflect so well the rural life in this unspoilt corner of England. Features on farming, walking and wildlife, together with the exploits of newsworthy villagers fill its pages.

I read the romantic tale of Land Army girl Sybil Fletcher and farmer's son Bill Nelson who fell in love during the second World War and six children and sixteen grandchildren later are celebrating their golden wedding. I also heard how Sydney Banks has tended the gardens at stately Holker Hall for 44 years and why Lakeside resident Josi Slapko believes in ghosts. I found two whole pages devoted to rural news and gossip from such marvellously named villages as Lindale-in-Cartmel, Grayrigg, Newbiggin-on-Lune and Old Hutton. For an outsider even the adverts can prove fascinating for they provide an insight into this agricultural world that is far removed from so many of us these days. Prime cattle steers, heifers, bulls and spring lambs are for sale at Ulverston Auction Mart, peacocks and in-kid goats can also be acquired for a modest price, while dogs and cats are available from the Wainwright Shelter which is largely financed by the late author's royalties.

3

I am writing these words with my notebook perched on the wall of one of England's most romantic ruins from which I have a spectacular view through Lakeland's southern gateway. Few visitors venture up here to Kendal Castle, for they are too anxious to experience the splendour of Windermere, Ullswater or Hawkshead. Yet a leisurely stroll up this grassy hillside is more than worthwhile for it is the perfect introduction to Lakeland. From this modest elevation the magic of the countryside seems to cry out, while this ancient structure built by Norman hands, remembers secrets from some of the most tempestuous episodes in our history.

What remains of the castle is a complete curtain wall which is surrounded

The romantic ruins of Kendal Castle

by a deep ditch, three towers and part of the gate-house, the earliest of these dating from the 13th century. Ivy clings in part to the stout walls, a handful of sycamores with bursting buds have found a hold in a sheltered spot and a solitary crow has taken it upon himself to act as a guardian. Looking down to the valley below I can see the grey rooftops of Kendal spreading outwards in hushed silence, following the line of the river along which the town was first built. Beyond curves the rising green of open fields, the wooded tops of limestone hills and to the north, lit by beams of soft light, my first view of the Lakeland mountains. The craggy outline of these high summits above Kentmere fill the distant horizon, their gullies highlighted by the silver of glistening snow that the spring sun has so far failed to melt.

Turning once more to the castle whose manicured lawns have just received their first mowing of the year, my thoughts have begun to move back nearly five centuries. For it was here, according to Sir Danial Fleming writing in 1671, that Katherine Parr, the sixth wife of King Henry VIII was born in 1512. Others have since disputed the fact, but few are willing to utter their disbelief around

Kendal for the locals have taken Queen Katherine to their hearts, naming both a school and a street in her honour.

Kendal's Norman castle, which was originally built of timber then rebuilt of stone, was first occupied by the Parr family in 1380. Katherine's mother was Lady Maud Greene, who came from an aristocratic family who lived in Green's Norton in Northamptonshire. She was married to Sir Thomas Parr in 1508 when she was still a child of 13 years old. Her husband held an important position as Master of the Wards and Comptroller of the King's Household, so the couple probably lived most of the time in London. Katherine was their first child who was born in the fifth year of their marriage, followed later by William and Anne. But in 1517, Sir Thomas died so Lady Maud and her three children came back here to Kendal, where it is believed they lived in this castle, also spending periods with relatives in Northamptonshire.

Katherine is reputed to have been an intelligent child who worked diligently at her lessons, becoming particularly accomplished in foreign languages. But her future seems to have been already written in the stars for an astrologer predicted that she would one day sit on the throne of England. However, she had been born with a remote Royal lineage for she could boast John of Gaunt as one of her ancestors and was actually the forth cousin, once removed, to King Henry VIII.

Lady Maud was devoted to her children and was anxious to ensure they had a secure future. So in 1529, when Katherine was seventeen years old, she was married to Lord Edward Borough whose father was the chamberlain to Anne Boleyn. He was not an old man, as has been sometimes suggested, but he is said to have been in poor health. Sadly, in 1531 her mother died, to which was added the tragic loss of her husband the following year. She received a moderate inheritance and probably returned north to live once more in Kendal.

At this time she had family links with nearby Sizergh Castle, for it was the home of her step-son Lord Henry Borough who was married to Lady Katherine Strickland. During a visit there she was introduced to a rich widower, Lord Latimer of Snape Castle in Yorkshire, who was to become her second husband. A few years after their marriage in 1533 the tempestuous period of the Dissolution of the Monasteries began, during which her new husband was one of the northern lords who became involved, under duress, in the uprising known as the Pilgrimage of Grace. It is said that astute Katherine advised him not to take any further part in the rebellion when it seemed doomed to failure, thus perhaps saving his life. However, her contentment was short-lived for in 1542 she was widowed for a second time.

King Henry VIII, to whom Katherine was destined to become linked, was 21 years older that her, having been born in 1491 and crowned in 1509. As Katherine's father had held an important position at court it is likely that Henry,

King Henry VIII and his sixth wife, Katherine Parr, who was born in Kendal.

together with many prominent figures of the day had known her from child-hood. She now began to spend her time in both Kendal and London, becoming involved in the social life of the court where her sister Anne was married to a courtier named William Herbert. It was at this time that she came to the notice of the handsome Sir Thomas Seymour, the brother of Henry's third wife Jane Seymour, who having heard of her widowhood had an eye to marry her himself. It is said that he rented a house near Kendal so that he could pursue his courtship, but in reality he became an intermediary between Katherine and Henry.

Henry's kingship had started triumphantly, he was not yet eighteen, well educated, full of life, 'the handsomest prince in Europe' and he had inherited a kingdom that was peaceful and financially sound. It seemed unlikely in his early years that he would become the 'most married' of all English kings for his first marriage to his brother's widow, Catherine of Aragon, lasted for eighteen years from which was born a daughter, Mary. He then quite suddenly decided that this marriage was 'illicit' and should be annulled which the Pope refused to allow. So ignoring the authority of Rome, for which he was excommunicated, he went ahead and married Anne Boleyn, only later did

Archbishop Cranmer declare that his first marriage had been invalid. Anne Boleyn bore him another daughter, Elizabeth, but this relationship was quickly growing cold. Henry accused her of being unfaithful which led to her inevitable execution on Tower Hill.

When Henry married Jane Seymour in 1536 it was hoped it would prove more long lasting for it is said that he was devoted to her. She quickly became pregnant, providing him with a much sought after male heir, Edward, but sadly she died giving birth. Two years later, for diplomatic reasons, he married Anne of Cleves whom he called the Flander's Mare and quickly divorced. He then married Catherine Howard, who was the cousin of Anne Boleyn, and who followed a similar fate for she too was executed.

One would assume that knowing Henry's past record it was an apprehensive Katherine Parr who took her royal marriage vows in July 1543, but she seems to have been in complete control of her new position. She quickly gained her husband's trust to such an extent that he made her Regent and gave any children they might have the right of succession after Edward. She also became a worthy step-mother to the young Edward, Elizabeth and Mary, whose welfare she actively organised.

However, it was her ardent Protestantism which almost led to her downfall, for surprisingly Henry did not share her outspoken views. A document which accused her of heresy had been drawn up by Chancellor Wriothesley and signed by the King. Pikesmen were summoned to Hampton Court, but using her highly developed feminine wile, she combined flattery and diplomacy on Henry to successfully escape arrest. But of course he was now quickly degenerating, he was grossly obese, had ulcerated legs and in January 1547 he died of venereal disease. His terrible autocratic reign of thirty-eight years, which had begun with such promise had ended in despair, for his personal extravagance had emptied the treasury. His best known epitaph is perhaps the rhyme learned by school children which describes the fate of his six wives:

Divorced, beheaded, died;
Divorced, beheaded, survived.

The death of Henry had left Katherine even richer, his will stated that she must receive a thousand pounds in money and over three thousand pounds in jewels and goods. She was now also free from the terrible burden of living with the ever-present threat of the axe. Moving to Chelsea Palace she was re-united with her former admirer, Sir Thomas Seymour, who became her fourth husband just a few months later. But sadly, what at first seemed to be a love match proved to be yet another unhappy episode in her life. Her new husband, in the fashion of the corrupt court in which he lived and worked, was unfaithful to her. It is said that she even caught him in the arms of the young Princess Elizabeth.

At the end of August 1548 Katherine, then aged 35, gave birth to her first child, a daughter named Mary. But complications followed the birth, leading to her death one week later from puerperal fever. Her funeral took place at St Mary's Church at Sudeley in Essex, amidst a large crowd of mourners which included her brother William and the claimant to the throne, Lady Jane Grey. William later supported Lady Jane Grey in her battle for the crown which almost resulted in his execution, only his relationship to Katherine saved his neck. Mary Seymour, known as 'the Queen's Child', was cared for by the Duchess of Suffolk, but is believed to have died in childhood.

"This is the second widest Parish Church in England, the largest is in Great Yarmouth."

I had descended the green hillside from Katherine Parr's birthplace to reach Holy Trinity Church which lies on the bank of the Kent. A quietly spoken man who was a steward had greeted me at the entrance and we began to chat. He told me how there was probably a place of Christian worship here as early as the 8th century. We then talked of its early history and he pointed out to me some of its many treasures.

Here I gazed at the flag captured by the Border Regiment during the China War, I saw a memorial to the artist Romney and a 13th century coffin lid, then I looked at the helmet of 'Robin the Devil'. Apparently Major Robert Philipson of Belle Isle in Windermere, came here during the Civil War to seek out his arch enemy, Cromwellian officer Colonel Briggs. He hastily rode his horse into the church and during the skirmish that followed he lost his helmet which has remained here ever since. The episode was later used by Sir Walter Scott in his poem *Rokeby*.

But inevitably, like most visitors, it was to the Parr Chapel that I was drawn. Here I looked on the ancient tomb of William Parr whose grand-daughter was destined to reach such fame, and I saw the carved maiden's head emblem that King Henry VIII had given to his last wife.

"Why do you think Katherine Parr took such a risk in becoming involved with Henry?" I asked the steward as I was about to leave the church.

"Well, perhaps she regarded it as the ultimate challenge of her day? And don't forget, she did survive."

4

There are places in Britain which remain serene and unspoilt because nature has given to them a great advantage: they are not on the road to anywhere else. These include peninsulas like St David's in Wales, fishing villages such as Mullion Cove in Cornwall and Staithes in Yorkshire, and the tidal islands of

Lindisfarne, Sunderland Point and St Michael's Mount which can only be reached by road twice a day. Visitors seldom arrive in these communities by chance so they largely escape both the busyness and change that mass tourism can bring. In Lakeland it is a handful of half-hidden valleys which have been blessed in this way, for they have been hemmed in by mountains. Kentmere, I discovered, is fortunate in being one of these, for access by car is only possible up a single narrow lane which comes to a sudden end at the valley head.

On a day when the bright spring sunshine was at last lifting the chill of winter, I left the cars and the coaches and the buses behind to speed on their way to Windermere. Entering the tranquillity of Kentmere from its gateway at the village of Staveley, I was able to catch a passing glance of the infant Kent which was gushing with the water of melted snow. Slowly I drove up this lovely silent valley, the narrow lane fringed by moss-laden dry stone walls. I had to stop a couple of times to allow anxious ewes with new-born white lambs to make their escape from the lane into which they had wandered. This allowed me time to admire the fresh greenness of the lush fields that spread outward from the river and to see my first close-up view of the Lakeland mountains. The summits of Kentmere Pike, Knowe and Harter Fell much loved by fell-walkers, soared into the sky on my right to be met by Ill Bell, Yoke and Frostwick. It is strange to think that two thousand years ago the eyes of Rome would gaze down on this serene English valley. From their elevated road which we now call High Street that crosses these lonely mountains tops, the soldiers would perhaps curse their luck at having to spend yet another winter guarding their northern frontier of Hadrian's Wall.

It is from the becks that pour off High Street that the River Kent, whose name means appropriately 'from the hills', is first born. It feeds a a small reed-fringed mere which lies among flat pastureland from which the valley takes its name. This was once much larger, but in 1840 it was partially drained to secure more valuable grazing land. However, this robbed a number of mills which lay downstream of their water supply, so a new reservoir which remains at the head of the valley had to be built. In the fifties two large dug-out boats, which had been fashioned from oak, were discovered in the mud of the drained mere. Believed to be over 600 years old, one of these was claimed by the Maritime Museum at Greenwich.

I was surprised to find the small car-park, which lies close to the village church, was almost full for I had not seen a single car on my journey up the valley. But the occupants had no doubt made an early departure to the hills, for this is a convenient starting point for climbers and walkers.

Healthy-looking poultry from a nearby farm were happily foraging for food on the sloping hillside watched by a pair of chirping jackdaws who have made

The rugged splendour of Ill Bell sweeps down to Kentmere

their home in the small church tower. I left my car and walked to the dry stone wall at the edge of the car park to look down on the special loveliness that is Kentmere. Below me lay a huge emerald field, flat as a bowling-green and spreading outwards to meet the fells, it was dotted with the white heads of slumbering lambs. I could see the homes of this scattered community sheltering up narrow tracks and along steeply rising lanes that disappear into the mountains. Prominent among these is Kentmere Hall, which is now a farmhouse, for like Sizergh Castle it boasts a pele tower which is six centuries old. A tale told locally is that a giant of a man, Hugh Hird who came from Troutbeck, helped to build this house using his enormous strength. Alone he lifted a massive beam which ten men had previously failed to move!

For centuries Kentmere Hall was the home of the Gilpin family who had many prominent members. These included Richard Gilpin, a soldier who killed a fierce wild boar which had caused havoc in the valley, and John Gilpin, whose hilarious ride through London was immortalised in the famous poem written by William Cowper.

Two builders were busy at work repairing the church porch which had suffered from the ravages of winter, lying as is does on the top of an exposed hillside. They smiled as I avoided their scaffolding that partially blocked the entrance, then I entered the simple church which is dedicated to Saint Cuthbert. My eyes were immediately drawn to the altar and beyond to the clear glass of the east window, for through it lay a magnificent panorama of the curving hills stretching to the sky. The architects were quite right in not using stained glass for no man-made design could hope to compete with this splendid living picture.

I walked towards the pulpit to read two memorial plaques which are attached to the whitewashed wall. One remembers the generosity of Admiral Wilson who paid for the church to be restored in 1866 and the other outlines the life of Bernard Gilpin who was born at Kentmere Hall in 1533. He was educated at Oxford where he became a Fellow, then later he became caught up in the turmoil of the Reformation. After initially being a defender of the Roman Catholic Church he later became one of its strongest attackers, his followers calling him 'The Apostle of the North'. When the catholic Queen Mary came to the throne he was in danger of losing his life for his outspoken views, but fate saved him. Due to him breaking a leg he was unable to stand trial, then Mary died before he had recovered and luckily for Gilpin the new Queen Elizabeth was a Protestant!

The parish magazine which I bought at the door informed me that a new vicar was due to be inducted here at Kentmere. The Reverend Geof Watson will be carrying on a religious tradition in this secluded valley which many believe began in the 9th century. It is said that the monks of Holy Island wandered for seven years through the northern counties carrying the body of their beloved St Cuthbert together with the head of St Oswald. They were ensuring that their precious relics did not fall into the hands of the pagan Vikings. Each place where they stopped to rest was regarded as being holy and a church was eventually built which was dedicated to one of the saints. As Kentmere lies on the route of their known journey it is likely that the relics were brought here before they eventually found a permanent resting place a century later in Durham Cathedral.

As I drove back down the valley towards Staveley, the hills shimmering in the bright sunlight, it was hard to imagine the atrocious weather of just a month ago which led to a terrible tragedy. It happened during the famous 12-mile long Kentmere Horseshoe fell race, which took place over the gale-lashed mountains which were shrouded with mist. Experienced athlete Judith Taylor from Blackburn, the mother of two grown-up children, failed to return to the finish. Mountain rescue teams searched for seven hours before, sadly, her body was discovered by a rescue-dog below Hayeswater Dam near High Street.

5

Windermere, the longest and best known of all the English lakes, is separated from Kentmere by eight miles of rich green countryside. Here secluded lanes lined with dry stone walls, dip and dive through a mosaic of small woodlands, low hills and marshy valleys. Here I saw wide eyed lambs limping their first uncertain steps as they gazed out in wonder at a new world. In small sloping fields which ended in a tangle of silver birch and orange bracken chaffinches chatted excitedly as they flitted from branch to branch. The Lyth Valley, which penetrates the southern end of this attractive terrain is the meeting place of two rivers, the Pool and the Gilpin. Lying almost at sea level it was once subjected to heavy flooding, but now an efficient series of dykes successfully lead the rain water away.

The valley is overlooked on each side by the high points of Whitbarrow Scar and Scout Scar. By Lakeland standards these wooded limestone summits are small, yet they attract many walkers for they allow spectacular views in all directions. Below lie the ancient villages of Levens, Brigsteer, Underbarrow and Crosthwaite together with scores of secluded farmsteads which hide in a sea of waving damson blossom in early springtime. The western flank of Whitbarrow Scar descends through woodland to the River Winster and the quiet village of Witherslack. Here in 1612 was born John Barwick, a man who joined Cromwell's army during the Civil War but was really spying for the King. Eventually his clandestine activities were uncovered and he ended up being horribly tortured in the Tower of London. However, he managed to survive and after the Restoration was rewarded with the position of Dean of St Pauls. But he never forgot the village of his birth, he left a large sum of money which paid for a new church in 1671.

The mallard ducks which live off the crumbs of charity from Lakeland visitors were pleased to see me when I drove into the car park at Beech Hill for the rain had driven away all but one vehicle. This was a small school bus whose occupants, teenage boys and girls, were apparently oblivious of the soaking they were getting, for they were laughing and chatting as their hair became flattened by the torrent of water. After ten minutes the worst of the downpour had eased so I was able to venture over the rise for my first view of Windermere. Embraced by a circle of white drifting mist the silver line of the lake spread out below me. The surrounding mountains, having vanished into the clouds, had left behind them a strange monotone landscape cocooned in an atmosphere of romantic splendour. Every small vestige of our present century had temporarily been erased leaving the mind free to conjure up images of the past. The ghosts of Wordsworth, Coleridge and Southey could return with confidence on a day such as this.

Windermere, which was originally named Vinand's Mere after the Viking chief who lived here, is a long narrow lake which stretches from north to south for ten and a half miles, reaching a maximum width of one mile. The point where I was standing lies about four miles from the southern tip of the lake where the water pours into the lovely River Leven at Newby Bridge. The most northerly point is known as Waterhead, which lies on the edge of Ambleside, with the tourist town of Bowness-on-Windermere lying half way up on the eastern bank. How deep the water really is has been a matter of debate and curiosity among travellers for centuries. The earliest simple surveys were carried out towards the end of the 18th century, followed by a more thorough one in 1895 when Dr Mill systematically lowered a weighted rope from a rowing boat. But more sophisticated techniques using echo sounding equipment have now revealed the lake to be about 65 metres (213 feet) at its deepest point near White Cross Bay, which is mid-way between Bowness and Ambleside.

A rare fish which loves these deep waters is the char, which is related to the trout but which lives below 14 metres (45 feet). It is not large, growing only to about 250 mm (10") in length, but it is delicious to eat. During the 17th century when char-pie and potted-char became a fashionable delicacy among the rich, a lucrative trade was established between Windermere and London. Some experts believe the fish was trapped in the lake during the Ice Age while other feel it was more likely to have been introduced here by the Romans. The right to catch it has always been jealously guarded, originally being held by the monks of Furness Abbey near Barrow. Today only a handful of fishermen using a rod and line from small boats are allowed this unique privilege. Two other unusual fish which are also found in Lakeland are the vendace, which lives only in Derwentwater and Bassenthwaite, and the schelly which is a type of freshwater herring which move in shoals across Ullswater.

After giving way to the demands of the ducks by feeding them a few crusts from my sandwiches I continued northwards along the wooded banks of the lake in the direction of Bowness. As I approached the town the rain began to pour as only Lakeland rain can, allowing me a misty view of lovely Belle Isle which lies off a promontory named Cookshott Point. This, the largest of the islands on Windermere, is conveniently positioned just a quarter of a mile from the shore. It is believed to have once been the home of the head of the Roman military garrison which existed at Ambleside. No doubt he came here as a temporary escape from his responsibilities and perhaps to dream of returning to Rome. After the Conquest it became the seat of the Lord of the Manor of Windermere, then later the Philipson family who occupied it during the Civil War. Although Major 'Robin the Devil' Philipson showed remarkable spirit when he rode into Kendal Church others had little fight in them, for after a single canon ball landed on the island the family immediately surrendered.

But it was in 1774 that the owner, Mr English, decided to build a unique residence on the island whose design caused a great deal of controversy. Built on the highpoint, he chose a unique round house which was influenced by the

This unique Round House was built on Belle Isle on Lake Windermere in 1774.

classical Italian style. In the staid Georgian society of the time the design came
in for a great deal of criticism. William Wordsworth said it resembled a 'pepper
pot', but it later became one of his family's favourite retreats. However, Mr
English was happy to rid himself of the publicity; it had cost him around £5000
to build but it was sold within six years for a mere £1700!

One of Lakeland's oldest families, the Curwens, bought the island together
with the mansion as a wedding gift for their beautiful daughter, Isabelle. She
had married a well known agriculturist, John Christian, who was the cousin
of Fletcher Christian who is remembered for his part in the infamous mutiny
on *HMS Bounty*. However, he chose to take the Curwen family name, as his
wife was the sole heiress and they did not want the ancient Curwen name to
be ended. He also changed the name of the island from Longholme, as it was
then known, to 'Belle' Isle which was his abbreviation of 'Isabelle'; a gesture
which enhances what many believe is the most romantic place in Lakeland.
Over two hundred years later the Curwen family still live here, but now they
have the advantages of mains water and electricity which has been laid across
the bed of the lake.

Bowness, in spite of the dismal weather, was busy with traffic. Day trippers
in raincoats and plastic hats had arrived from Leeds, Birmingham and Cambridge, determined to see the Lakes in a day. Smiling Japanese tourists,
sheltering beneath huge red and yellow umbrellas, were strolling in a bewildered fashion through the ascending main street. They were looking in the
Hole in th' Wall tavern which was once visited by Dickens, they were admiring
the small cottages which hide in narrow alleyways and they were buying prints
of Heaton Cooper watercolours to hang on their walls back home in Tokyo.

"I guess we've just time to see the Washington coat of arms in the Parish
Church," said one elderly American to his plump wife, who was gazing
adoringly at a cream cake in a baker's shop window.

Those who come to the Lake District for solitude and natural beauty
sometimes talk scathingly about Bowness, for them it is a place to avoid. The
huge influx of whistle-stop visitors together with the tourist shops which have
sprung up to cater for their needs, they argue, has created a potential monster
which could destroy the area. But in spite of the strict National Park regulations
which make such expansion most unlikely the battle between commercialism
and preservation rolls on. This battle really began in 1847 when the railway
arrived here, allowing for the first time large numbers of people to see the once
remote countryside which they had only read about. The hamlet of Birthwaite,
which lies three miles up the hill from the ancient settlement of Bowness, is
where the Windermere railway station was built. A village, then a small town,
completely distinct from Bowness, quickly developed close to the station
which became known as Windermere. This was confusing for visitors, for they

now had both a town and a lake of the same name, so they are now often referred to as Windermere Village and Lake Windermere.

In the same year as the railway arrived the impressive Rigg's Windermere Hotel was built to accommodate visitors, it became a base for coach excursions to more remote areas. Wealthy businessman who were also attracted by the improved transport, began to build their opulent mansions set in splendid landscape gardens. Many of these have survived to find a new role as hotels, nursing homes or in the case of Brockhole as the National Park Visitor Centre. One of the great characters who made his home in Windermere during the last century was J.B. Baddeley. He was a very strong walker whose famous guide-book of Lakeland became the bible for all visitors who came here. His grave, which lies in Bowness cemetery, was appropriately covered with stones from the summit of Scafell Pike.

Eventually, like all visitors who come to Bowness, I found my way down to the relative tranquillity of the lakeside. Here I sauntered along The Promenade, admired the sheltered slopes of the emerald parkland known as The Glebe and gazed across the silver surface of the lake to the pier. For this is of course nautical Windermere, a place of lapping water, over-fed swans, brown varnished rowing boats, powerful motor launches and sleek yachts.

"I never fail to be surprised by the whims of visitors," the friendly man in the steamer ticket office confessed to me. "Often when the weather is the most foul we have the largest number of bookings for the lake."

As I looked across to the pier from which the public launches now run, my thoughts drifted back to the last century for it was then owned by businessman H.W. Schneider who lived at his majestic home of *Belfield*. With aristocratic panache he would walk down to his splendid steam launch, *Esperance*, followed by his butler who was carrying his breakfast on a silver tray. During the journey down the lake he would eat his meal, then at Lakeside he would board his private train which would speed him in style to his sumptuous office in Barrow!

2

Bowness-on-Windermere to Keswick

I find the place where Ambleside began, admire Stock Ghyll
Force, explore Bridge House then head for Grasmere. I learn about
Wordsworth's early life, see his grave, eat some gingerbread, and
walk around Grasmere Lake to reach Dove Cottage. I see wrestling and fell-running at the Grasmere Sports, look at Helvellyn
from Thirlmere, meet Malaysians at Castlerigg Stone Circle, visit
Keswick Museum, then enjoy a slide show in the Moot Hall.

1

In the sunshine of early morning, I took that lovely lakeside road which winds
it way above the wooded shoreline of Windermere, heading north towards
Ambleside.

"What a flippin' old coach that is. Bump, bump, bump, and no toilet on
board." Two boys, one plump with ginger hair and the other smaller with eyes
like Bambi, had alighted from a motor coach which had just arrived at
Waterhead from Blackburn. They uttered their protest out of earshot of their
teacher as they anxiously dashed into the Gents.

Walking from the car park I caught a glimpse of one of the white ferry boats
as it pushed its way through the reedy water to reach the pier at this, its northern
terminus. I then entered Borrans Park, whose soft green turf sweeps down to
the very edge of the water. Here black-headed gulls were gliding through the
cool air, watching a group of laughing picnickers who were sitting above the
shoreline.

Passing a small tree which bore the poignant memorial notice, *Hiroshima,
6 August 1945*, I reached the place where Ambleside really began. Here, on a
flat peninsula formed by the clear waters of the Brathay and the Rothay and
the lake, lies the remains of the Roman fort of Galava, whose name is said to
mean 'rigorous stream'. It was first excavated by the famous Professor R.G.
Collingwood, who was an authority on Roman Lakeland.

I strolled past the foundations of the gateways and the granaries, then into the green outline that was once the commander's house. Here I stopped to ponder on what might have been talked of by the generations of powerful local leaders in the world of two thousand years ago. Perhaps the strategy of policing this corner of Cumbria, which stretched to the very end of the Roman Empire at Hadrian's Wall, would have taken up most of their time. In the early days of the Roman occupation this would have been no easy task for the native Brigantes were the biggest tribe in Britain. The Romans may have sought spiritual consolation from Mars, the God of War, who was much favoured by soldiers. But I wonder what the reaction was in AD 306, when news that Constantine had proclaimed himself Emperor at York quickly reached this fort? For unlike many of the other scheming Emperors, who reputedly persecuted followers of Christ, Constantine embraced the Christian faith.

It was around AD 79 that the fort of Galava was first built here from wood and turf, to house 200 soldiers. During the reign of Hadrian, AD 117-138, it was rebuilt of stone on a much more ambitious scale to accommodate 500 men. Hadrian came to Britain in AD 121, and may have visited this fort which had an important role guarding the road which linked the coastal port at Ravenglass to the walled town of Carlisle. Like all such forts it would have attracted a large civilian population who probably lived in part of what is now modern Ambleside. These people made a comfortable living supplying food and services to the fort which was in existence for over three centuries.

Just a few tumbled stones set in carefully excavated trenches is all that now remains of Galava. Yet, in this unchanging landscape of crag and mountain and lake, I was able to look on much the same scene that would have greeted Roman eyes so long ago.

Ambleside was surprisingly quiet. Visitors could stroll with pleasure along its narrow pavements, looking in shop windows filled with walking boots, rucksacks, waterproofs, postcards of Striding Edge bathed in elusive sunshine and videos showing the exploits of the late Alfred Wainwright. After finding a parking spot for my car, which in itself is an achievement in central Lakeland, I joined them in an exploration of the town.

Wandering up Church Street I came to the Old Stamp House whose elevated entrance is reached by a flight of stone steps. Here from 1813 to 1843 William Wordsworth, no doubt reluctantly, turned his quill from writing poetry to the more mundane job of accountancy. Like many literary figures his income from writing had to be supplemented from other sources, so he took up a position as a local tax administrator known as the Distributor of Stamps. But earlier this century it was not the association that Wordsworth had with Church Street that attracted local children here, but another Lakeland character named Mary Dugdale. In her small cottage she produced a mouth-watering toffee known as Ambleside Clag 'em which helped to keep many a dentist in business!

Around the corner I stopped to look at the impressive Salutation Hotel, which stands close to the Market Cross. This replaces the old Salutation Inn that according to Victorian travellers lacked even basic comforts. However, it was here that Keats stayed during his celebrated excursion into Lakeland. He would have seen a small but thriving market town, which after gaining its charter in 1630, had become a popular centre for the sale of Herdwick sheep. But of course even by the beginning of the last century the tourist industry had begun in Ambleside, while today visitors often outnumber the resident population of 3000 people.

After browsing in a small second-hand book shop whose volumes appropriately rested in a bookshelf once owned by Wordsworth, I strolled up quiet Cheapside towards Stock Ghyll Force. Here, only half a mile from the centre of the town, I watched the cascading mountain water twist its silver course down a moss-laden rocky gully. Overlooked by the green foliage of spring the scene looked like a miniature Amazon, only the jaunty progress of a dipper giving away the true scale. This attractive beck rises high on Red Screes overlooking Kirkstone Pass. The falls, which are in three stages, drop over 70 feet taking the fast-moving water down the valley to join the Rothay. This torrent was used from the 14th century to provide the power to drive five watermills, producing woollen and linen goods, bobbins and the grinding of corn.

Returning to the centre of Ambleside I strolled along to the town's best known landmark, the unique one-up-and-one-down house that has been built on a small bridge which spans Stock Beck. It is believed that Bridge House was constructed during the 16th century by the Braithwaite family in the grounds of their home, Ambleside Hall. The hall has long since gone but this strange building has remained to puzzle generations of visitors.

"Some say it was originally built as a summer-house which at the same time allowed the family to cross over the beck, but it has been put to many different uses over the years," said the National Trust guide whose stall took up most of the tiny lower room.

I walked up the stone steps which led me to the equally small upper room which gave me an elevated view of the endless line of cars which pass this way. Up to 1843 when the Rydal Road was constructed, the house lay in a magnificent rural setting, becoming a popular subject for many artists including Turner. At this time it was probably used as a counting house for the goods produced in the nearby water-mills. It then became the home of Charity Rigg and his wife who somehow managed to bring up a large family of six children in just two rooms. In the early years of this century a cobbler took up residence here, the upstairs room became a temporary pigeon loft, then later it was turned into a gift shop.

The curious design of Bridge Hose has puzzled generations of visitors.

In 1926 its importance was at last fully realized when it was purchased by a group of local people for £450. They then passed it over to the care of the National Trust, which thirty years later turned it into their first Information and Recruitment centre.

As I headed towards a small café hidden down one of Ambleside's quieter streets, I thought what a splendid novel is waiting to be written about the chequered history of Bridge House.

"Won't be a minute, just working out my VAT. It's been quiet today."

A smiling, swarthy man was busy working out his tax returns on a Tandy computer which was wedged on the side of the counter of his café-come-bakers shop. When he later returned with my pot of tea and scones we began to chat about business in the town. He told me that the recession was still badly effecting the tourist industry leading to many owners being in financial trouble.

"It's the high class hotels which are suffering the most," he confided. "One manager I know has had to cut his prices to the same level as hotels which have far less facilities. But at the moment he just needs to fill the rooms and hope that the business will soon pick up."

Before leaving Ambleside I wandered around the corner from the café, into the quietness of St Mary's Parish Church; an imposing building which was designed by Sir Gilbert Scott in 1854. Here I looked inside the Wordsworth Chapel whose stained-glass memorial window was funded by subscriptions given by both American and English admirers of the poet. This now attracts tourists from all over the world who come to Lakeland on the Wordsworth trail. A glance in the Visitor's Book revealed that in a single week people from the USA, Japan, Australia, Canada, France and Greece had paid homage here.

A surprising feature of the building is a unique, colourful mural than spans one wall. It was painted in 1944 by Gordon Ransom to show the splendour of Ambleside's ancient Rushbearing Festival which is celebrated each July.

2

There are certain places in England which once visited, stay in the mind forever; St Oswald's churchyard in Grasmere is one of these. For here in spiritual serenity lies the body of Lakeland's most revered poet, William Wordsworth. His tombstone, simply inscribed, lies with those of his family in the village he cherished most, for he once described Grasmere as the 'loveliest spot that man hath ever found'. But as I stood in the hazy sunshine I was thinking that Wordsworth was more than a mere creator of fine words, for in a mystical way his very soul seemed to resound with the magic of Cumbria's countryside.

He was born on the 7th April 1770 at Cockermouth, the son of John Wordsworth a lawyer, and Ann Cookson who was the daughter of a linen draper from Penrith. William had three brothers, Richard, John and Christopher, and one sister, Dorothy, who was just over a year younger than himself and to whom he grew increasingly devoted. The family lived in a splendid Georgian house in the centre of the town, which was owned by his father's employer, Sir James Lowther.

As a child William was high-spirited and at times difficult to control, with a violent temper, but in contrast he had an inborn love for the beauty of landscape. His early education took place at a dame school in Penrith and at the local grammar school in Cockermouth. But the bliss of family life came to an abrupt end in 1778 when his mother sadly died of pneumonia. The children were then sent to live for long periods with various relatives, Dorothy living permanently in Halifax, was separated from her brothers for nine years.

But in 1779 William and his brother, Richard, found temporary contentment when they began studying at Hawkshead Grammar School. In this lovely Lakeland village the two boys were lodged in the home of Ann Tyson and her husband Hugh, who were both in their sixties. Their board was paid for by their grandparents, and here they remained for eight years, returning home only at holiday times. The boys were allowed complete freedom to roam around the local countryside by Dame Tyson, who became a substitute mother to them, at a vulnerable period in their young lives. But more grief came to them in 1783 when their father, after catching a chill while journeying through Lakeland in winter time, died at the early age of 42.

Under the influence of his mother's brilliant brother, William Cookson, who was a Fellow of St John's College in Cambridge, Wordsworth became an undergraduate there in 1787. During his first year he seemed to enjoy the social and academic experience, but then he became disillusioned. The subjects he was forced to study seemed inappropriate, he disliked the pressure of examinations and he discovered that the veneer of respectability of the university hid a corrupt regime. But he was able to make life bearable by, wherever possible, reading works which interested him and by visiting his friends and relatives. These included his beloved sister, Dorothy, who now lived in Norfolk and his childhood friend from Penrith, Mary Hutchinson. He also made his first foreign walking tour through France in the summer of 1790, before his final examinations which resulted in him receiving a rather poor, unclassified degree.

At this period he was filled with what seemed an uncertain future. His writing had barely begun and the possibility of taking holy orders, which was the normal practise for many graduates of St John's, held no appeal to him. But inwardly, in spite of his less that spectacular success, he somehow suspected that he had special talents and this was also felt by others who knew him, including his sister. However, finance was also a problem, for the Wordsworth children were owed a huge sum of £5000 by the Earl of Lonsdale, for work carried out by their father. The family eventually sued the rich landowner and won the case, but this left William with a dislike of the English aristocracy which lingered with him for many years.

In 1791 he undertook another tour through France, a country which was going through the trauma of the Revolution. Here he saw at first hand the poverty and cruelty which had brought about the overthrow of the ruling classes, of which he applauded. But it was a love affair with a young catholic girl named Annette Vallon which was to dramatically overshadow any political thoughts. Their passion led to her becoming pregnant, and the birth of a daughter named Caroline on the 15th December 1792. William, now penniless was unable to support her, so he returned to England with the intention of returning with some money and marrying the girl, who he seemed at the time to sincerely love. But shortly afterwards war between France and England came, making travel between the two countries impossible, and slowly over the next few years his desire to return diminished. Although his close family knew about this liaison, it was only in 1922 that the secret was disclosed to the public, after being uncovered by some clever research carried out by a Wordsworth scholar.

His literary ambitions were now coming to the forefront, in 1787 his first sonnet had been published anonymously in a magazine and now his first books appeared. These two slim volumes, *An Evening Walk and Descriptive Sketches*, were published by Joseph Johnson in 1793. The next few years found him living with Dorothy at Racedown, near Crewkerne and then at Affoxden in Somerset, and the beginning of his famous association with the brilliant Samuel Taylor Coleridge, the radical Robert Southey and many other literary giants. It was a vibrant, exciting period which fired Wordsworth's genius, saw Coleridge writing his epic *The Ancient Mariner*, and the two collaborating in the *Lyrical Ballads*. However, it was also a period of financial worry and at times, of failure. Both men saw their hopes of success in drama dashed when their plays were rejected by Covent Garden.

But it was when William and Dorothy returned home to Lakeland in 1799 that his work really began to flourish. For eight pounds a year they rented one of a cluster of small cottages known as Town End here in Grasmere and now known world-wide as lovely Dove Cottage. Coleridge and Southey, who were brother-in-laws, followed, creating a literary conclave in Lakeland which was later to draw in many of the great names of their day. Here Wordsworth wrote his much loved *The Daffodils, The Green Linnet*, his long, autobiographical poem, *The Prelude*, and his famous ode, *Intimations of Immortality*. From here too, he wandered in utter contentment with his sister and his friends to every corner of Lakeland, recapturing childhood memories and becoming completely enthralled by the magic of the landscape. Dorothy, who is now acknowledged to have had a mind equal to her brother and who was the inspiration behind many of his poems, vividly recorded their daily events in her famous Journals. It has been suggested in the past by one Wordsworth scholar, that William and Dorothy had an incestuous relationship, but this accusation is only based on flimsy evidence and speculation.

In October 1802 William Wordsworth married his childhood friend, Mary Hutchinson at Bromptom Church, Scarborough. The couple returned to live in Dove Cottage with Dorothy, and with improved finances, for the money owed to them by the Lowther family had at last been paid. In 1803, John, the first of five children was born here and further good news came when William acquired the patronage of the wealthy, Sir George Beaumont. But two years later sadness returned when he learned of the death of his brother, John, who was Captain of the East Indiaman, The Earl of Abergavenny. He was among three hundred men who drowned when the ship hit rocks in a gale off Portland Bill.

The Wordsworths lived for nine years in Dove Cottage, then in 1808 they moved to Alan Bank, a larger residence which lies across the valley. This was needed to accommodate their ever growing family, together with Mary's sister, Sara Hutchinson, and always a houseful of literary friends. These now included the rich and talented Thomas De Quincey, who took up the tenancy of Dove Cottage.

They again moved home in 1811 to The Rectory in Grasmere, close to St Oswald's Church. But this proved to be an terribly unhappy period during which two of their children, Thomas and Catherine, sadly died. This led them to take up residence in the imposing Rydal Mount, a lovely mansion set in acres of gardens which was to become their home for almost forty years. But this they did not own, merely renting it, for although he was now one of England's greatest poets his income was small. However, his financial position did again become more stable when he was given the government position as Distributor of Stamps for Westmorland, which paid a regular salary.

Over the next two decades, although he was often the butt of much satirical humour due to his eccentric ways and despite many poor reviews, his fame as a poet continued. His works sold well, if not in vast numbers; he enjoyed ice skating in winter and walking up the mountains in summer, and always the joy of exploring new places. In 1843, following the death of his fellow poet Southey, his talent was officially rewarded when he was appointed Poet Laureate.

William Wordsworth, unlike many of his contemporary poets, lived a long and mainly happy life. He died, perhaps appropriately, on St George's Day, 23rd April 1850 at the age of eighty. His devoted sister Dorothy, who had suffered from poor health for two decades, died in 1855 and was followed four years later by Mary. But the dazzling influence of the Wordsworths and their friends seems to have created an aura which lives on as strongly as ever in each corner of Lakeland. It has even been suggested that the area should be re-named as Wordsworthshire!

I strolled away from the Wordsworth graves, then after looking for brown trout in the clear waters of the meandering River Rothay which skirts the churchyard, I went inside of this ancient building. In *The Excursion*, Wordsworth described St Oswald's church as:

> Not raised in nice proportions was the pile,
> But large and massy; for duration built

Visitors were quietly staring upwards, admiring the timbered roof and then reading the memorial tablets which remembers the village's worthies. But I am told that August is the best time to come here, when the ancient Rushbearing Festival is celebrated. Many believe it began as a pagan ceremony associated with the Roman Floralia which was later adopted by the early Christian church. What seems to have been a practical way of keeping the once bare earth floor of the building, warm and fragrant, by laying down rushes, has clearly a deeper meaning. For it has become associated with a celebration of the victory of good over evil. This being epitomised in Grasmere by the glorious death of Saint Oswald, a Christian King who died fighting the pagan King Penda in AD 642.

Today it is a flowery and colourful event, which draws in the crowds to enjoy a day of laughter, music and Christian worship. It begins as a long procession of local children carrying banners and Traditional Bearings of woven rushes depicting religious themes, who are accompanied by six Rush Maidens in dresses of green and white who hold a Rush Sheet. As they wind their way through the village streets they are joined by the Bishop, clergy, churchwardens and a band and choir. Their arrival here at the church, which has been decorated with rushes, marks the start of the Rushbearing Service. This includes special prayers and the singing of Rushbearing Hymns, which includes:

> To-day we come from farm and fell,
> Wild flowers and rushes green we twine,
> We sing the hymn we love so well,
> And worship at St Oswald's shrine.

Also associated with the event is the distribution of Rushbearing Gingerbread, a local delicacy which is marked with the stamp of St Oswald. This tradition goes back at least to the beginning of the last century and is now made by the local Helm Bakery.

And it was just beyond the lychgate, in what was once the village school, that I purchased a mouth-watering piece of another type of gingerbread which has tempted tourists for over 140 years. This business was started in 1854 by Sarah Nelson, a local lady who sold her home-made confectionery from outside her cottage. As more visitors came to Grasmere, often to visit the nearby Wordsworth graves, it slowly began to flourish and has now become an essential part of the tourist trail. Gerald and Margaret Wilson who own the business, and are only the third family to occupy the shop since the days of Sarah Nelson, now have requests for their gingerbread from many parts of the world.

I continued my stroll around this lovely village, which in spite of its popularity remains largely unspoiled. In the English Lakes Perfumery, from which permeated a score of different exotic aromas, I could hear the chatter of a party of Americans who had arrived by coach. I wondered if they were aware that they were following in the illustrious footsteps of two of their fellow countrymen. For both Emerson the great philosopher, and Woodrow Wilson who became the 28th President of the United States, once explored the streets of Grasmere.

With the smell of wood smoke filling the air and a hint of drizzle on the fellsides, I joined the pathway with follows the shoreline of placid Grasmere

Lake. This small spoonful of silver set in a green vale provides one of Lakeland's loveliest waterside walks. For two hours I revelled in its tranquillity, watching gulls glide over the water, looking upwards to the gullies of Stone Arthur and Seat Sandal, and thinking of the laughter of the generations of walkers who have passed this way. From the elevation of the Loughrigg Terrace I gazed down to the wooded banks of the Rothay, and beyond to the beauty of Rydal Water, once known as Routha Mere, which was being guarded by a soaring buzzard.

Returning by the old road, which lies between Heron Pike and the northern end of the twin lakes, I ended my walk as all pilgrims to Grasmere should, at Dove Cottage. Joining a group of young Japanese students I looked at the manuscripts, furnishings, pictures and a thousand and one pieces of memorabilia which chart the lives of William and Dorothy and Mary. It was here in 1956 that the famous travel writer, H.V. Morton, came with the great-grandson of the poet, the Reverend C.W. Wordsworth. Sitting beside a plaque of his famous ancestor, it was as if William Wordsworth had returned to Dove Cottage, for the clergyman's profile was almost identical with that of the poet.

3

On an overcast August day, which the weathermen said would remain unsettled, I returned to Grasmere. At Ambleside I had joined a slow trail of cars whose occupants were dressed in wax jackets, tweed caps and appeared unusually fit and tanned. This was a clue to their destination, for today was the third Thursday following the first Monday in August, which every Cumbrian knows is the traditional day for the Grasmere Sports!

It seemed like every policeman in the county had been called in to try to control the traffic, but their task was too much.

"I give up," exclaimed a pretty, smiling policewoman as she directed me on to the sports field off the A591 road. Behind her a never ending line of cars, coaches and buses, disappeared up the road to Dunmail Raise.

I paid my entrance fee, then a steward directed me down a steep grassy slope where I parked my car. Seconds later I was joined by another car, whose driver would have been better occupied taking a Grand Prix circuit. He speeded down the hillside, braked at the last minute and almost demolished the rear of the pink Bouncy Castle. With around five acres of land on which to park he had decided to place his car about three inches from my own car door. This inevitably led to an heated exchange of words.

The flat green sports field, which nestles on the edge of Grasmere Village is overlooked on all sides by the rising fells. The actual sporting events, which consist of Cumberland and Westmorland wrestling, hound trails, short and middle distance races, leaping and fell races, take place in a large central arena. Adjacent to this are rows of trade stands protected by canvas awnings, a funfair, a craft marquee, bookmakers, refreshments stalls and dozens of other attractions which, I discovered, give these Old English Games a splendid carnival atmosphere.

It was probably the Vikings who started it all, for they are known to have been keen wrestlers. They settled here in Cumbria over a thousand years ago, as well as in Iceland and in northern France, where this sport is also part of the local culture. It later became a feature of the village celebrations prior to the Rushbearing ceremony held in St Oswald's church, and wrestling bouts also took place during the annual Sheepfair.

Fell runners at the start of the Senior Guides Race.

Fell running, of which the Senior Guides Race at Grasmere is the premier English event, has also a long history. One of the earliest records tells how King Malcolm of Scotland, during the 11th century, chose his messengers for their ability to race up to the mountain tops. Here in Lakeland it was the hardy local men who guided the wealthy Victorian tourists up to the summits of the fells, who first began competing. The winners of what is still called the Guides Race, could boast that they were the toughest in Lakeland and hopefully demand a higher fee.

The modern Grasmere Sports which began in 1865, was organised in the early days by some of the village's leading residents. But as the event grew in popularity it became necessary to employ a Sports Manager. The first man to hold this position was Myles D. Dickinson in 1936, and the present holder is Dr. Chris Lane of Ambleside. The Earl of Lonsdale, who is the High Sheriff of Cumbria, is the President of the event.

Before the sports got underway I joined the fascinating mixture of humanity that had been drawn here to Grasmere. We wandered around the crowded avenues of stalls, being tempted to purchase perhaps a packet of Cumberland sausages, a pair of real leather gloves or take a years subscription of Cumbria Magazine. Two polite young men who pilot Tornado Jets, were explaining to a small group of local people why low-flying through Lakeland is really necessary. The four pretty girls who were looking on in starry eyed admiration, self-consciously giggling, needed no convincing.

"Want, want, want. You're always wanting something," shouted a short tempered young mother to her two small children who had been tugging her hands towards a toy stall.

Two men, who had a huge open sided lorry piled high with coloured towels, seemed to be doing a roaring trade.

"You won't get a better bargain in the whole of Cumbria, luv."

"Aye, but they 're all foreign," came the bitter reply from a grey haired man in the crowd, who I suspect may have suffered redundancy from a textile mill.

Farmers with weather beaten faces like tanned leather, Japanese families who had just been to Dove Cottage, painfully thin athletes with figures like greyhounds, and quick witted groups of retired women from Yorkshire, all mingled together in the wonderfully cosmopolitan crowd.

There were also dogs. Bright eyed collies who would have been more at home among the high crags of Helvellyn or Scafell. Overfed labradors always ready to sit down, ever-curious Yorkshire terriers which every child wanted to pat and yapping hounds, waiting for their big moment later in the afternoon.

Peter Shawcross, from a falconry and conservation centre in the Yorkshire Dales, was creating a lot of attention for he had a large, burgundy coloured hawk perched on his arm. Nearby, sitting like a king on a throne, was a magnificent eagle, its cruel eyes scanning the crowd with aristocratic arrogance. Its partner, a fluffy short-eared owl with a speckled breast, seemed much more placid, having accepted its confinement with quiet dignity.

In the craft marquee men and women who had spent the dark days of winter perfecting their artistic skills, could now sit back, hoping that their goods would find appreciative customers. Framed photographs, which caught the subtle moods of Lakeland's changing seasons, glistening minerals made into earrings and necklaces, and ornately carved walking sticks adorned the stalls.

People looked with admiration at the work of these dedicated artists, which include a husband and wife team who produce superb hand-made rocking horses. John and Dorothy Woods from Westhoughton in Lancashire are typical of this new generation of cottage workers. Individuals who are attempting to reverse the effects of the Industrial Revolution by working not in a factory, but in their own home. It is refreshing to discover that in this age when computer controlled machines churn out goods by the million, such individuals still have the ability to follow in the footsteps of our ancestors. It seems that the traditions and skills of those craftsmen who built the great cathedrals of York, Durham and Canterbury, perfected the furniture of Chippendale and Sheraton, or the porcelain of Wedgwood, have not been completely forgotten.

"Ladies and gentlemen, the sports are about to begin," came an announcement over the loud speaker.

The musicians on the rostrum who were playing a jaunty Irish tune quickly ended their number. Men standing in the beer tent began to drain their pint glasses of Jennings bitter and plump ladies sitting in the refreshment tent reluctantly ate their last chicken sandwich. We all then made our way to the perimeter of the sports arena.

Wrestling, which is the oldest of all the sporting events held here in Grasmere, got quickly underway in a corner of the field. Strangers like myself, whose only knowledge of the sport are the theatrical bouts seen on television were happily surprised; Cumberland and Westmorland style wrestling I found to be much more attractive from a spectators point of view. The contestants wear a traditional costume which consists of a sleeveless vest, long tight trousers which are tucked into their stockings and dark coloured velvet trunks which are embroidered with attractive patterns.

The bout begins with the contestants facing each other, supervised by a referee looking on. They then grip their opponent around the body, resting their chin on his right shoulder. A contest of strength now follows with the two interlocked men slowly moving around the grass. Suddenly the swift action begins as one man tries to throw the other. If any part of a contestants body other than his feet touch the ground or if his grip is broken, then he loses the bout.

We were entertained first by the wrestling of young boys who were under 15 years old. As the afternoon progressed the age and weight limits increased, ending in the final meeting of the titans, huge Lakeland giants who looked as if they could easily carry a sheep under each arm!

While the wrestling bouts continued the other athletic events were also taking place in the arena, accompanied by the light-hearted banter of the official announcer. His comments over the loud speaker system, spoken in a splendid north-country accent, created an atmosphere of jollity.

"If you see the police walking about in pairs, don't worry. It doesn't mean there's trouble, they just get very lonely."

Later, as a number of presentations to the winning contestants took place, the rival announcers vied for the attention of the crowd in hilarious fashion.

"Please let me finish before you present the cups. This happened last year and now its happening again!"

The excited barks of the hounds as they jumped from the back of Range Rovers to be led towards the arena, heralded the start of an event which is unique to Cumbria. Hound Trailing, which evolved during the last century, is said to have first become popular among the former supporters of cock-fighting. The trail-hounds, which at first glance look similar to foxhounds, are in fact quite different. They are leaner, having been specially bred for their speed in climbing the steep fellside, but require less stamina. Their performance is attributed to a diet which is kept a strict secret by their trainers, but is said to be similar to that once fed to fighting-cocks. Still known as cock-loaves, it has as its basis eggs, raisins and sherry.

In a scurry of activity, watched by officials from the Hound Trailing Association, the animals were released to follow an invisible trail of aniseed and paraffin oil. It was fascinating to watch their seemingly effortless progress, unaided by any human intervention, up the steep fellside. But the exciting climax came on their descent into the arena after having completed the arduous course circuit. At this point the close bond between the hounds and their trainers became apparent. Responding to individual whistles, shouts and hand signals, the hounds were coaxed in a final sprint past the finishing line, to the claps and cheers of the delighted spectators.

During the afternoon the sky began to grow progressively darker as the scurrying clouds slowly covered the high summits of Seat Sandal and Greatrigg Man. By the time the Senior Guides Race had begun a soft drizzle had descended to the valley.

"This rain makes the fellside very slippy, but these tough athletes can cope with any conditions."

We watched as the runners sped from the arena then crossed the main road, before beginning their steep ascent up the mountain, while the announcer continued his knowledgeable commentary.

"This is the main event of the day ladies and gentlemen. Remember the winner becomes the English Hill Champion, which for fell-runners is like winning a gold medal at the Olympics. What? Oh I'm told its better than winning a gold medal at the Olympics."

Slowly the winding snake of runners fought their way up what seemed to be almost a vertical slope. They passed over a dry stone wall then curved around the rocks to finally reach the summit of Butter Crag from which fluttered a flag. The shouts of the excited crowd roared across the field as the names of the leading athletes were received from the stewards. This led the bookies into frenzied activity as they shouted to encourage possible punters who might still want to bet.

"I'll still give you six to one on McGovern and he's among the leaders."

The runners had taken around nine minutes to reach the high-point, but their lung bursting descent took only around three. They seemed to tumble down the fell like a human waterfall. Soon they were speeding across the road to the finishing line.

"Yes its John Atkinson who has taken this years title in a time of 13 minutes and 19.6 seconds. Will you also please give a big hand to local veteran runner A. Riley who is now approaching the field. Its a big day for the Riley family for both his daughter and his son have successfully competed today."

Reluctantly I left one of Lakeland's finest social gatherings.

4

It was mid-morning when I took the road northwards, climbing up that lovely incline which is familiar to all Lakeland visitors – Dunmail Raise. There is a marvellous feeling of excitement about this highway, it fills travellers with eager anticipation. Perhaps this is something to do with its long history, for it is probably Lakeland's oldest crossing point. The Romans came this way, as did the Norsemen, for King Dunmail was their leader. It is said that he was defeated in battle here in AD 945 by King Edmund of England, and some people believe that a cairn of stones at the summit of the road mark his burial place. During the 18th century the first trickle of early Lakers wound their way up Dunmail Raise from Grasmere, then later, with northern common-sense, it became the last road in Britain to resound with the hooves of the Mail Coach, for no railway was going to ruin this landscape.

From my car window I could see on my left the greenness of rough pastureland watered by the infant Rothay, quickly ending in the bronze of the steeply sloping fells. Helm Crag, known as the Lion and the Lamb, Gibson Knott and Steel Fell are the picturesque names of some of these summits which stretch unending to the west for over twenty miles. Herdwick sheep were feeding with determination behind dry stone walls, while groups of walkers in bright anoraks of red and blue pitted their stamina against the rising hillside. On my right the mountains seemed to be steeper and higher, for the rugged bulk of Fairfield, Dollywagon Pike and Nethermost Pike are the giant stepping stones which lead to the king of these summits, Helvellyn.

I descended towards the wooded valley of Wythburn, then took the narrow lane to the left which hugs the western shore of Thirlmere. Overlooked by towering crags, conifer woodlands and cascading becks, the silver water of the lake was glinting like a precious stone in the bright sunlight. Leaving my car on the roadside I walked towards a gap in the overhanging trees to gaze across the lake at the curving profile of Helvellyn, which looked surprisingly gentle from this vantage point. In the quietness two chaffinches and an inquisitive robin hopped in my direction along the perimeter wall, checking if there was any chance of a crust.

Any stranger who comes to Thirlmere will undoubtedly say that it is beautiful, but behind its present face lies a story of protest and heartache. For when Wordsworth and his friends came here and carved their names upon a boulder, they would have seen a different, more pastoral landscape. This changed a century ago when an army of workmen arrived at this spot to build Manchester's first Lakeland reservoir. It took a decade to erect a dam, destroy a cluster of ancient cottages and drown part of the old road. What had been two small natural lakes named Wythburn Water and Leathes Water, were linked together to create the new, three and a half mile long Thirlmere, whose level was raised by a massive fifty-four feet. A marvellous feat of engineering then took this water by aqueduct for ninety-five miles to the thirsty city, but left only sad memories for those who had seen their community destroyed.

The lovely Vale of St John looked fresh and serene in the crisp air. Soft beams of sunlight were lighting up this quiet green valley and casting giant shadows in the gullies of the high fells. I drove past the rugged face of Castle Crag, then followed the by-way which mimics the twisting path of St John's Beck. When I arrived at Castlerigg Stone Circle I expected to be alone, but this was not the case, for I discovered that the fame of this 3,000 years old Bronze Age monument has spread to foreign parts. As I joined the pathway which leads across the boggy turf up to the impressive stones, I was joined by a colourful group of eastern visitors. This amphitheatre from a past age was transformed by their laughter and chatter, for they seemed to be utterly delighted by its presence. One man, who was dressed in a white turban and a red, flowing cloak, began to prance between the upright stones, giving the lead for others to follow. · ·

Unable to decide from which country they originated, my curiosity got the better of me, so I approached one of the younger men. Wearing a brightly coloured balaclava which covered his ears, his friendly bearded face grinned out at me, looking like a Himalayan Sherpa.

"We are from Malaysia," he answered, "and are on a tour of Britain." In perfect English he then went on to tell me how they all loved England, but were finding it very cold.

For half an hour we strolled around the site, as he told me about life in his fascinating homeland. The cold breeze, the snow topped mountains, and the chatter of foreign tongues around these pagan stones, created a unique and memorable atmosphere. As I reluctantly waved the laughing group farewell, I wondered what Keats, who came here in 1818 with his friend Charles Brown, would have written of such a meeting?

As I walked through the door of the small hotel which stands in the bustling centre of Keswick, I was greeted by the smiling lady owner.

"I hang my head in shame," she said in a broad Northumbrian accent, "I told you on the phone that it was going to be sunny and its starting to rain! I'm usually correct with my predictions, but you can't win every one."

However, the cosiness and warmth of the hotel bedroom more that made up for the impending dismal weather. Sipping a cup of coffee I stared out over her large garden which was filled with the remnants of last seasons vegetables and the yellow of newly arrived daffodils. Blue tits hung upside down from her washing line, blackbirds scavenged beneath the hedgerows and a solitary jackdaw glided silently over the rooftop. But overshadowing the whole scene was the huge towering bulk of Skiddaw, its deep-cut gullies disappearing into a ghostly grey mist. Beneath it lay the lovely green hill of Latrigg, whose curving ridge was being traversed by a group of walkers who looked like black ants in the falling light.

On my way to spend the last hour of the afternoon in Keswick Museum, I stopped to read a sign which gave a list of some little-known Lakeland facts which might win many a pub quiz night. Did you know that Robert Southey wrote the first *History of Brazil* and *The Three Bears*, and that Lord Nelson gave him the signal gun from *HMS Victory*? That Keswick is Norse for Cheese Farm and that in 1597 the plague killed a tenth of its population? That Frederick Myers, a Keswick Poet once swam across the river below Niagara Falls and it was at Keswick that Beatrix Potter first drew Squirrel Nutkin? And of course everyone knows that George Washington paved his porch with St Bees sandstone and that the book, *Gulliver's Travels*, was inspired by White-haven!

This collection of little known facts was a fitting introduction for my tour of the small museum which I discovered contains a miscellany of fascinating objects. With surprise I learned that as early as 1785 Keswick boasted a museum of curiosities which was established by a local man named Peter Crosthwaite and from which the present collection evolved. Here I gazed at Southey's clogs, the key to Greta Hall, the dress shoes worn by Ruskin at Queen Victoria's coronation and the diary of Thomas De Quincey. Beneath a glass cabinet I looked at Sir Hugh Walpole's original manuscripts together with letters written to him by T.E. Lawrence, Joseph Conrad and John Masefield. Nearby stood cases of stuffed birds, climbing gear once owned by the Abraham Brothers, geology specimens gathered by Jonathon Otley and the 650-year-old grotesque form of a mummified cat! But pride of place is given to a huge plaster relief map of Lakeland which was created by local artist Joseph Flintoft during the last century, and which once had pride of place in the Moot Hall.

Keswick, a pleasant market town of old inns and narrow streets, which lie snugly between the banks of the River Greta and the placid shore of Derwentwater, is an ideal base from which to explore Lakeland. In every direction there are mountains and valleys and lakes, radiating out in alluring temptation. An indecisive mountain walker who glances at his map here, is faced with a bewildering choice of delights. Should he climb Skiddaw and Blencathra, Helvellyn or Scafell, Cat Bells or Eel Crags? Why not a more modest walk through the woods to Watendlath or perhaps a saunter around the edge of the lake? But its almost lunchtime, too late to travel far and the smell of steak pie coming from the kitchen of the George is irresistible. Perhaps another day!

Lying in the centre of Keswick is the Moot Hall, a building which gives the impression that it might have been stolen from Switzerland. It was built in 1813 in this Alpine design to pander to the guide book writers of the time, who constantly compared Keswick to the mountain villages of Europe. It was originally used as a court house in which the Court Leet and Petty Sessions were held, but it also doubled as part of the Market. In the clock tower is an

The Alpine-style Moot Hall is situated in the heart of Keswick.

ancient bell which was brought here from the ancestral home of the Radcliffe family who lived on Lord's Island in Derwentwater. The family, who were the Earls of Derwentwater, lost their land in 1715 for supporting the Jacobite Rebellion.

Today the bottom part of the building contains the Tourist Information Centre, but it was in the cool of the evening that I climbed to the second storey to attend a slide lecture entitled *Lakeland In Winter*. This was presented by Ray McHaffie, who is one of Lakeland's most experienced climbers, a great character and surely an inspiration to many young people. For escaping from the prison of a broken home in the early fifties he found excitement and adventure among the Lakeland mountains. Exchanging the empty promises of the Teddy-Boy gangs, which were in fashion at the time, he discovered he had a natural ability for rock-climbing. This led to him pioneering over 200 new routes and forty years on his love of the Lakeland Mountains is still as strong. He now works for the National Trust, supervising the rebuilding of upland footpaths.

For over an hour I sat in the audience of bearded climbers, retired couples and enthralled youngsters, looking at his superb colour slides of Lakeland's snow-laden mountain tops. We saw hair-raising scenes of ice-climbing up frozen waterfalls, we looked at the incredible beauty of pink skies over Great Gable, and we heard of the horror of mountain accidents.

"We call Helvellyn the Killer Mountain. Each winter six or seven bodies are brought down by the Mountain Rescue teams. And its nearly always from the same spot – below Swirral Edge.

Well I must end now, I've got to be up early tomorrow. We're repairing the highest footpath in England which is on Scafell. And it involves a seven mile walk to work – all up-hill!"

5

For Lakeland visitors like myself, who cannot resist delving into the unwanted cast-offs of others, Keswick I discovered has a host of charity shops. Following in the great tradition of jumble sales, flea-markets and car-boot sales, which are now firmly established in every town in England, the charity shop success-fully directs its profits towards the needy. Here in a marvellous Aladdin's Cave of miscellany, one persons junk is miraculously transformed into another persons treasure.

As I gazed upon the splendid assortment of second-hand clothes, sadly discarded books, old radios and cracked pottery, I began to speculate on their forlorn journey to this 'last chance saloon'. Had those terrible red gloves been received with a contrived smile from Auntie Joan four Christmas's ago and immediately hidden away in a drawer? Perhaps the dust of Great Gable is still ingrained in the half worn soles of those walking boots, but why are they here? Can ageing limbs no longer manage the steep fellside slopes or even worse? Had middle-aged grandmothers, now pleasantly rounded, once danced in mini-skirts to the music of the Beatles from that old transistor radio? I opened a well preserved volume of H.V. Morton's *In the Steps of the Master* which was inscribed 'To mother with love from Veda, Keswick, July 1943.' A once treasured book purchased half a century ago in the dark days of wartime Britain and filled with unknown memories was now seeking a new home. I bought it for a pound.

Hiding beneath the bookshelf in a tattered brown cardboard box I discovered half a dozen dog-eared copies of one of Lakeland's great success stories, that splendid little magazine, *Cumbria*. Now over forty years old this Lakeland institution plops on to 16,000 door mats each month, then with north country thrift, is passed on to at least five times as many readers. It began life as an amateur publication which had been founded by a group of members of the Youth Hostels' Association under the editorship of Leslie Hewkin. Deciding that its success demanded a more professional approach they contacted Harry J. Scott who had a small publishing company at Clapham in Yorkshire from which the very popular magazine, *The Dalesman*, was issued. The proposal to pass on the publication was quickly accepted and the first edition of the new series was published in April 1951. At this time the Lake District embraced parts of the counties of Lancashire, Cumberland and Westmorland, so the magazine's title anticipated by over thirty years the boundary changes of 1974 which was to create the new county of Cumbria.

As I browsed through the pages of the twenty-year-old copies of the magazine I quickly became absorbed in the features, which is surely the secret of its success. For its well written tib-bits from so many aspects of Lakeland life appear ageless and highly readable. Much of this success can be attributed to the guidance of W.R. Mitchell who for almost four decades was first a writer and then the editor of both *Cumbria* and *The Dalesman*. A native of Skipton, he began his writing career as a cub reporter on the *Craven Herald* in 1943, before joining the staff of the magazines five years later. In the early days, working on a very tight budget the luxury of a car was out of the question so he travelled by train and on foot, building up an unrivalled knowledge of the people, wild life and landscape of the north-west. After writing tens of thousands of words for the publications Bill Mitchell retired in 1987, but he still continues to contribute to both magazines as well as adding each year to his astonishing list of over sixty books which he has written about life in Lakeland and the Yorkshire Dales.

Author W.R. Mitchell who, for many years, was the editor of the much-loved *Cumbria* magazine.

I later bought a current copy of *Cumbria* to compare it with the earlier editions. Due to the advances in printing most of its illustrations are now in glorious colour and it contains more pages, yet essentially it remains the same. A much loved publication which uniquely reflects the special richness of Lakeland in a way that appeals to both residents and to visitors alike.

3

Keswick to Caldbeck

I go to Friar's Crag in late evening where I see the sun set over Derwentwater, remembering John Ruskin and St. Herbert. I reach the summit of Skiddaw in a gale, visit Southey's grave at Crosthwaite, then leave Keswick. I discover the splendour of Cockermouth, see Wordsworths's birthplace, find a link with Pitcairn Island, and end up in John Peel Country.

1

Fell walkers and climbers, having reluctantly descended from the mountains, were now earnestly discussing their exploits in the many old inns which hide among the alleyways of Keswick. Their evening conversation was littered with such names as Napes Needle, the Corridor Route, Black Sail Pass and Pillar, in the same way as a Londoner might mention Fleet Street or the Edgware Road. After enjoying a large plateful of cod, chips and peas in Ye Olde Golden Lion, which stands adjacent to the Moot Hall, I joined the groups of strollers who had wandered down to the shoreline of Derwentwater.

I stood on the end of the little wooded peninsula of Friar's Crag gazing out over the supreme loveliness of the lake. The air was warm and still, the sky had taken on the soft blue of late evening. As the sun began its descent the cotton-wool clouds had a mantle of gold that was quickly turning to rose pink. On the opposite shore the fells of Cat Bells and Maiden Moor were silhouetted like velvet, giving the impression that they were not real at all, but like a stage set fashioned from cardboard. Below me the mirror surface of the water was only broken by the wash of a solitary rower as he energetically propelled his boat towards Derwent Isle.

This small wooded island has had a chequered history. It was originally known as Hest Holme then when it came into the ownership of the monks of Furness Abbey in the 13th century it was called Vicar's Island. Following the Dissolution of the Monasteries it was given to John Williamson who in turn sold it to a band of German miners who had settled in Cumbria. Later it became

Derwentwater, where Saint Herbert built his island hermitage during the 7th century.

the property of the powerful Radcliffe family who lived in a mansion on nearby Lord's Island. One of the Radcliffes died on Bosworth Field, then a later member was created the Earl of Derwentwater by King James I. The family became strong supporters of the Stuarts which led to the last Earl losing his head for his involvement in the rebellion of 1715. He is said to have spent his last night in Keswick at the George Hotel which is the town's oldest inn. Following his execution on Tower Hill a magnificent and rare display of the Aurora Borealis appeared in the north. People quickly associated this event with the earl's death, so the Northern Lights became known locally as Lord Derwentwater's Lights.

Friar's Crag is said to be the place from which pilgrims were rowed across the water to visit the shrine of St Herbert which lies on the small island which still bears his name. He was a close friend of the most brilliant English Christian of the period, St Cuthbert, but the two men had entirely different personalities. St Herbert was a solitary man, having chosen a hermit existence on the island where he could devote himself to a life of prayer. St Cuthbert had risen to become a great bishop whose skill at preaching had fanned the fire of Christianity in the north. But their common faith drew them together, each year they would meet on Lindisfarne to discuss their doctrine of eternal life.

On one occasion St Herbert heard that his bishop was coming to visit Carlisle, known then as Lugubalia, so he decided to make his annual devotion in the city. The two holy men met to discuss their business, but the humble Herbert was shocked to hear the final words of Cuthbert.

"Remember brother Herbert, that whatever ye have to say and ask of me, do it now, for after we depart home we shall not meet again, and see one another corporally in this world, for I know well the time of my dissolution is at hand, and the laying aside of this earthly tabernacle draweth on a pace."

When Herbert heard this he fell at Cuthbert's feet begging him that "they might depart home for heaven together." The bishop immediately began to pray and according to the Venerable Bede, who recorded the tale, their wish was granted for both men died on the same day, March 19th 688.

In 1374 a mandate was issued by the Bishop of Appleby which ensured that St Herbert would never be forgotten. He ordered that the Vicar of Crosthwaite must visit the island each year on St Herbert's day, which is the 13th April, to hold a commemoration service.

Half hidden among the foliage of Friar's Crag I stopped to look at the memorial to John Ruskin who regarded this spot as among the three most beautiful places in all of Europe. Words written beneath his portrait recall his childhood memories:

'The first thing that I remember as an event in life was being taken by my nurse to the brow of Friar's Crag on Derwentwater'.

With darkness falling fast I took the pathway back towards the town. As I passed the mobile Century Theatre I could hear the laughter of the audience who were being enthralled by the humour of Alan Ayckbourn. I paused in the churchyard of St John to read an inscription to the author of the classic novel *Mist Over Pendle*, Robert Neill, who shares a final resting place with many other literary figures including Sir Hugh Walpole.

2

Although grey trailing clouds were hiding the tops of the high fells the day was bright, with patches of sunshine occasionally lighting up the rugged outline of Borrowdale. Leaving the Carlisle road on the outskirts of Keswick I followed a meandering narrow lane that ascended above the town. Shrouded by woodland it came to an abrupt end at a small car park that overlooks the lovely green slopes of Latrigg. It was no surprise to find half a dozen cars already parked, for this is the popular starting point for the ascent up Skiddaw, which as Alfred Wainwright remarked, boasts 'probably the first path up a Lakeland mountain'.

Skiddaw is special in many ways. Rising up to 3054 feet (931m) above sea level it is the forth highest in England, its rocks are said to be the most ancient, but more that this it is a friendly, much-loved giant. Its gentle curving profile, whose rearing heights dominate the landscape with their ever changing hues, welcome the stranger. It has no savage crags or daunting ravines like Scafell or Great Gable, its attraction lies more in its bracken fringed uplands, its murmuring becks and its magical atmosphere of remoteness.

As I was lacing up my boots I received my first 'Good morning' from three healthy looking women who, together with a black labrador and a young eager collie, were also about to climb Skiddaw. One of the most rewarding parts of walking in the mountains is this sense of comradeship that is instantly apparent. Strangers who would not give each other a second glance, when say walking along Oxford Street in London or Princes Street in Edinburgh, when meeting on a remote Lakeland path will immediately strike up a conversation. It is as if throwing away the shackles of 'civilization' suddenly brings about a transformation in the normal reserved British character. No doubt this fascinating change in human behaviour has been explained somewhere in the works of Desmond Morris.

After walking for about ten minutes I came to a fine carved cross which sits on a stone plinth close to the path. Sitting appropriately in this amphitheatre of hills it is a memorial to three members of the Hawell family who worked at Lonscale during the last century. They were all shepherds and noted breeders of Herdwick Sheep. While grand and famous men of their generation are now so soon forgotten, this wind swept monument still remembers these tough Cumbrians. Their simple epitaph reads:

> Great Shepherd of Thy heavenly flock
> These men have left our hill
> Their feet were on the living rock
> Oh guide and bless them still.

Beyond this point I discovered that the path reaches its steepest gradient; a lung-bursting struggle for many. On the right the hillside falls quickly away into a deep-cut valley through which flows Whit Beck. Fringed with hardy conifer trees, it then rises majestically upwards on the far side to reach the grassy summit of Lonscale Fell. The great bulk of its slopes hid from me the most formidable of all the mountains in the Skiddaw range, Blencathra. Also known as Saddleback, its craggy spurs provide a magnificent backcloth for motorists driving from Keswick to Penrith.

Continuing up the well worn track I passed the site of what was once known as the Skiddaw Hut, a place where Victorian travellers took refreshment. This was a forceful reminder that I was following in the steps of the famous, for this mist laden mountain became a magnet for these early tourists who sometimes ascended on the back of a pony. Although English explorers of the last century had a reputation for understatement, those of earlier generations tended to exaggerate the terrors of travel. But one of the most charming accounts of this ascent is given by Mrs Ann Radcliffe in her Description of the Scenery in a Ride over *Skiddaw*, which was written in 1794. Her route was followed in 1802 by Charles and Mary Lamb, who being town dwellers, found it hard-going but eventually managed to reach the summit. 'Mary was excessively tired when she got about half-way up', Charles recalled in a letter to Thomas Manning. He went on to describe the view as: 'Oh, its fine black head, and the bleak air atop of it, with a prospect of mountains all about, making you giddy'. However, a decade later John Keats was able to climb the mountain before breakfast, but perhaps he was a very early riser!

Robert Southey wrote a fascinating and extremely humorous account of an ascent of Skiddaw made in 1815. This was to light a victory bonfire to celebrate the successful Battle of Waterloo. He and his family were accompanied by the Wordsworths, James Boswell, son of Dr Johnson's famous biographer, together with a large group of friends and neighbours. The intention was to toast the victors in rum diluted with water, which had been carried up in separate containers. However, William Wordsworth, who had a reputation for being clumsy, inadvertently kicked over the water barrel which spilled away. He tried to hide his guilt, but this was discovered by the group who gathered around him singing: "Twas you that kicked the kettle down! 'twas you sir, you!" Consequently the rum had to be drunk neat, which resulted in the best mountain top party ever seen in Lakeland. It ended with one of the group riding his pony down to Keswick facing back-to-front!

I continued the steep climb which at last eased out into a lesser gradient as I reached the 2000 feet contour. I was now ascending the edge of Jenkin Hill whose summit was partially covered in thick mist. Down this slope suddenly appeared a tall limping man who gave the impression he was most happy to be descending. In a loud Scottish accent he boomed out, "Be careful, its blowin' a gale up there and you can only see five yards. I almost lost my way". Then he quickly turned, striding with determination down the track.

Just before walking into the clouds beneath Skiddaw Little Man, I turned around to scan the marvellous Lakeland panorama. Far below I could see the green of Latrigg, the grey rooftops of Keswick and the sunshine lighting up the splendour of Borrowdale and the Newlands Valley. Derwentwater appeared as a splash of silver, dotted here and there with the black of its islands. Only the lower slopes of Cat Bells and Eel Crags were visible, their summits being enveloped by a bank of cloud which continued southwards to hide the high mountains around Honister Pass. Turning eastwards I could see the lovely St John's in the Vale, and the towering uplands that end in Helvellyn. For ten minutes I gazed out on the sweeping landscape which lay before me like a map, trying to identify half hidden peaks. I then reluctantly walked into the swirling mist, which like a drawn curtain swept away the view.

The wide path now led up the eastern flank of the mountain, with occasional breaks in the cloud revealing a vast perspective of hills and sky, completely devoid of human habitation. Quite suddenly as I reached the exposed ridge the wind changed from a pleasant breeze into a raging gale, it was like walking from summer into winter. Visibility was down to a few yards, figures of walkers, whose anorak hoods made them look like ghostly monks, battled to stay upright. I fought my way to the high point, but any hopes I had of staying there to eat my picnic had long since been dashed. My ungloved hands were blue with cold, and moisture from the clouds began to condense into large globules on my clothing. Having reached the summit I quickly turned around to retrace my route, thinking that the Scotsman had been quite right.

After a descent of just a few hundred feet both the wind and the clouds had completely disappeared. In the lee of the hillside I was at last able to eat my sandwiches and drink my coffee in comfort. But soon I was joined by the young collie which I had previously seen with the three women walkers. Obviously made ravenous by its climb it almost demanded a share of my food. In spite of calls from its owner it refused to budge until I had fed it two ham sandwiches which it gulped down in one second flat. Sitting on the sheltered vantage point I had a splendid view of Lakeland's unique mosaic, a colourful panorama of mountains, lakes and valleys which stretch to the sky. I could well understand why George Smith, who became known as the Skiddaw Hermit, once chose these slopes for his home.

It is said that it was in the 1860s that shepherds first found signs that someone had been living in one of their remote fellside huts. At first they were unable to track him down, then by chance they came across him near to a remote waterfall. But they were surprised, for instead of a rough tramp which they had expected to find, the Skiddaw Hermit turned out to be a talented artist who was capturing the view on his canvas. It was later revealed that he had been born about 1825 in Banffshire, the son of a respected family. But his artistic temperament had made him unsettled, he became a wanderer; a way of life generally viewed with suspicion by landowners. For a time he lived here on the side of Skiddaw, gaining the respect of the local people. He was able to eke out a meagre living by painting portraits in both water-colour and oil, but sadly none of these works have ever been traced. One day he quite suddenly departed from Skiddaw as quickly as he had appeared, but then he turned up in the Ambleside area, where he regularly worshipped at the local chapel. There he again won respect as a honest eccentric, for although he was very poor he never resorted to begging. Sadly his mind eventually failed and the man who is forever remembered as the Skiddaw Hermit died in a Banff-shire asylum in 1873.

As I made the final descent to my car I passed a group of elderly walkers who were resting near a stile.

"Is it windy on top?" a small grey haired man asked me, with a twinkle in his eye.

"Just a bit," I replied.

"What! Just a bit? You're joking. We've been up there too!"

3

Fortified by a delicious Lakeland breakfast of eggs, bacon, sausage, tomatoes and piles of hot toast, I took the road to Cockermouth, but made a short stop to see Keswick's oldest building and the resting place of Robert Southey.

"Do come in. We're an army of Mrs Mopps who try to get the church cleaned as early as possible so that we don't upset visitors, but you've caught us out!"

Stepping over buckets and mops I accepted the invitation of a jolly woman who had greeted me at the door of Crosthwaite church, which is one of the most delightful in all of Lakeland. Situated within easy walking distance of the town centre it lies in a green meadow which is framed on all sides by the rising mountains. Chaffinches sing from the trees, robins hide beneath hedgerows and young rabbits speed irreverently over ancient gravestones. It was due to the foresight of St Kentigern that such a marvellous site was chosen for this church, for here he planted his holy cross in 553 AD.

I stood beside the white marble figure of Southey which lies here in splendid serenity, his head resting on two pillows, his right hand holding the pages of a book, with a panel bearing an epitaph written by Wordsworth. This superb sculpture which captures so well the likeness of the dead poet, was fashioned by John Lough of Hexham who began as a stonemason's apprentice. Artistic ambition spurred him on to London aboard a collier-brig, then later to study in Rome. Other examples of his work include a statue of George Stephenson which stands in Newcastle and another of Queen Victoria outside London's Royal Exchange.

It is mainly literary scholars or those of a curious nature, who come here to visit Southey's resting place yet this should not be the case. For although much of his prolific output is now seldom read, as I discovered at Keswick Museum, he was the author of the classic children's story, *The Three Bears*. So for this alone, we all should make a pilgrimage here.

He was born in Bristol in 1774, the son of a linen-draper. As a child he attended the famous Westminster School but was expelled for writing an essay on flogging which upset the authorities, however he then managed to get a place at Balliol College, Oxford. After leaving university and making several unsuccessful attempts to quality as a lawyer, his literary leanings led him into a close friendship with Samuel Taylor Coleridge. The two friends married two sisters and in 1803, following in the steps of Wordsworth, they came north to Lakeland. At first they shared a home here at Greta Hall in Keswick, but Coleridge left shortly afterwards leaving Southey to support both families.

Lakeland was his home for over forty years, where he gained fame by writing an immense amount of both poetry and prose. His presence here drew in many other literary visitors including Wordsworth, Hazlitt, Shelley, De Quincey, Scott, and Charles and Mary Lamb. He later became an inspiration to several younger writers including Charlotte Bronte and Carlyle. In 1813 he accepted the position of Poet Laureate for which he had been recommended by Sir Walter Scott who had declined the position. Sir Robert Peel later offered him a baronetcy which he refused, but he was grateful for an extra £300 a year on his pension.

In 1837 he was grief stricken by the death of his wife, which together with overwork, led to his mental breakdown. Although in 1839 he married the poetess, Caroline Anne Bowles, he never fully recovered and he died of 'softening of the brain' four years later. Today he is chiefly remembered for *The Battle of Blenheim, The Inchcape Bell*, and *The Holy Tree*, together with his lives of Nelson and Wesley, and of course *The Three Bears*.

In the hush of morning I stood beside Southey's tomb which lies in the shadow of the church he attended for so long. Here I read a notice which states that it had been 'Restored by the Generosity of the Brazilian Government in 1961'. This surprising connection is because, between 1810 and 1819, he wrote the first *History of Brazil*, which is still regarded by students as being a valuable volume.

Also buried here at Crosthwaite is Canon Rawnsley, who died in 1920. He was one of those amazing figures whose tremendous energy helped to shape the present face of Lakeland. As well as carrying out his spiritual duties he had a lively interest in art, literature and the preservation of the British countryside. He was the friend to many great writers of his day, he helped the young Beatrix Potter to get her first works published, but will forever be remembered as one of the founders of the National Trust.

4

If a curious stranger had taken a look inside my car, which was parked near Crosthwaite church, he could have easily assumed I was consulting a medieval document to which time had been unkind. However, he would have been quite wrong, for I was merely consulting my much-loved copy of the one-inch Ordnance Survey Tourist Map of Lakeland which has visibly suffered from the passing of time! I remember quite clearly buying this map over thirty years ago, deciding with youthful optimism to get the more expensive cloth edition, then looking with horror as it was almost destroyed on its very first excursion up a Lakeland mountain.

It began when some friends of mine, who had arranged to take part in a long walk from Penrith to Windermere over the mountain tops of High Street, invited me to join them. As I could not make the start of the walk I arranged to meet them part way along the route, on the summit of Kidsty Pike which overlooks Haweswater. With my new map proudly in my rucksack I began the ascent in light drizzle, starting from Kirkstone Pass, close to Brothers Water. However, as I climbed upwards the drizzle turned to light rain, then the light rain turned to heavy rain, until when I reached the summit I was met by a deluge of such proportions that I could barely stand. The wind blew up into a fierce gale, the torrent of water poured unceasingly and clothed in completely inadequate waterproofs I waited in the biting wind for my friends who never arrived. For having more common sense than I had, they had abandoned their walk.

On arriving home I emptied my sodden rucksack, with horror removing from it my new map which was now a terrible mushy mess which seemed destined only for the dustbin. But after two weeks of continual drying my worst fears were happily not realised, for miraculously it could still be read. True, the paper cover had fallen completely away, it looked perhaps ten years old, it would never quite fold in the same way again, but the permanent waviness gave it a sort of unique character. Since its first baptism so long ago it has matured even further and become a real friend, for together with a number of equally dog-eared volumes of Wainwright's classic guides which I received as a 21st birthday present, it continues to successfully guide me across Lakeland.

I drove in the slanting morning sunlight through the green valley along which runs the little River Derwent, to reach the western shore of Bassenthwaite Lake. On my right, across the silver water, rose the towering bulk of Skiddaw, while on my left the wooded slopes of Thornthwaite Forest hid the curves of Whinlatter Pass. Bass Lake, as it is affectionately known is a favourite spot with anglers who come here to catch pike and eels. I am told that on occasions that other fisherman, the rare osprey, is sometimes seen lifting a meal from the water. When the young Alfred Tennyson came here to Lakeland in 1835 it is said that Bassenthwaite was his inspiration, for it became the lake of Excalibur in his classic Morte d'Arthur.

Continuing under a canopy of sycamore and ash the landscape began to quickly flatten out so that in a short time the fells were behind me. I was now driving along a lane which might have been in Devon, for on each side lay rich green pastures, fringed with low hedgerows and banks of wild flowers. This graceful sweeping countryside led me down to the point where the River Derwent and the River Cocker converge to produce a splendid setting for what many regard as Cumbria's most attractive town, Cockermouth.

I stood in a quiet corner of Main Street watching the warm sun slowly awaken this ancient town. Across the broad road on which Wordsworth played as a child, old men, bronzed and with the gait of farmers, stood chatting. They spoke of cattle and sheep, of border collies, of hound trailing, and of Rugby, stopping at intervals to look in silence at the latest batch of visitors to descend on their town. Laughing through a mouth of blackened teeth one old character hobbled away uttering his farewell in a rich Cumbrian accent that only his friends could understand. Soon, I suspect, he would be drinking a pint of Jenning's strong dark bitter in his favourite inn and reminiscing once more about life in the twenties.

Dodging the cars I managed to reach the safety of a small island in the centre of the road on which stands a large Victorian statue. A plaque relates that it is of Richard, the Sixth Earl Mayo, who was the local MP from 1857 to 1868. He then took up one of England's most powerful positions as Viceroy of India, but his success was destined to be short lived, for he was assassinated by a convict in the Andaman islands in 1872. His statue also came under threat in 1964 when a petrol tanker ploughed into it, but the sturdy memorial survived while the tanker was wrecked.

Few visitors to Cockermouth realise there was a time when it was part of Scotland for the border, following the Conquest, was often in dispute. This is why no mention of the town is made in the Domesday Book, but a castle, built originally of timber about 1134, finally helped to settle the matter. This was replaced by a more substantial stone structure a century later, much of the material being taken from the nearby Roman camp at Papcastle. Forming the seat of the Barony of Allerdale, in the early days it was occupied by the Lucy family but later it became part of the estates of the very powerful Percies who became guardians of this border country. It was held for Parliament by this family during the Civil War, being besieged for two months during 1648, then later partially demolished. In the 18th century, when the Percy direct line ended, it passed to the Wyndham family who continue to play a prominent role in British politics, using part of it as an occasional residence.

I continued my stroll up the spacious street which still retains a strong rural feel about it, for fields and trees and flowers are ever visible down inviting alleyways. When Camdem came here in 1582 he found 'a populous, well-standing market town, neatly built, but of low lying situation between two hills, upon one of which is a church, and on the other, against it a very strong castle.'

If he had been here just fourteen years earlier he would have witnessed a most colourful scene for into the town came a cavalcade bringing Mary, Queen of Scots. With sixteen loyal followers she had arrived the previous day at Workington by ship after escaping from the Battle of Langside across the Solway. Almost every person in Cockermouth turned out to greet the twenty-six-year-old, who most Roman Catholics considered to be the rightful Queen of both England and Scotland. She found Cumbrian hospitality at Cocker-mouth Hall, which was the home of a wealthy merchant named Henry Fletcher. Such was the state of her dress due to the rigours of her weary journey that he insisted she accept a length of rich crimson velvet for a new robe. But this sad Queen, of which one historian said: 'no historical personage outside scripture is better known', was destined to die so cruelly at Fotheringay in 1587. However, the small act of kindness shown by Henry Fletcher was not forgotten. When Mary's son, James I, finally came to the throne of England he rewarded the merchant's grandson with a knighthood. The family still lives in Cumbria, headed by Lord Inglewood of Hutton-in-the-Forest.

Those of us who are used to seeing the portrait of Wordsworth as a solemn faced, whispy haired, old man, which is shown on the cover of many of his works, are perplexed when we come to Cockermouth. For here lived a Wordsworth who is unfamiliar to us, for the boy who probably fished for tiddlers in the Derwent, played hide and seek with his sister and brothers around the castle and heard tales about Mary, Queen of Scots, had not yet received the heavy mantle of genius.

I stood in silence at the end of Main Street gazing at the elegant Georgian building in which he was born on the 7th April 1770. Visitors are often surprised at the beauty and size of the house, for with its nine impressive bays it is regarded as the finest of its type in Lakeland, being tastefully preserved by the National Trust. However, the family was far less prosperous than this image portrays, for his father was merely a lawyer who worked hard as the Earl of Lonsdale's agent. The Wordsworths possessed no great fortune, but were wealthy enough to live in comfort among the bustle of the town, but did not own the house.

Here the high-spirited William lived until 1779, when following the tragic death of his mother, he went to live in Hawkshead. Here too was born his beloved sister, Dorothy, but the fame that the couple were to later receive completely overshadowed the success of other members of the family. Their brother Christopher, who was an outstanding scholar, is largely forgotten, yet he rose to become Master of Trinity College, Cambridge. His three sons were equally brilliant: Charles became the Bishop of St. Andrews, Christopher became Bishop of Lincoln, and John followed his father as a lecturer in Classics at Cambridge.

Another young boy who would have walked the streets of Cockermouth around the same time as William Wordsworth was Fletcher Christian. He was born in a farmhouse close to the town in 1764, then grew up to become the leader of the infamous Mutiny on the Bounty. He lived the rest of his life on remote Pitcairn Island but his descendants sometimes come here to Cockermouth to return to their roots.

After admiring a bronze bust of the poet which stares forever at his birthplace, I strolled down narrow Low Sand Lane to the quiet banks of the Derwent. I then wandered for an hour in the hot sunshine, joining the morning shoppers beyond Cocker Bridge in the heart of the old town which hides beneath the castle. Here, in what was once Cumbria's main commercial centre, I explored fascinating alleyways once known as 'wents', looked at splendid Georgian houses, and discovered ancient coaching inns. Many of these have a unmistakable nautical look about them, for the sea is less than ten miles away.

William Wordsworth was born in this imposing Georgian House at Cockermouth in 1770.

As I looked at Cockermouth's oldest hotel, The Globe, I remembered that it was here that John Dalton used to stay when he returned to his hometown. But such is the wealth of talent in this amazing corner of Cumbria that his presence probably went largely unnoticed. I can well imagine the locals around the bar saying: "What's all the fuss about? Wordsworth's lad can write fine poetry but young Dalton's only discovered something called the Atomic Theory"!

5

From Cockermouth I took the old road eastwards which skirts the edge of wooded Elva Hill to reach Ouse Bridge, where the Derwent takes a wide curve as it leaves Bassenthwaite Lake. This quiet by-way passes beneath a curtain of foliage giving glimpses of lush green fields which spread outwards towards the rising summit of Skiddaw. It then changes into rougher heathland, brightened by the gold of gorse, as it ascends towards the remote villages of Uldale and Ireby. Here, where the unfenced road dips and dives across a wild expanse of sweeping pastureland, I paused to enjoy the stunning view. For the northern fells of Lakeland had now ended, giving way to a rolling landscape of wide skies and distant horizons. Aspatria, Wigton and Carlisle remain the last guardians of this corner of England before Hadrian's Wall and the hazy blue hills of Scotland are reached.

It was at Wigton in 1939, continuing Lakeland's great literary tradition, that best-selling author and television presenter, Melvyn Bragg, was born. After attending his local Nelson-Thomlinson Grammar School, he continued his education at Wadham College at Oxford, then joined the BBC in 1961. His first novel, *For Want of a Nail*, was written when he was twenty-three years old and first published in 1965. He chose the splendour of his native Cumbria as the setting for this story which traces the early life of an only child. His later works of fiction which also have Lakeland as a backcloth, include *The Second Inheritance (1965)*, *The Cumbrian Trilogy (1969-80)*, *The Maid of Buttermere (1987)* and *A Time to Dance (1990)*. He has also written many non-fiction

works and screenplays, including acclaimed biographies of Laurence Olivier and Richard Burton. But it is his marvellous *Land of the Lakes (1983)*, and his *Cumbria In Verse*, which appeals most to lovers of Lakeland.

In 1978 when he first became the presenter of the popular ITV arts programme, *The South Bank Show*, his face became familiar to millions of people and he is now regarded as one of Britain's leading figures in the art world. But in spite of living in Hampstead with his wife, writer Cate Haste, his roots still remain firmly here in Cumbria, where he returns whenever possible to walk over his native hills.

Best-selling author and TV presenter Melvyn Bragg was born in Wigton

The road now descended slowly to bring me into the quietness of Caldbeck village, which seemed to be sleeping in the warm sunshine. After parking my car under the shelter of a tree I wandered into the churchyard, like most visitors do, to seek out a large white tombstone which sits on the soft turf. Here, as I stood reading the inscription, I began to think how strange are the twists and turns of life. For the name of the man who is buried on this spot became known in every corner of the world, often by those who have never even heard of Lakeland. For there was a time whenever people came together for a good old fashioned sing song, be it in a school assembly hall, a pub or at a regimental dinner, that a rendition of the rousing hunting song *D'ye ken John Peel*, was almost obligatory. But being immortalised by these catchy words has led to many wrong assumptions about John Peel. For the traditional image is of an immaculately turned out huntsman wearing a red, or to be precise hunting-pink coat, white breeches and gleaming leather boots, mounted on a thorough-bred horse. However, although this may be true for the pastoral Shire counties of England, hunting during the early part of the last century here in Cumbria, was somewhat different. Peel's attire was coarse rather than elegant, his horse was small and sturdy, he often followed his hounds on foot, and he endlessly chased the fox over the toughest terrain in the country.

The exact date of John Peel's birth is not known, but he was baptised here at Caldbeck church on the 24th September in 1777. His father was William Peel who was a horse dealer and his mother Lettice Scott, came from a local family who were regarded as being 'better-off'. As her parents had not approved of her choice of husband the couple had eloped across the nearby border to wed at Gretna Green in Scotland. They were destined to have a large family of thirteen children.

In was among this remote farming community, full of long-horn cattle, Herdwick sheep and sturdy horses, that the young John Peel grew up. The rising fells lay on his doorstep, so from childhood he would have become familiar with these windswept summits together with the wild animals which lived on the sheltered slopes. These included badgers, hares, rabbits and what was to become his main adversary, the fox. But the foxes which inhabited this corner of Lakeland were of a different breed than those found today. Known locally as greyhounds, they were larger, tougher and covered with a thick silvery coat to protect them against the northern winter. They also had an acute sense of smell and hearing, with keen eyesight and amazing stamina. When hunted it was not uncommon for them to speed over these rough uplands for up to seventy miles.

Being raised in this rural masculine community of hard drinking, tough farmers it is likely that John Peel got a taste for the local pastime of hunting from an early age. But he quickly grew into manhood, reaching a height of over six feet and his marriage in 1797 closely mirrored that of his parents. His bride, eighteen-year-old Mary White, came from a prosperous local family who had been opposed to the wedding. But, following the well-trod path to Gretna Green they had an anvil ceremony which finally settled the matter. This was followed by a more conventional marriage service in Caldbeck church which for the sake of respectability had been insisted upon by the bride's mother.

However, John Peel seems to have made a good choice for Mary brought with her a gift of land which raised an annual income of almost £500. This provided a large degree of independence allowing him time to pursue his ever growing obsession with hunting. Soon the large nosed, tall figure of Peel, dressed in a long grey coat and wearing a top hat became a familiar sight around the district. With a whip in one hand and his dented horn in the other, often riding a pony and surrounded by his beloved hounds, he chased foxes and hares over a territory stretching from Carlisle to Penrith. Although he is reputed to have hunted at least twice a week for half a century, he still found time to run his small farm and raise a family of six sons and seven daughters.

It is likely that the colourful antics of Peel would never have been known outside this northern part of Cumbria except for the chance endeavours of two men, John Woodcock Graves and William Metcalfe.

Graves had been born in Wigton but after being married for a second time he came to live in Caldbeck were he worked as a wool weaver. Here, he and Peel soon became hunting and drinking companions. It was while the two men were sitting around the fireside during a snow storm in 1832, reminiscing about their hunting exploits, that Graves was suddenly prompted to write a song about the coarse huntsman who had become his idol. An old woman, 'Granny', was also seated in a corner of the room nursing Graves's eldest son while quietly singing the Scottish rant *Bonnie Annie*. Graves quickly penned his ballad, then for the first time, using the tune that Granny had been singing gave his friend a rough rendition of what was to be refined as:

D'ye ken John Peel with his coat so grey?   (Chorus)
D'ye ken John Peel at the break of day?
D'ye ken John Peel when he's far, far away –
With his hounds and his horn in the morning?

'T' was the sound of his horn called me from my bed,
And the cry of his hounds has me oft-times led
For Peel's view halloa would awaken the dead
Or the fox from his lair in the morning.

D'ye ken that bitch whose tongue was death?
D'ye ken her sons of peerless faith?
D'ye ken that a fox, with his last breath,
Curs'd them all as he died in the morning?

Yes, I ken John Peel and Ruby, too,
Ranter and Royal and Bellman as true,
From the drag to the chase, from the chase to the view,
From the view to the death in the morning.

And I've followed John Peel both often and far,
O'er the rasper fence and the gate and the bar,
From Low Denton-Holme up to Scratchmere Scar,
Where we view for the brush in the morning.

Then here's to John Peel with my heart and soul,
Come fill – fill to him another strong bowl,
And we'll follow John Peel through fair and through foul,
While we're waked by his horn in the morning.

Both men instinctively knew that a masterpiece had been casually created. Peel was reduced to tears while Graves later recalled that he had prophetically said, "By Jove, Peel, you'll be sung when we're both run to earth."

The villagers of Caldbeck first heard the ballad in the local pub, The Rising Sun, which is now named The Oddfellows. The following year its composer had a quarrel with the manager of the mill where he worked and as a result impetuously decided to emigrate to Tasmania. There he put his brilliant mind to a variety of jobs, ranging from journalism to the design of textile machinery and of course hunting, but kangaroos instead of foxes. He died in 1886 at the age of 91 and was appropriately buried at the side of the River Derwent in Hobart.

John Peel had continued his prolific hunting activities for over twenty years after Graves had left England. In his characteristically selfish way, he always put the chase before any family event, even the birth or the death of his own children. He hunted with both the local gentry and the labouring classes, living up to the words of the ballad that had made him a local legend. It is said that his death in 1854 at the age of 78, had resulted from injuries sustained while hunting. His burial in this quiet corner of Cumbria attracted 3000 mourners, it is recorded that even his hounds let out a 'deep-mouthed cry' as the funeral procession passed their kennels.

Strangely, it was to be a lay clerk at Carlisle cathedral, William Metcalfe, who was to bring lasting fame to Peel. When he heard the ballad being sung at a dinner party he attended he was captivated by the number. However, he decided that musically it left a lot to be desired, so he sat down to write an improved version. This delighted the audience at its first public performance in Carlisle in 1869, then gained national recognition when he later sang it in London. It immediately became a success, quickly spreading the name of John Peel to the furthest corners of the world.

In more recent times some anti-blood sports followers have come to despise the life of John Peel and all he represents. These fanatics even came here to Caldbeck with the intention of digging up his bones, but they were caught and ended up in jail. However, in spite of this opposition the foxhounds and hunters of Lakeland still keep up the tradition by speeding over the fells and occasionally becoming completely outfoxed. In 1975 the Blencathra pack were chasing their quarry towards the edge of a crag when it suddenly changed direction. The leading hounds were unable to stop, seven of them plunging over the sheer cliff. Of these, two fell 160 feet to their deaths, four were brought to safety and one required the aid of Keswick Mountain Rescue Team to haul it from a ledge. The wily fox, during the confusion that followed, managed to make its escape!

Before setting out to find St Mungo's Well I discovered that another Cumbrian celebrity shares with John Peel, a final resting place here in this lovely churchyard. I read the inscription on the moss laden gravestone of Mary Harrison which gives no clue to the fact that she was the famous Beauty of Buttermere. For after the fame and intrigues of her tempestuous youth, which I will relate later, she found quietness and respectability as the wife of a Caldbeck farmer.

I took a path from the churchyard down to the river which dashes its silver path through this enchanting village. Close to an ancient pack horse bridge I found the well, which with Cumbrian pride, was being cleaned by a healthy looking local woman. Her hands protected with yellow rubber gloves, she was industriously tearing out the weeds and removing the lichen from stones which surround Caldbeck's first link with Christianity.

"These weeds seem to grow so quickly, but we do like to keep it in good condition," she told me.

It is said that St Mungo, who was also known as St Kentigern, brought his Christian faith here towards the end of the 6th century. The clear fell water which bubbles from this well was used by him to baptise those who had renounced their pagan gods. What little is known about his life was written in the 12th century by a monk from Furness Abbey. It relates that Mungo was the Bishop of what is now Glasgow, but he was forced to leave the area by the king who was opposed to his teachings. It was while escaping to the security of Wales that he is said to have stopped here at Caldbeck, lighting the flame of faith which still flourishes in the Back o'Skiddaw.

I walked across the bridge which both John Peel and Mary Harrison would have known well, then I sauntered along a secluded lane admiring the cottage gardens and listening to the bird song. Returning to the cool of the 'church of Blessed Kentigern of Caldbeck' I learned about its 800 years history, then I headed down a bumpy road for refreshments to the marvellously restored Priest's Mill. This old watermill, which was built by the local rector in 1702,

Caldbeck's ancient church and Holy Well was founded by Saint Kentigern, also known as Saint Mungo

stands among the lush foliage of the riverbank. For over two centuries it ground corn, then in 1933 it became a sawmill before the floods of 1965 brought to an end its working life. Here in an elevated restaurant, I sipped a glass of elderberry wine, ate a delicious piece of Homity Pie and salad, while watching a dipper fight its way upstream beneath a canopy of sunlit beech trees.

In a small second-hand bookshop which forms part of the mill, I spoke to a woman from Cockermouth who is one of the charity volunteers who work here. I detected that her accent was Lancastrian and not Cumbrian, but was surprised to find out that she was born just three miles from my own home in Bolton.

"I'm a widow now. I came to live up here with my husband over thirty years ago and our children were born here and they have married into Cumbrian families. But in many ways I still feel that I am an outsider."

We then spoke of the beauty of Lakeland, which to the casual visitor seems to be unchanging. Yet she told me that this was not the whole story, for there is a constant battle going on to fight new developments which many residents feel threaten the very character of the area.

After taking a final look at the 14 feet diameter water-wheel which has been painstakingly restored, I reluctantly returned to my car, for Caldbeck is one of those sleepy places that strangers find difficult to leave.

4

Caldbeck to Watendlath

I drink tea in a Quaker Meeting House, look for a phantom army, ponder about King Arthur then enter Cumbria's Transylvania. I learn of Vampires at Croglin, a Cockatrice at Renwick, then visit Long Meg and her Daughters. In Penrith I see the Giant's Grave and hear about border warfare, before following in the steps of Sir Hugh Walpole into hidden Watendlath.

1

There is a strangeness about this corner of Lakeland that lies to the north of Skiddaw; it seems to be a land which the rest of England has forgotten. Bathed in soft sunlight it exudes an atmosphere of utter peacefulness, a place, I suspect, where the locals have never even heard of sleeping pills or tranquillisers. With no other car in sight I was able to drive at a snails pace, stopping wherever I desired to stare at a grazing cow, puzzle at a feature of the landscape or to take in the scent of foxglove in a cottage garden. Hesket New Market was also sleeping. I was the only visitor admiring its impressive wide street of 18th century houses, looking across its manicured village green to the Market Cross and wondering how its Bull Ring has managed to survive.

Although I had the feeling that I was driving to the east, my map indicated that I was actually moving south. This illusion was because the road along which I was travelling closely follows the side of the fells, its imperceptible curves had changed my direction. Here is the place where the Lakeland mountains end and the lush Border Country begins. On my right rose the steep flank of Carrock Fell, ending in its 2174 feet (663 m) high summit which was once a hill fort. In 1857 Charles Dickens and Wilkie Collins, who were wandering through Lakeland, made an unlikely ascent of this mountain. Their adventure was recorded in a magazine feature entitled *The Lazy Tour of Two Idle Apprentices*.

Screes formed from craggy outcrops line the slopes of Carrock Fell and large boulders have fallen into the valley, littering the green turf as if some

Sheep graze on the quiet roadside beneath the grassy slopes of Carrock Fell

giant has been playing a game of bowls. Colouring this tumbled landscape, which is devoid of hedgerows, are masses of gorse whose shimmering gold looks breathtaking in the sunlight. Sheep wander at liberty here, turning the grass into a lawn by their continual feasting, watched only by jet-black crows who glide with ease on the air currents.

It is hard to imagine that both Caldbeck and Hesket New Market were once regarded as industrial settlements, but this was two centuries ago when both farming and industry could survive in harmony. Here small mills, which took advantage of free water power, ground the farmer's corn, manufactured woollen goods, produced paper and bobbins, and importantly brewed the local ale. But as early as the 13th century miners had wound their way up these remote fells, for they had discovered the area was rich in minerals. It is said that twenty-two different types are to be found on these slopes. Those which were mainly in demand were lead, copper and the less well-known barytes, which can be used in the manufacture of paint, glass and ceramics. Mining reached its height here during the 17th century, then gradually declined, ending in 1960 when the last mine closed down.

I stopped at a small cluster of buildings known as Mosedale, which lie in a curve of the River Caldew in the shadow of the towering fells. A small sign which was swinging in the breeze, told me that cups of tea and coffee were being served; an invitation which I could not resist. But I soon discovered that this was no ordinary tea-shop, for this refreshment room was really a Quaker Meeting House on whose door lintel was carved the date 1702, and I was the only customer.

"Can I help you?" said a young woman, smiling with enthusiasm, as I was filled with indecision. Should I have a scone or a chocolate biscuit with my tea? When at last I made up my mind we began to chat.

"I have come up from Chester for a week to look after the tea room." she related, "It is so unbelievably peaceful here. There is no way that I feel lonely. On bank holidays we can get as many as a hundred customers, but normally its only a handful so I can easily cope."

We then began to talk about how the Quaker religion first became established here in 1653, when George Fox came to nearby Mungrisdale. A local farmer named George Peacock, who became one of the members, owned the simple building which is now the Meeting House. Then in the early 18th century his son, Hugh, formally gave it to the Society. The emphasis that Quakers place on religion in daily life, their lack of appointed ministers and their belief that there is 'that of God in everyone', appealed to a small but dedicated group. This flourished for two centuries, but as the number of Quakers in the area declined their meetings in the building eventually ended.

For a period travelling preachers of other denominations used the building, then it was later used as a chapel-of-ease for Mungrisdale Parish Church, finally closing its doors in 1968.

"A group of Friends from Carlisle began restoring the building in 1971 and now volunteers like myself act as caretakers through the season. We spend two weeks here – looking after the coffee shop, welcoming visitors and generally enjoying the unique atmosphere of the place."

I sat on a heavy wooden bench sipping my cup of tea in the quietness of the room. Looking around at its flagged floors and whitewashed walls it was easy to picture in my mind the Quakers of 17th century Mosedale, gathering here in silent worship. The ancient farms in which these Quaker families once lived are remembered on the wall by copies of the date stones, the oldest one being 1610. But the unusual pillars which support the roof of the building are reputed to be much older and may well have pagan connections. A tale told locally relates how General Wade, the famous road builder who came from Mosedale, had them brought here in 1724. They are said to have come from a Roman temple dedicated to Mithras, which was discovered near Hadrian's Wall.

Four more visitors were just arriving as I stepped out in to the sunshine which lit up this secluded hamlet.'

"Grand day. Glad I'm not working," came the greeting from a cheerful, bright-eyed man who seemed to be enjoying the fruits of his retirement.

Mosedale sits at the end of a narrow valley which penetrates deep into the heart of the mountains around the high summit of Skiddaw. It is guarded on one side by Carrock Fell and on the other by Bowscale Fell, with the River Caldrew flowing between the two. From here a six mile trek up a contouring path leads to what is considered to be the remotest residence in Lakeland, Skiddaw House. This house, which appears to have originally been a short row of terraced cottages, is now used as a youth hostel. But for generations it was the home of shepherds who would spend months on end, alone among the wild hills. Its dramatic, isolated setting prompted novelist Sir Hugh Walpole to use it in two of his books, *The Bright Pavilions and The Fortress.*

2

My suspicions that I had entered an enchanted land were confirmed when I reached Mungrisdale, for here the fells which soar upwards like huge green pyramids, are alive with tales of the supernatural. Overlooking the village I could see the slopes of Souther (pronounced 'Souter') Fell. This impressive ridge, which rests in the shadow of the high summit of Blencathra, is almost entirely surrounded by the little River Glenderamackin. It was during the early 18th century that a series of strange events occurred on this hilltop which became the talking point in every inn in Lakeland.

It was on Midsummer-eve in 1735, that it first became apparent that something strange was happening around Mungrisdale. Daniel Stricket, a servant who worked for William Lancaster, reported seeing the eastern edge of the fell covered with soldiers. He watched them marching over the craggy uplands for over a hour. They appeared to be coming from a high point at the north, then vanishing close to the summit. He concluded that it was some form of ghostly army, for in places the fellside was almost sheer and intersected by gullies, making it impossible for normal troops to march over such terrain. But when he told the local villagers they just laughed, and would not take the tale seriously.

However, two years later at exactly the same time of the year, Lancaster himself witnessed a similar event. He at first thought that the two men he saw on the fell with their horses were merely out hunting. But shortly afterwards he glanced up to see a vast number of soldiers marching five abreast, with mounted officers riding alongside. Fortunately he had time to summon other members of his family, who were also able to watch the manoeuvres of the phantoms.

For the next few years the claims of the family still went largely unbelieved, so to put the matter at rest, on Midsummer-eve in 1745 they gathered together twenty-six reliable people. As this crowd anxiously scanned the slopes of Souther Fell the army suddenly appeared. But this time it was larger than ever, there were also carriages, and the men appeared to be solid, not transparent like ghosts are often depicted. The march continued until nightfall, when it became hidden by the darkness. But a search next day revealed not a single footprint or hoofmark on the fell.

The witnesses all swore on oath, in the presence of a magistrate, the details of the strange happening. This led to another local man, Mr Wren of Wilton Hall, confessing that both he and his manservant had seen another apparition two years earlier. This was a man and a dog who appeared to be chasing some horses at an amazing speed, over a slope which was so steep that no normal horse could ever find a footing. When they went to the spot, half expecting to find the bodies of both the man and the animals, there was no trace of either.

This odd event, having now been seen by so many, could no longer be disputed by those who did not believe in ghosts, so a 'logical' explanation was sought. One theory put forward was that the Jacobite Army was gathering together in 1745 on the western coast of Scotland. Somehow, by some strange freak of the weather, their images were reflected here on Souther Fell. But of course, this would not explain why the phantom army had appeared in previous years and at exactly the same time? However, this is far from being the only place in England in which ghostly soldiers have been seen. It is said that just two months after the famous Battle of Edge Hill, during the Civil War, a group of men witnessed a complete re-enactment in the sky. The slopes of Helvellyn were also brimming with military apparitions the night before the Battle of Marston Moor and in recent years, a full regiment of phantom Roman soldiers marched through a cellar close to the Minster in York!

Victorian tourists, who came here to Mungrisdale to hear about ghosts, were also asked by the guides, 'Would you like to see the stars at mid-day?' Unable to resist the temptation they were taken by carriage up a bumpy track to Bowscale Tarn which lies high on the fellside. Due to its great depth, and that it is almost entirely surrounded by towering crags, if the air is still then reflections of the stars can be seen in the water during daylight.

Although my destination was Penrith, which lies only about ten miles to the east of Mungrisdale, I decided to make a detour northwards to learn more of the romance of this special corner of Lakeland. Throwing off the shackles of our present noisy age, I dipped down flower scented lanes, passed 17th century farms fringed with sycamores, and saw a rapid transition from rugged fell to lush meadowland. With the misty blue outline of Scotland in my windscreen I passed though sleepy villages, paused on elevated viewpoints and then began to ponder on whether this was really a landscape once known by King Arthur?

Facts and fantasy intermingle so much in the great Arthurian legends that it has become almost impossible to decide where fiction ends and truth begins. Since childhood we are told of the noble King's exploits, of the magic of Merlin, the romance of Camelot and the Isle of Avalon, of the beautiful Guinevere and of the Knights of the Round Table. There is little doubt that Arthur really did exist and that he won many bloody battles, but over the centuries writers have felt free to weave their own fiction around his lifestory. Geoffrey of Monmouth who wrote during the 12th century began this romanticism, to be followed later by Sir Walter Scott and Lord Tennyson. The south-west of England is claimed by some scholars to be Arthur's kingdom; Tintagel is said to be his birthplace, Cadbury Castle is Camelot and mystical Glastonbury the site of Avalon. However, some Lakeland folk dispute these claims, producing an impressive array of traditions that link Arthur and his knights with the north.

They say that Arthur was born not in Tintagel but on the site of Pendragon Castle, a Pele Tower which stands near the village of Mallerstang. The present ruined structure dates from the 13th century, but the strategic site is much older, and was probably occupied in Arthur's time. Legend tells us that his father was Uther Pendragon, who was the Lord of the isolated area. Apparently he attempted to build a moat around his fortress with little success, for he was unable to divert the river. This event is still remembered in a local rhyme:

> Let Uther Pendragon do what he can,
> But Eden will run where Eden ran.

Poems written by the ancient Celtic bards mention that Arthur fought twelve great battles against pagan foes. These were fought mainly in the north from Lincolnshire up to southern Scotland, but their exact location is open to speculation. Four are known to have been fought close to the River Dublas, which some historians believe is the present River Douglas in Lancashire. Bassenthwaite, here in Lakeland, is a possible site of his sixth battle, while Chester, known as the 'City of the Legions', is where the ninth battle took place.

Arthur's final battle is believed to have taken place in AD 539 at Camlan, where both he and his adversary, Mordred, met their end. This is said to be Camboglanna, a Roman fort on Hadrian's Wall at Birdoswald. The Cumbrian coastal town of Ravenglass has a strong tradition that links it with Arthur's court, making it a possible location of the enchanted Isle of Avalon. But it is here, to the north of Penrith, that is said to have been the home of the noble knight, Lancelot. Near the working village of Lazonby once lapped the quiet waters of Tarn Wadling which has now been drained. Local people will assure you that this is the setting of the wonderful tale of Gawain and the Green Knight.

3

It was hard to believe that the dappled green countryside through which I was driving had once been thickly wooded. But at the time of the Conquest this patchwork of fields which stretches from Penrith to Carlisle, formed part of the vast Inglewood Forest. It became notorious as the abode of outlaws such as Adam Bell and William Cloudeslie, whose exploits challenged those of Robin Hood. It still remains sparsely populated, a place of wide skies which look down on inviting hamlets and farms nestling beneath low hills. Croglin, which I discovered among a maze of roads to the west of Alston, is a peaceful village which seems typical of this outpost of Lakeland. But strangers are amazed to learn that it has become known as the Transylvania of Cumbria, for here once lurked a rare species in England – a vampire!

When Dublin born author, Bram Stoker, first published his classic horror story, *Dracula*, in June 1897 he unleashed a popular interest in the cult of the undead which continues to this day. Stoker's *Dracula*, who arrived at Whitby harbour during a violent storm, had captured the imagination of millions of fans. The exploits of the infamous Count, portrayed by such actors as Bela Lugosi and Christopher Lee, together with his adversary, Dr Van Helsing, forever associated with Peter Cushing, have thrilled generations of filmgoers. From the popular Hammer Films that still appear on our TV screens, we have become familiar with the corpse rising from the grave when darkness falls, ever searching for living blood. The only weapons which seems to defeat the fictional vampire is the shadow of the cross, a stake through the heart and perhaps a clove of garlic. So popular has the tale become that the novel has never been out of print, Dracula societies have been formed in both Britain and America, and tourists flock to Dracula's castle in Transylvania. But many years before Bram Stoker penned his masterpiece, the villagers of Croglin were fighting their own local Dracula.

Croglin's vampire is said to have made an appearance in the eighteen seventies, but the date is subject to dispute. Some people believe the tale was first recorded around this time, but the event took place much earlier. However, when the vampire first began its exploits there were two villages at what is now Croglin. The larger one, Croglin Magna, lay about two miles from Croglin Parva, which was the site of the happening. This small community, which no longer exists, consisted of a handful of houses, a church and graveyard, with a small manor house nearby known as Croglin Grange.

The Grange was owned at this time by the Fishers, but as they had other estates they sub-let the building to tenants. The family who took up the lease one warm summer consisted of two brothers and a sister named Cronswell. Apparently they settled happily in the village, quickly making friends with the local people and enjoying the quiet rural atmosphere. Sadly, their peace was destined to be short-lived.

One hot evening the family had enjoyed a hearty dinner followed by a relaxing hour on the verandah, which allowed a fine view of the surrounding countryside. Eventually, after darkness had fallen and the bright moon had ascended, they decided to retire to bed. The two men quickly sank into a deep sleep, but suddenly they were awakened by a horrible piercing scream which came from their sister's bedroom. They rushed to her door, forced it open, and the older brother was just able to catch a glimpse of a weird, emaciated man leaping out of the window. He took up the chase, following the strange character which pranced across the lawn, but unfortunately he lost it when it vanished into the nearby churchyard. Returning home he found his younger brother holding their ashen faced sister, who was bleeding from a deep throat wound.

After being comforted and having her wound dressed, she related the details of her harrowing ordeal. Having retired to bed she had found difficulty in sleeping, so she began looking out through the unshuttered windows. In the moonlight she was amazed to see the silhouette of what appeared to be a deformed man, who was moving backwards and forwards across the lawn. But the most frightening part was that his eyes seemed to be glowing like beacons. Even worse was to follow, for the hideous figure had seen her, in an instant it had dashed over to her window and began scratching at the pane. Paralysed with fear she could only watch as it removed some glass, lifted the catch, then jumped into her room. It leapt on top of her, holding her head with its claw-like fingers, then sank its fangs into her neck. At this point she had at last been able to find her voice, letting out the scream which had summoned her brothers.

The next day the brothers told their local friends about the macabre incident and a thorough search was made of the area. No sign of the strange creature was to be found, so it was assumed to be an isolated attack by a demented madman. At the suggestion of a doctor the girl was taken on a holiday to recover from her shock, then the family returned to the house, the event now being almost forgotten.

However, in the spring of the following year the family were again reminded of their terrible experience when a local child was taken ill. The two years old girl, who had been fit and healthy, was now white-faced and frightened. More ominous was the discovery of a number of small wounds on the child's neck. The child's father, who was a friend of the Cronswells, decided to visit them at the Grange to ask their advice. They discussed the matter over dinner, which continued into the early hours, so the friend decided to stay the night at the Grange.

The brothers continued to chat with their friend, while their sister retired to bed. But their conversation was cut short by a horrific scream of terror which came from their sister's bedroom; the deformed creature had returned to scratch at the window. This time all three men clearly saw the wizened man running across the lawn. One of the brothers grabbed his loaded pistol which he fired at the figure, which flinched as the shot entered his leg. The men pursued it over the lawn then into the churchyard where it was seen entering one of the grave vaults. At this point they ended their chase, deciding it was wiser to wait until daylight.

Early next morning a group of local men were gathered together and told about the strange event. With apprehension they made their way to the ancient vault, which had not been used for years, then began to remove the stone slabs from the entrance; a scene of utter chaos met their eyes. Coffins, broken into pieces, had been scattered all over the vault floor, human skeletons had been thrown about, their skulls and bones piled high. As the shaking lanterns searched every corner it was noticed that only one coffin remained untouched, but the lid appeared to be loose. Fearfully, the lid was pushed open to reveal the brown shrivelled corpse of a man. They were just about to replace the lid when one of the brothers noticed a strange mark on the corpse's leg. Closer examination showed that it was a bullet wound of recent origin; they had at last found the terrible Croglin Vampire.

In a state of disbelief, the villagers carried the coffin and its macabre contents outside. A huge bonfire was quickly built, its flickering flames consuming the strange creature, returning Croglin Parva once more to rural peace.

Similar tales of vampirism have been recorded in many European countries for over 700 years, with historians and doctors putting forward various explanations. Some believe that 'rising from the grave' may have resulted from premature burial, where people not clinically dead have been interred. Even in recent years there have been horrific examples of 'corpses' having been certified dead, suddenly starting to breath. The other aspect of the vampirism is blood lust. This is an acknowledged medical condition which may result from either a physical deficiency or from psychopathic tendencies. An American doctor believes that some vampires may suffer from one of a number of rare hereditary diseases called porphyrias. These can lead to terrible disfigurement, extreme sensitivity to sunlight and the need to suck blood, which is the basis of many of the recorded vampire tales. It is estimated that at least 700 Americans are addicted to drinking human blood, with Los Angeles claiming to be the vampire capital of the world with 36 registered addicts!

Continuing my journey southwards through Cumbria's Transylvania I reached Renwick, a small village which rests in the shadow of the rising Pennine hills. Situated to the east of the River Eden, well away from the popular highways, this secluded community has been spared from any mass influx of tourists. Once known as the manor of Ravenwick it was the abode of the Staveley family during the 13th century, then after their line ended it was given to Andrew de Harcla. He had a spectacular rise in fortune, becoming the first Earl of Carlisle, followed by an even more spectacular decline when he was executed for treason. This led to the manorial rights reverting to the crown, who then gave them to Queen's College at Oxford, who have now held them for six centuries.

I stood outside the small village church which is dedicated to All Saints, pondering on the strange events which occurred here in 1733 when the church was being rebuilt. Apparently workmen, engaged on digging out the ancient foundations, noticed a disturbance among the rubble. Suddenly a weird creature pushed itself upwards then, in a flurry of wings, took to the air. The men ran for their lives, fearing that like nearby Croglin, they had disturbed a vampire.

The giant bat-like creature, later said to be a Cockatrice, flew in a fury around the village. But fortunately Renwick possessed a man named John Tallentine, who proved to be of strong spirit. On hearing about the creature he cut himself a staff from a rowan tree, renowned for its supernatural powers,

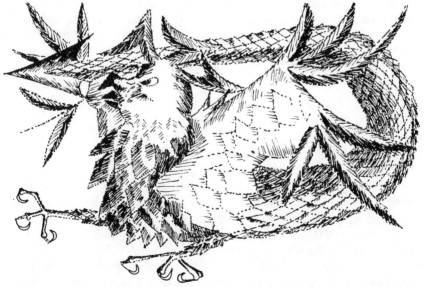

The giant bat-like creature known as a cockatrice, said to have been unearthed at Renwick.

then he set off towards the church. The Cockatrice saw him approaching so made its attack, swooping down like a prehistoric pterodactyl. A vigorous fight followed, the creature digging its talons into Tallentine's face and arm, but eventually he won the day. In a bloody climax the creature was beaten to death and John Tallentine became the hero of Renwick.

Just another local legend? Maybe, but in *A Directory of Cumberland* which was published in 1847 it is recorded that all local landowners around Renwick paid a prescription in lieu of tithes. The exception being the Tallentine family, on account of the ancient owner having slain a Cockatrice.

The curious origins of the fabulous creature known as the Cockatrice, which was mentioned by early Greek writers, seemed to have originated in ancient Egypt. Over the centuries it gained a reputation for having the power to kill by its mere glance. Having hatched from a cock's egg it was a hybrid monster, having the head, wings and feet of a cock, with the rear of its body being like that of a serpent, with a barbed tail!

My day of history, legend and fantasy ended appropriately near the village of Little Salkeld where I walked in the fading light among the stones of Lakeland's Stonehenge. This impressive circle of 59 stones, the second largest in England, is known as Long Meg and her Daughters. It has enchanted generations of tourists, including Camden who decided that the Romans must have built it, and Wordsworth who associated it with the Druids.

Meg is reputed to have been a witch, who danced with her coven on the Sabbath day, which resulted in them being turned into stone. However, if anyone counts the number of stones correctly the spell will be broken and the witches will return to human form. It is said that a local farmer, disputing the tale, told his men to blast the stones away. As they began the task a violent thunderstorm suddenly filled the sky, which they took as an omen; they refused to proceed any further, so thankfully this monument to our ancient history remains.

4

I stood under the shelter of my umbrella, looking across the Market Square in Penrith, which in spite of the dismal day was bustling with activity. I saw women strolling past the Victorian clock-tower, loaded down with shopping-bags, laughing, talking, and no doubt exchanging the latest gossip. I saw sombre faced, weather-beaten farmers who had driven in battered Landrovers from their isolated homes in the Eden Valley to purchase supplies. And I saw excited groups of angelic school children who were discussing the finer points of their latest computer games. This small attractive town of red-sandstone buildings gives a stranger like myself the impression that it has always been a place of tranquillity, but I was to learn that this is far from true. For many of these residents of Penrith who today pass their lives in relative peace, can number among their ancestors those who fought and suffered for centuries in bloody, border warfare.

The name Cumbria is said to mean 'the land of the Celts', a people who first arrived in the north-west around 400 BC. The Brigantes, who were one of these Celtic tribes, later settled in the area around Penrith, becoming tough hill farmers. But by 79 AD the might of Rome, under the leadership of Julius Agricola, had advanced northwards bringing these tribes under his control. Within half a century the frontier of Hadrian's Wall had been established just twenty miles away from the present town, creating an artificial borderline which for over a thousand years would be a source of conflict.

After controlling their northern frontier for over three centuries the Romans were finally forced to abandoned Hadrian's Wall in 383 AD when their empire began to decline. Immediately the Picts began raiding from the north, followed later by the Anglo-Saxons from the east. This eventually led to the establishment of a new kingdom, known as Strathclyde. It stretched from the present Scottish lowlands down to North Wales, part of which was Cumbria, a semi-independent homeland for both Celts and Angles.

By the 9th century the kingdom was being claimed by both the Anglo-Saxon kings and the Scottish kings, while the Norsemen who had already colonised Ireland and the Isle of Man, were beginning to pose a threat. Penrith, whose Celtic name means 'ford by the hill', was by this time the capital of Cumbria. In 945 AD Dunmail, who is believed to have been the last Celtic king of Cumbria, was defeated by the forces of King Edmund at Dunmail Raise. This led to the Celts of Cumbria being exiled to Wales, leaving a vacuum which was filled by a large influx of Norse settlers.

Cumbria remained part of the Kingdom of Strathclyde until 1070 AD, when the advance of the Normans, following their triumph at Hastings, brought it under English rule. But this was an uneasy peace for the border country and particularly for Penrith, which proved vulnerable as it lacked natural defences. Although the Scots had at first reluctantly agreed to concede the territory, later generations began to claim it back. This led to centuries of conflict, ranging from isolated raids to all-out warfare. The town was completely burned down in 1314, then overrun by 30,000 Scots in 1347, who took all the able-bodied men as prisoners. Not until the Union between Scotland and England in 1610, following the establishment of King James I as the monarch of both Scotland and England, could the people of Penrith rest soundly in their beds.

I continued my stroll in the rain into Cornmarket, passing the ever-cheerful stall holders of the little open-air market which now gathers twice a week around the impressive Market Cross. Unperturbed by few customers and the dreary weather, they were laughing and joking among themselves. For centuries this was the place where farmers came to sell their harvest from the back of their horse drawn carts. The host of ancient inns which surrounded the site became associated with the sale of different crops. So a farmer with a load of barley would head for the front of the Griffin, while wheat would be sold near the Black Lion and rye at the Black Bull. Afterwards, no doubt, the transactions would be celebrated in the appropriate bar.

Overlooking the open market place named Great Dockray I stopped to look at an ancient row of cottages and the famous Gloucester Arms Hotel. Once this was Dockray Hall, which became a residence of King Richard III, when he was still the Duke of Gloucester. In spite of the claims of early historians who labelled him a 'cruel monster, deformed in body', he seems to have been well thought of in Cumbria, having gained a reputation for gallantry. Penrith was particularly grateful to him, for his northern campaigns led to a thankful lull in the raids by the Scots.

Penrith, I discovered, has a series of inviting alleyways which like those at Kendal are known as 'yards'. These narrow passageways once provided a means of escape from raiders, then they became the doorways to small workshops which housed the craftsmen of the town. Those remaining lead the walker into quiet backwaters in which hide sturdy stone houses, just two minutes walk from the bustle of the market.

A stroll up Castlegate brought me to two features of the town which were both of prime importance at different points in history: the castle and the railway station. Now a handsome ruin which sits on a manicured hill, the castle was originally a simple Pele Tower built as a refuge for Penrithians. In 1399 a thick curtain wall was added by the powerful William Strickland, who later became the Bishop of Carlisle and the Archbishop of Canterbury. Further extensions during the 15th century created an impregnable royal fortress, fit to protect Richard, Duke of Gloucester.

As well as being largely responsible for the building of the castle, Bishop Strickland also organised Penrith's first water supply. He had constructed what is now known as the Thacka Beck, a link between the River Eamont and the River Petterel. This brought much-needed drinking water into the heart of the old town, but in later years became polluted by small industries which grew around its banks.

The nearby railway station, although hardly regarded as one Penrith's romantic attractions, is of significance for it represents one of the great engineering feats of the last century: the first western railway link between Scotland and England. In the 1840s many doubted that trains would ever climb the steep incline needed to traverse notorious Shap Fell. At this time the line ended in Lancashire, with those passengers bound for Scotland continuing their journey by sea from Liverpool or via the new port of Fleetwood.

But the London and North Western Railway Company had other plans, for they knew that a route through to Scotland would be highly lucrative. Following a Royal Commission of 1844 which approved their proposed link from Lancaster to Carlisle, which passed through Penrith, they appointed engineer Joseph Locke to mastermind the plan. This involved the largest financial investment ever made in such a project, employing a massive workforce of 10,000 men using mainly picks and shovels, but aided by up to a thousand horses.

The string of jokes which begin with, 'There was an Englishman, an Irishman and a Scotsman', may well have originated from this period for the navvies employed on the scheme are said to have been chosen equally from each race. The rivalry between these gangs of tough, hard-working and hard-drinking men was legendary; fighting was an everyday occurrence, ending often in severe injury and sometimes death. The men would leave their camps at the weekends and pour into the nearest town or village, taking over all the pubs and bringing chaos to a perplexed rural community. In 1846 this resulted in a huge riot in Penrith involving 2000 men, which ended only when troops were called in. However, in spite of the challenge of both the workforce and the fells, Locke completed his task in just two years. To save time and money he had decided not to build a tunnel at Shap, as was originally planned, but to make do with a very steep gradient. This pushed the locomotives of the time to their very limit, but allowed the vital line to be opened in December 1846.

I returned to the town centre where I wandered for an hour around prosperous Micklegate and Devonshire Street; walking in the footsteps of both Bonnie Prince Charlie, who stayed here in '45, and the grandfather of William Wordsworth who once owned the Old Moot Hall.

"Say, could you tell me how we can get to Kes-wick from here, then on to Cocker-mouth?"

A small, bright-eyed American man, together with his attractive wife were gathered around the counter in the Tourist Information Centre, which is housed in an imposing Elizabethan building which was once a school. The attendant took out a map, then began to trace the route with his finger.

"I'll give you a selection of brochures on both towns – but don't miss seeing the older parts of Penrith. We have a Town Trail you can follow if you have time."

In the quietness of St Andrew's Churchyard, which is fringed by rows of splendid Georgian houses, I went to look at Penrith's oldest Christian remains. Close to the North Door stands the Giant's Thumb, a weathered Norse Cross which dates from the early years of the 10th century. It is said to have been erected by Owen Caesarius, King of Cumbria, as a memorial to his father. But it is the nearby Giant's Grave, which has been the cause of most speculation over the centuries, for traditionally this is the last resting place of King Owen himself.

The rain had now ceased but the sky remained dismally grey as I pondered on the origins of the Giant's Grave. It consists of an unusual arrangement of four hog-backed tombstones which have been grouped in pairs, with two upright stone crosses at each end. This is said to represent the wild boar which Owen often killed in Inglewood Forest, for he had a reputation as a slayer of both men and wild beasts. During the 16th century the site was opened to reveal several large bones of a man and a broadsword; this may be when King Owen first gained a reputation for being a giant. In 1722 when the church was being partially rebuilt, the church wardens considered breaking up the ancient stones, but thankfully the local people opposed the plan, so an act of 18th century vandalism was averted.

I strolled around the interior of this lovely sandstone church which has been at the heart of Penrith for a thousand years, gazing on the many memorials which chart its vibrant history. Then before I reluctantly left the town I bought a fascinating booklet which has the title, *A Hired Lass in Westmorland*. Written by Isabelle Cooke, who died in 1981 at the age of ninety, it records in her own honest words her life as a country girl at the turn of this century. Her work began here in Penrith in 1906, when she stood in Burrowgate at what was known as the Hirings. Here she found her first job, working as a farm lass for a wage of £9 for half a year!

The sky was at last beginning to shed its dullness, with patches of blue appearing over Beacon Hill which dominates the town. I took this to be a good omen for my journey would now continue eastwards into the splendour of Borrowdale.

5

What image is seen on the front of thousands of postcards, adorns scores of Lakeland calendars, helps to sell boxes of biscuits to whistle-stop tourists and is used to illustrate almost every book ever written about Cumbria? The answer is of course, that marvellous view of Derwentwater, the Vale of Keswick, and the rising bulk of Skiddaw from Ashness Bridge.

I stood with a small group of visitors on the side of this little river which rushes white over the rocks then disappears beneath this most photographed of all bridges. A beaming Japanese student had his Pentax poised to take yet

Skiddaw and Derwentwater from Ashness Bridge – one of Lakeland's best-known views

another shot which would be shown to his friends back home, while nearby, a tall lean man almost toppled into the water as he eagerly sought the best vantage point. But most of us just gazed down this sublime hillside in silence and with adoration, for in spite of its familiarity the view was no anti-climax. For even the most gifted writer or the very best landscape photographer can never hope to convey the true splendour of this spot; it is one of those magical corners of Lakeland that is beyond description.

I was returned to reality by a traffic jam which had suddenly appeared at the entrance to the small car-park which has been created in a woodland glade. A middle aged woman, who was driving her husband, seemed full of indecision. Should she turn right off the road and into the car-park? Perhaps it would be better to park beside that tree on the left? But Watendlath is only a few miles away? No, I will park here, but that is rather a sharp turn?

Quite oblivious to the chaos her stationary Fiesta was causing it was around five minutes before she finally made her move. Barely missing a jutting out boulder, she at last came to a halt off the road and we all breathed a sigh of relief. But quite remarkably, not a single car-horn was heard during the whole episode. I smiled to myself, thinking what a different response there would have been had this happened in Italy!

The Watendlath road is narrow and winding, rather like driving along a woodland footpath. It rises alongside rocks and ferns, almost touches the branches of silver birch trees, turns blind bends shrouded with foliage then emerges between stout dry stone walls. On the right it is overlooked by the modest summit of Grange Fell; this is bordered by a sparkling beck which tumbles down the hillside to form the Lodore Falls. The road at last comes to a dramatic end in the best-known hidden valley in Lakeland.

There is a marvellous feeling of secrecy about Watendlath, like no other spot in Cumbria. It is the type of place in which Robin Hood might have sought refuge had he decided to venture north. In the 12th century it came into the possession of the powerful Fountains Abbey, but since the 1960s it has belonged largely to the National Trust. Watendlath's small farming community, which look after their Herdwick sheep in this elevated stronghold, welcome visitors. They greet today's walkers and fishermen with a smile, as their ancestors greeted Wordsworth and Coleridge nearly two centuries ago. Some people come here on a literary pilgrimage, following in the steps of *Judith Paris*; others come to fish for pike and perch in one of Lakeland's most perfect tarns; but most are drawn by the magnetic atmosphere of peace and remoteness which is the essence of this hanging valley of Watendlath.

It was a perfect day to wander around this cluster of cottages and farms which rest on the reedy shore of the tarn. I passed the whitewashed walls of the 'Home of Judith Paris', nodded half a dozen 'Good Afternoons' to the

Fishermen enjoying the tranquillity of remote Watendlath Tarn.

walkers who I met, then I crossed a hump-backed bridge which led me to the solitude of a small hill. Here I sat in the warm sunshine, encompassed by the fells which guard this tranquil green bowl. Sheepdogs were scampering around the hamlet watched by an anxious tethered goat, swifts were soaring over the silver water catching flies, while two fishermen and a fisherwoman were busy, endlessly casting their lines. I suppose it was inevitable that this idyllic setting would eventually spawn a great novel. This happened in 1930 when Sir Hugh Walpole's hugely successful Judith Paris was first published; Watendlath had at last been immortalized.

Hugh Seymour Walpole first came to live in Lakeland in 1924 when he was 40 years old, by this time he was already a well established member of London's literary set. He had been born in Auckland, New Zealand on the 13 March 1884, where his father was the Canon of the cathedral. When he was five years old his father took up a position teaching religion in a New York seminary and Hugh was sent to England from where his parents had originated. He lived at first in Cornwall, then later in Durham where his father returned to become the Principal of Bede College. After leaving King's School in Canterbury he completed his education at Emmanuel College in Oxford, where his desire to become a writer first became apparent. While still an undergraduate he completed the draft of two novels, one of which eventually became his first published book in 1909, *The Wooden Horse*.

Following the example set by his father, he began his career as a Church of England lay reader, then as a teacher in a boy's school. But his real ambitions lay in the literary world, which inevitably led him to Fleet Street where he began to review books for the Evening Standard. At the same time he was also pursuing the difficult steps of trying to establish himself as a novelist. His first four books gave him little financial reward, but with *Fortitude (1913)*, came the first hints of the success which was to follow.

As a young man he was handsome and impressive, but he was never destined to marry. Well liked for his amiable personality he quickly became a welcome member of the middle-class literary society which flourished in London at this time. When the horrors of the First World War began to dawn he joined the Red Cross, serving in Russia where he gained an award for heroism under fire. It was there that he met up with journalist, Arthur Ransome; two men who would eventually leave their mark on Lakeland.

By the early twenties he was a well-established, prolific writer who did not confine his work to the novel, but wrote travel, biography and later wrote plays. He had already received official recognition for his talent, being awarded the CBE and was enjoying the social whirl of the metropolis. However, another side of his nature, which yearned for peace and solitude, was becoming forcefully apparent. Motivated by this urge to be alone, he decided to seek a country retreat in which he could escape with his 'dogs and his books'. His search ended, like many great literary figures before him, among the mountains of Cumbria.

Enchanted by the splendour of Lakeland he found 'a little paradise on Cat Bells', which was to become his new home. This was a stone house named Brackenburn which lies six miles from Keswick, on the Portiscale to Grange road. The magnificent view from his study window, across the silver of Derwentwater, became his inspiration. As early as 1925 his mind had begun to dwell on thoughts of a new writing project. But this, he decided, would not be a single book, it would be a saga. He would stake his reputation on capturing with his pen the spirit of life among the fells and lakes of Cumberland. It would be a tale of the fortunes of an English family spanning three centuries.

But he had many other diversions and commitments which stopped him immediately starting work. Still part of literary London, he also needed to spend time in the capital to keep in the swim of things. At this time he had become a close friend of Yorkshire writer, J.B. Priestley, and the two men co-operated in a joint novel, *Farthing Hall*. This proved to be a milestone in Priestley's career, leading him on to a huge success with *The Good Companions*, which he dedicated to his friend.

In 1927, despite the shock of discovering he had developed diabetes, Walpole began the draft of the first book in the series he had long planned. Its title was *Rogue Herries*, which began the colourful story of a family living in 18th century Cumberland. Although the characters came from his imagination, the historical events which shaped their lives were factual and the countryside was that which the writer had come to know and love. He was later to confess that one of his few regrets was that he 'hadn't been born a Cumbrian'.

Rogue Herries, which was well received, was completed in 1929 and published the following year. His second and most popular work in the series, *Judith Paris*, followed in 1931. It is said that he found the perfect setting for the book, when he came here to Watendlath on a picnic with his brother and sister. In later years, when the *Herries' Chronicle* had gained an army of followers, a dispute arose as to which was really the heroine's home. Two friendly rivals in the hamlet each maintained that theirs was the location chosen by Walpole. But with the diplomacy for which he was noted, he said her house was not based on any particular dwelling!

The *Herries Chronicle* continued with *The Fortress (1932)* and was completed the following year with the publication of *Vanessa*. All these volumes have proved to be so popular that they have remained continually in print since their publication. Walpole's intention of recording 'scenes from the life of an English family during two hundred years of English change' has been proved, by the passing of time to be immensely popular.

Hugh Walpole continued to live and write in his Lakeland home for the rest of his life. The sales of his books rewarded him with wealth, which he invested in antiques and the world's greatest collection of Sir Walter Scott's manuscripts. In 1937 he received a well-deserved knighthood, but sadly died four years later at the early age of only 57. His death followed a heart attack and a diabetic coma, believed to have been brought on by the hectic schedule of a 'War Weapons Week' which was being held in Keswick in June 1941. His final resting place is as he wished, in the tranquillity of St John's churchyard in Keswick, at the heart of his adopted homeland.

I stood on the shimmering green hillside gazing down at the dappled beauty of the valley, the sunlight reflecting in a ring of gold on the surface of the tarn. Lifting my eyes to a fellside path I could see the figure of a girl slowly descending to the hamlet. I wondered if she was aware that she was following in the steps of one of Lakeland's greatest fictional characters?

5

Watendlath to Gosforth

I pass through the Jaws of Borrowdale remembering an Easter adventure, I learn about plumbago, then traverse magnificent Honister Pass. In Buttermere I meet a sheep named Lucy, learn about Lakeland's most famous romance, then I gaze up at Haystacks, thinking of Alfred Wainwright. I reach the Irish Sea at St Bees, discovering the start of the Coast-to-Coast walk, and end in Viking Gosforth where I learn of a wartime tragedy.

1

I descended from the seclusion of Watendlath, reaching the main road that skirts the wooded shore of Derwentwater. Here I was surprised to see not one, but half a dozen gleaming Rolls Royce cars, making their majestic way into Borrowdale. It seemed appropriate that these, the supreme examples of automobile engineering, should be seen in this valley which many regard as being the loveliest in Lakeland. I later learned that these cars were part of the Rolls Royce Round Britain Rally, which was passing through Cumbria. They were following in the illustrious treads of a 1911 Argyll, which is reputed to have been the first car to have ever been driven up Borrowdale. It was purchased brand-new by the Simpson family of Hazel Bank and driven by their coachman turned chauffeur, Jonathan Hind.

As I drove slowly up the valley I could see on my left soaring grey crags entwined with foliage, reflecting a wildness rarely found in England. But on my right there was a more tranquil scene, for here lay the placid waters of the lake, mirroring the gentle outline of trees and rocks and fells. Just beyond the point where Derwentwater ends I passed the plush Lodore Swiss Hotel; this once witnessed a historic meeting between those two, much-loved men of the Lakeland mountains, W.A. Poucher and Alfred Wainwright. Close to this spot lies the hidden cascade of the Lodore Falls. This is a waterfall whose torrent is only truly impressive after rain, but quickly returns to a mere trickle, to the disappointment of many a tourist. One puzzled visitor is said to have asked where the falls were, only to be told he was actually sitting on them!

Shepherd's Crag, much loved by rock climbers, loomed majestically over the narrowing road which brought me into the quiet village of Grange-in-Borrowdale which straggles the River Derwent. This is the largest of five villages which nestle in the green of this valley; the others being Rosthwaite, Stonethwaite, Seathwaite and Seatoller. The name 'thwaite', which appears so frequently in these parts, means a 'clearing'. The Norsemen are believed to have first created these settlements during the 10th century, then later much of the land became the property of the powerful Furness Abbey. When King Henry VIII closed the Abbey its estate was seized, then later sold off by agents to rich families. However, the romance of Borrowdale seems to have been largely unaffected by this wheeling and dealing, with the valley folk pursuing their hard-working lives in idyllic seclusion. One marvellous tale tells how they had the idea of bringing perpetual springtime to their valley by keeping a cuckoo a prisoner here. Sadly, this much thought-out scheme must have failed, for Seathwaite is the wettest spot in England!

I strolled from the small roadside car-park, in the steps of generations of curious visitors, to see the famous Bowder Stone. Here a group of delighted walkers were scrambling up the ladder to the top, while below a couple, unperturbed by the mud, were attempting to shake-hands through a gap at the base. Although the Bowder Stone is thought to have gained its name from Balder, who was a son of the Norse God Odin, there is surprisingly no legends attached to this extraordinary boulder. But what geologists do tell us is that it

The finely balanced bulk of the huge Bowder Stone in Borrowdale

did not topple down from the mountain top, like most visitors wrongly assume, for it is not a local rock. They believe it was most likely carried here to Lakeland from Scotland, by the glaciers of the Ice Age.

I wandered around the eighty-nine feet circumference of this finely balanced stone, which is said to weigh 1.970 tons, then I too climbed the ladder to the top. Standing thirty-six feet high, this elevated platform gives a fine view through the trees to the upper reaches of the valley and beyond to the rising fells. But my enjoyment of the landscape was seriously halted by a thought which suddenly occurred to me. Could my weight be all that is necessary to over-balance this huge Caledonian monster and tumble it on a journey that was interrupted 20,000 years ago? Quickly I descended the ladder and returned with sweating palms to my car!

The Bowder Stone lies on the slopes of Grange Fell, which was bought by the National Trust in 1910. It stands as a memorial to King Edward VII, who had died in the same year, remembered by the summit which is named King's How in his honour. Here where the valley narrows to form the Jaws of Borrowdale, on my right I could see the rising heights of Castle Crag. This former hill-fort now also belongs to the National Trust; it was given as a memorial to Lieutenant John Hamer and all the other Borrowdale men who died during the terrible carnage of the First World War.

As I passed Rosthwaite I smiled to myself, remembering an episode from the past which I always associate with this gateway to the Stonethwaite and Lang Strath Valleys. It began at Eastertime, almost thirty years ago, when I arrived in the Langdale Valley with a friend named David Kaye. We each were burdened with a huge rucksack which contained a mass of ancient camping equipment, for our youthful masterplan. The idea was that we would ascend to above the 2000 feet contour, then camp there for four days, leaving any heavy gear in the tent. This meant we would be able to casually stroll just a short distance to such high summits as Scafell Pike, Scafell, Glaramara, Bow Fell and Crinkle Crags; in theory, we would be as free as birds!

Having made the journey from our hometown of Horwich in Lancashire, by a series of monotonous bus journeys, we arrived at last in the Langdale Valley in late afternoon. We then began the terrible slog up the steep path of Rossett Gill, our backs almost breaking under the heavy loads. But we kept reassuring each other that it was all worthwhile, once we had established our camp we would soon forget this hardship. At last, with the sun about to set we reached the dark waters of Angle Tarn which lies below Esk Hause. As the cold wind was now blowing strongly on the exposed ridge, we decided to descend a few hundred feet into the valley of Lang Strath to pitch our tent.

This was when we hit our first problem, for we searched in vain for even the smallest patch of ground which could be described as remotely flat. As it was now almost dark we finally had to compromise our high ideals, placing our ancient tent, which looked like a veteran of the El Alamein campaign, on the least sloping bit of the fellside. This meant that our inadequate sleeping bags were destined to be sliding forever towards the side of the tent, but this was the least of our problems.

The isolated valley was by this time bathed in an inky darkness, there were thick clouds, no moon and the wind was getting fiercer by the minute. Our next priority was to cook a hot meal, which created another major problem. Our brass, pre-war primus stove was duly assembled and filled with fuel from a large bottle which formed part of our back-breaking supplies. But outside of the tent, due to the gale which was now blowing up, it proved impossible to light. We then attempted to ignite the wick, sheltered inside of the tent, which in itself was barely large enough to hold two people. On we struggled, gently coaxing and then cursing the small blue light. At times it looked promising, then it would suddenly flare up into a huge yellow flame which threatened to engulf the whole tent. We responded by quickly turning off the fuel while at the same time pushing the infernal stove out through the tent flap. Eventually, too tired and too hungry to try any more, we ate a meal of dry biscuits and cold soup. Then prepared to sleep fully clothed in our sloping sleeping bags, listening to the wind blowing hard and the first patter of rain on the tent roof.

Wearing all of our outdoor clothing including our woollen hat and gloves, we then attempted to sleep on the hard ground in the ever lowering temperature. As the hours dragged on we drifted in and out of sleep, menaced by drops of icy water which kept dripping onto our faces. When at last the blackness began to lift we suddenly became aware that the tent roof had sunk down to just two inches above our heads.

"The guide ropes must have come loose," exclaimed Dave. So as I was the nearest to the tent door, I undid the flap and pushed my head outside. I then gasped in disbelief, for the valley looked like a scene from an Antarctic travelogue. Unknown to us, over a foot of snow had silently fallen during the night, which the wind had blown into huge drifts. Our tent, which had been completely covered, was almost at the point of collapse with the weight of snow!

As the first light of dawn was breaking we began to pack up the tent, then abandoning any supplies we could to lessen our load, we started the treacherous descent to Rosthwaite. We arrived in the village at about five am; two cold, wet, and weary figures whose masterplan had failed due to poor equipment and our inexperience of Lakeland's Easter weather. As we travelled back home to Lancashire, we decided that next time our accommodation would be in a hotel in Borrowdale!

2

Beyond Rosthwaite I drove along the twisting road which curves westwards, cutting across the upper part of Borrowdale and crossing over the River Derwent. Glancing to my left I could see the emerald of the narrowing valley, served by a lane which ends at the lonely community of Seathwaite. Nearby stands the celebrated Borrowdale Yews; yet another Lakeland feature which was immortalised by Wordsworth's pen. Here too lie the disused Borrowdale Lead Mines, which since the 16th century produced the highly valuable mineral known as Plumbago or Wad. This high grade graphite, which is one of the world's softest minerals, was first used by Keswick's pencil makers, then later was in great demand for use in firearms. It was so greatly prized that the miners, like those in the diamond mines of South Africa, were searched at the end of each shift to ensure that they had not stolen any. Armed men guarded the precious mineral, and tales are told of gangs of thieves making bloodthirsty raids on the plumbago storehouse. This colourful episode in Seathwaite's history finally came to an end in the middle of the last century when the mine became uneconomic. Today Seathwaite has returned to rural tranquillity, being best known to walkers as the much-loved gateway over Sty Head to the summits of Great Gable and Scafell.

Passing the hamlet of Seatoller I now began the steep ascent up the winding road which is the start of Honister Pass. Here sheep were wandering at liberty off the boulder strewn fells, for there are few walls to restrict them. At Honister Youth Hostel, which sits high on the roadside in a landscape of green slate, I saw young walkers starting out on their days excursion. The bright reds, blues and purples of their clothes bringing a refreshing feast of colour to this isolated spot. Then suddenly I had reached the high point of the road, with the breathtaking panorama of Honister Pass spreading out below me. From here the road plummets down in a silver twisting line, hemmed in by towering blue-grey crags, creating one of Lakeland's most stunning views.

I then began my descent of this English Glencoe, which quickly opened out in spectacular fashion to reveal the brown curve of high ridges which sit on both sides of the road. The great bulk of Fleetwith Pike overshadowed the scene on my left, while on the opposite side lay the craggy summits of Dalehead, Hindscarth and Robinson. Quickly, the distant line of pale blue which lay before me then began to expand, showing the full splendour of Buttermere Lake surrounded by the shimmering green of fields.

Buttermere village, I discovered, is one of Lakeland's unspoilt gems which sits alone in an amphitheatre of magnificent mountains. Fringed by small woodland glades it lies mid-way between Buttermere Lake and Crummock-water at the junction with the ascending road to the Newlands Valley. The cluster of buildings consist of two hotels, a youth hostel, a church and a group of farms. Its community of about fifty people rely mainly on raising sheep or feeding hungry tourists for their living. I walked in the hot sunshine from the small car-park, which was nearly full, past the side of the Fish Hotel. Nearby lies a small café where I bought tea and scones which I decided to eat at a table outside. But no sooner had I begun my snack than I felt a sharp nudge in my back. Turning around I found myself staring straight into the piercing eyes of a fully grown herdwick ewe who was demanding my attention. She made it perfectly obvious that she wanted some of my scone, so together we ate our snack which she gulped down in two seconds flat.

"I hope Lucy isn't bothering you," said the woman who was serving in the café. "We hand reared her from being a lamb and now she feels its her right to demand food."

By this time Lucy had lost interest in me as all my scones had been eaten, so she had moved quickly on to seek out new arrivals. My attention was now drawn by a strange conversation that was taking place just outside the café entrance. A tall, thin walker was having great difficulty trying to communicate with a small oriental-looking man. Arms were windmilling through the air and shoulders were moving up and down with frustration, till finally the small man smiled and walked away up the Newlands road.

"Bit of a language problem," said the walker. "Its seems he's a student from Korea who has missed his bus to Keswick. But I just can't get through to him."

I then sauntered towards the old Fish Hotel where I got into conversation with the driver of the Mountain Goat Bus, who was sunning himself outside. He confirmed that this was indeed the birthplace of the 'Beauty of Buttermere', whose grave I had seen in Caldbeck churchyard.

"But strangely, they don't seem to make much of the connection nowadays," he confided.

It was here at Buttermere during the late 18th century, in what is now the Fish Hotel but at the time was an inn called The Char, that this famous Lakeland romance began. Mary Robinson, who became known as the Beauty of Buttermere, was the young daughter of the landlord, who helped her parents by serving travellers with ale and food. Her rare beauty was first brought to public notice in 1792 when a visitor, Joseph Palmer, wrote a book entitled *A Fortnight's Ramble to the Lakes*. In it he described his first meeting with her when she brought in his dinner; She was about 15 years old at this time.

'Her hair was thick and long, of a dark brown, and though unadorned with ringlets, did not seem to want them. Her face was a fine oval, with full eyes and lips red as vermilion. Her cheeks had more of the lily than the rose.'

Palmer's book improved business at The Char, for not only did tourists flock here to view the unsurpassed landscape, but they now had the added attraction

The Fish Hotel, formerly the Char Inn: birthplace of Mary Robinson who became widely known as the Beauty of Buttermere.

of being served by Lakeland's most beautiful girl. Mary, once looked upon as being merely an innkeeper's daughter, was now growing famous. Her looks also drew in curious celebrities including Wordsworth, Coleridge and Southy, together with a host of admirers. But in spite of her fame, she remained a modest girl who was still unmarried at the age of 25.

However, when a handsome and wealthy stranger arrived at the inn on a char fishing trip, all was to change. The Honourable Alexander Augustos Hope, who was the MP for Linlithgow and brother of the Earl of Hopetown, swept Mary off her feet. In a soft Irish brogue he talked of his travels in the Middle East, his military exploits in America, and of his estates in Cheshire and Derbyshire. In spite of a large age difference, for he was about fifty years old, Mary fell under his spell; she later had no hesitation in accepting his proposal of marriage. The ceremony took place in nearby Lorton church on the 2nd October 1802.

The event created a great deal of publicity in the press, but many Lakeland residents were a little suspicious about the credentials of Hope, including Coleridge. Why did he have an Irish brogue if he came from Scotland? Why was his speech, at times, vulgar and why did he not possess the restraint practised by men of his class?

But members of Lakeland's social circle, to whom he and his new wife had been readily accepted, quickly came to his defence. They argued that he was a full Lieutenant Colonel whose name could be seen on the Army List. His apparent lack of the ways of a gentleman, together with his accent, were explained by his many years of military service in which he had mixed with the lower classes. Did he not receive regular letters addressed to him as a Member of Parliament, and did his position not entitle him to the privilege of having his own mail sent post-free, to which he took full advantage?

Coleridge, however, was still unconvinced that Hope was genuine, so he passed on his suspicions to a London newspaper. Investigations which followed in Scotland revealed there was indeed a Colonel Hope, but he had been away on diplomatic business to Vienna all through the summer. Armed with this new evidence rumours spread fast and furious through the villages of Lakeland; was the husband of the Beauty of Buttermere indeed an impostor?

Faced with mounting publicity and doubt, fired by the fact that his lordly lifestyle was based mainly on credit, Hope began to answer his accusers with blatant lies. In panic he denied that he had ever claimed to be a Member of Parliament, or that he was even named Hope! But now it had become painfully obvious that the Beauty of Buttermere had been deceived, her affections had been manipulated by the words of a rogue. No longer able to sustain his sham identity Hope quickly departed from Buttermere leaving his heartbroken wife pregnant.

Further enquiries revealed that the true identity of the Honourable Alexander Augustos Hope was John Hatfield, a man who had no aristocratic roots but was a linen draper's salesman. Adding to Mary's despair it was then discovered that he had a wife and children living in Devon, and that he was a notorious fraudster with a prison record who carried the nickname of Lying Hatfield. He made his living by preying on rich young women, deluding them with a proposal of marriage he would then escape with their fortune.

A warrant was issued for Hatfield's arrest on three charges of forgery. This led to him being tracked down by the policemen of the day, the Bow Street Runners, near Swansea, then being transported up to Carlisle for trial. His bigamous marriage to Mary Robinson, although of paramount importance in the minds of the jury, was not an offence which carried a long sentence. But his forging of Parliamentary franks, which he used under the guise of being an MP to carry his letters free, carried a possible death sentence!

Although Mary was not required to give evidence, but simply to write a statement regarding her knowledge of Hatfield, the Prosecution emphasised the callous way in which she had been treated, which was of course already widely known. As a result Hatfield was found guilty of forgery and sentenced to death, but in the hearts of the members of the jury, was no doubt paying for his cruel treatment of the Beauty of Buttermere.

In spite of his impending doom Hatfield remained amazingly calm, seeming to revel in his last few days of freedom in the full glare of nationwide publicity. He even gave William Wordsworth a final interview, but refrained from seeing Coleridge whom he probably partially blamed for his exposure. On the 3rd of September 1803 he was taken to the place of execution, which lay close to the River Eden on the outskirts of Carlisle. Facing a crowd of thousands, smartly dressed in a black jacket and fustian pantaloons, he appeared less nervous than his Scottish executioner. Ensuring that the noose was positioned correctly on his neck, he faced the next world with incredible composure.

We can only guess at the heartache which the Beauty of Buttermere had to now endure, facing the impending birth of her child without a husband and in a blaze of publicity. She continued working at The Char for some years, but what became of her child is unknown, although some believe it was stillborn. In later years she was able to pick up the threads of her shattered life, at last finding permanent happiness as the wife of a Caldbeck farmer. She was blessed with several children, but died in 1837 at the early age of 58.

Following the execution of John Hatfield his dramatic tale of deception and betrayal was immortalized in a play which was performed in London. In 1987, Cumbrian born writer Melvyn Bragg, again adapted the story for his novel, *The Maid of Buttermere*, which became a best-seller.

3

I strolled from the warm sunshine into the cool of Buttermere's tiny church which is dedicated to St James-the-Great. A leaflet told me that the present building was erected in 1846 from stone which came from Sour Milk Ghyll and that one of its early unordained Readers was that great Lakeland eccentric, Robert Walker. Known in later years as Wonderful Walker, he was born at Seathwaite in the Duddon Valley, in 1709. One of twelve children he was very weak as a child, but surprising his parents he survived, then went on to become something of a scholar. He was taught how to read and write in Seathwaite village school, then in early manhood became a teacher at Loweswater. But he also continued his own education, mastering Latin and Greek, which allowed him at the age of 26 to take holy orders.

However, his early years of living on a very low income left their mark, for throughout his life he lived frugally, working with enormous vigour and vitality, and saving every penny he could. He married a domestic servant girl, raised a family of eight children and became the curate of Seathwaite, a position he held for nearly seventy years. He also served the church here at

Buttermere until 1736 for a fee of one pound; under a system known as Whittlegate, he would lodge free with a local family for up to two weeks.

But it was his non-stop activity which most impressed the Cumbrians of these isolated valleys, who themselves are renowned for hard work. For as well as carrying out his religious duties, together with teaching both his own and the other village children, he was a jack of all trades. He raised his own sheep, which he sheared, then he spun and wove the wool which he made into clothes. He also kept cattle whose hides he tanned for leather, he grew herbs which he used for medical purposes, and he kept bees for honey. Any excess produce was taken over the fells to sell at Ambleside or Keswick markets, and he also made some extra cash by labouring on farms and even selling his own made beer after the Sabbath service!

Proving the old adage that "hard work never did anyone any harm', Wonderful Walker lived well into his nineties, leaving a large sum of over two thousands pounds. He was im-

mortalized by Wordsworth who met him on one of his many Lakeland excursions, describing him as a Gospel teacher 'Whose good works formed an endless retinue'.

Today it is another Wonderful Walker who is remembered in this lovely church, by a simple marble plaque which sits on a window ledge. Following the wishes recorded on the memorial, I looked out of the window across the green of the valley towards the 1900 feet high summit of Haystacks. This 'Cinderella of Buttermere' as AW described it, together with the lonely Innominate Tarn, has become an intrinsic part of his lifestory. For the spirit of this man, whose name here in Lakeland is as well-known as that of Wordsworth, lives on in this magical landscape more than in any other place.

The Wainwright memorial

Blackburn-born Alfred Wainwright, author of the classic
Pictorial Guides to The Lakes

In 1993, while re-searching *A Journey Through Lancashire*, I visited the small terraced house in Blackburn where Alfred Wainwright was born on the 17th January 1907. Today No 331, Audley Range is the home of Kathleen Godfrey, who was happy to let the local Civic Society erect a blue commemorative plaque on the wall of the former Wainwright family home. Here Alfred, one of four children, spent his childhood in the poverty and privation which was all too common at the time. The Wainwright family had originated from Millhouse, near Penistone in Yorkshire, but AW's father who worked as a travelling stone-mason, had settled in Blackburn. Tragically, he later developed into an alcoholic, which transformed his normal good-humoured nature into that of a rough bully. This added to the desperate struggle of the family, drawing the children closer to their mother.

Living among the grey cobbled streets it was a challenge merely to survive, but in spite of the hardship, AW later recalled, people "had pride, courage, character, honesty and an observance of moral standards not seen today". He was also fortunate in living in Blackburn, for although it was a town of cotton mills and industry, wild moorland and windswept hills lay on his doorstep. The urge to explore such places came to him at an early age, for when not yet seven he took his first solitary walk up to the summit of local Darwen Hill. "None of my pals would come with me," he remembered. His artistic talent, the other attribute which was to play such a major role in his later life, was also becoming apparent at this time. He would painstakingly copy in great detail, cartoon characters from his much-loved comics.

Most of his pals were sadly destined to leave school at 12 years of age, then pursue poorly paid jobs in mills and factories. But showing above average intelligence, AW was given the opportunity to follow two extra years of education, which then secured him a job as an office boy in the Borough Engineer's Department in Blackburn. Three years later he was transferred into the Borough Treasurer's Department where he was persuaded to begin an accountancy course at night school. He found he enjoyed this new type of work, which also allowed him to show his skill with a pen by producing rows of meticulously shaped figures in the office ledgers. Importantly, when he eventually completed his accountancy examinations, he had also the security of a relatively well paid profession.

It was in 1930 that the tall, red headed AW first came to the corner of England which would change his life. Accompanied by his quiet cousin from Yorkshire, Eric Beardsall, he boarded a bus from Blackburn which took him on his first Lakeland holiday. From Windermere the two young men climbed in bright sunshine to the vantage point of Orrest Head, where they looked down on a magical landscape which left them spellbound. The splendour of the towering brown fells and the turquoise lake, framed with the emerald of woodland was a like a piece of heaven; life would never be quite the same again.

The two friends continued their personal exploration of the craggy uplands, which at times filled them with apprehension. The first summit reached was Froswick, followed later by a number of other inspiring mountains including Striding Edge and Helvellyn. When their holiday finally ended they had become completely enchanted by Cumbria, and only reluctantly did they return to the greyness of their working lives. However, there were some compensations for AW was a keen Blackburn Rovers fan, being a founder member of the Supporter's Club, and whenever possible he would watch the game. He could also enjoy his favourite meal of fish and chips, for which Lancashire was renowned!

The thirties brought inevitable change to AW's life, his father died, he was married to a local girl and then followed the birth of his son. However, his new domestic role did not diminish his love for the wild places of the north. Whenever possible he would take to the hills, exploring his local Lancashire moorland, with the occasional highlight of a trip to Lakeland. His hidden desire to be a writer became apparent in 1938, when he undertook a solitary walking tour from Settle in Yorkshire, up to Hadrian's Wall. He recorded his personal recollections of this walk in a manuscript which remained unpublished for nearly fifty years; unchanged, *A Pennine Journey* was at last published in 1986.

Another turning point came in 1941, when he heard that a vacancy had arisen in the Borough Treasurer's Office in Kendal. Always on the look out for the opportunity to move closer to his beloved Lakeland, he applied for the job and was successful. In spite of it meaning a reduction in salary, he quickly accepted the position, moving to a new home in the town. Now having easy access to the landscape which he knew was his spiritual homeland, he began a decade of intense personal exploration. Every weekend would see him catching the early morning bus from Kendal to a new part of Cumbria. He was unable to resist the urge to ascend every mountain summit, traverse every valley and discover every pathway; this he undertook with almost religious fervour.

By the early fifties he had gained an unsurpassed knowledge of the Lakeland mountains which he then wanted to pass on to others in the form of a guide book. But he was undecided how best to achieve this aim, for trying to concisely convey information about mountainous country is no easy task. For months he deliberated on the problem, then slowly he devised a solution which was unique: he would provide line drawings of the craggy mountain profiles, which he would intersperse with hand written text, giving any details he thought necessary. But after he had begun the task it soon became apparent that Lakeland was too great an area to cover in a single volume; he eventually decided it would require seven volumes to outline the main fells.

It was in 1952, when AW was aged 45, that he began, single handed, the work which was to make his name so well known throughout Britain. For a full ten years every minute of his leisure time was taken up with the project. It was during this period, he later recalled, his hair changed colour 'from red to grey and then to white'. The first volume, *The Eastern Fells*, was completed in 1955, being published by a local man, Henry Marshall of Kentmere. The pages, being produced entirely by hand required no type-setting, but were sent to Manchester to be engraved on plates, the printing was completed by Bateman and Hewitson in Kendal. The Westmorland Gazette later took on the entire publishing of the books, which unknown to them at the time, was to create a multimillion pound industry.

As AW never learned how to drive a car and never really wanted to, all his visits to the mountains were made on public transport. On fine days he climbed up to the high summits, making notes and sketches, and taking the occasional photograph. When the clouds were low, or Lakeland's famous rain poured down with determination, he would explore the paths and tracks in the valleys. Every two years a new volume was completed, being eagerly snapped up by the growing band of Wainwright fans, who did not even know what their beloved author really looked like. Rumours spread about his identity, but AW remained elusive; he was a private man who intended to remain so.

The final volume of his unique pictorial guides, *The Western Fells*, was published to much acclaim in 1966. His many readers decided he now deserved an award for what was a truly amazing achievement. One man started gathering signatures for a petition to Parliament, appropriately on the summit of Great Gable. As a result, Prime Minister Harold Wilson, invited AW to accept the honour of an MBE. The quiet man from Blackburn had reluctantly become part of the culture of the Swinging Sixties, which was more renowned for The Beatles, Flower Power, and James Bond!

Although he had now completed the works which had been his main aim in life, he was only 59 years old and most of his writing career lay before him. This began with his volume, *Fellwanderer (1966)*, which charted his adventures in the mountains and was followed by his guide to Britain's first long distance footpath, *Pennine Way Companion (1968)*. In this volume he made a promise to buy a pint of beer at the Border Hotel in Kirk Yetholme, for all those who successfully completed the 250 mile walk. Over twenty years this cost him £5000, which forced him to reduce the offer to half a pint!

His pen and ink drawings, which were a unique part of his books were now becoming admired in themselves which led him on to produce *A Lakeland Sketchbook* in 1969. This proved to be so popular that he went on to produce a whole series of similar works, covering Lakeland, Scotland, the Yorkshire Dales and parts of Lancashire. But it is perhaps his *Coast to Coast Walk (1973)*, which will forever be associated with his name. This pioneering route, which links St Bees in Lakeland to Robin Hood's Bay on the North Yorkshire Coast, is followed by thousands of Wainwright devotees each year.

In later years his second wife Betty, who is 15 years his junior, was able to drive him into the remote countryside which he loved so much. His books also took on a different format in 1984 when he teamed up with brilliant landscape photographer Derry Brabbs to produce stunning images of Lakeland. These coffee table volumes were published by Michael Joseph who now produce the full range of his works.

Unlike many successful authors who cherish the thoughts of high financial rewards, AW found reward enough in writing his books and living in his beloved Lakeland. He shunned personal publicity, generally preferred animals to humans, and only reluctantly agreed to appear on TV, knowing that this would boost his royalties which largely went to animal welfare. It has been estimated that the animal sanctuary which he supported near Kendal, has received over half a million pounds from his works, and he also donated £10,000 to Kendal Town Council for a special achievement award. In 1990, approaching his 84th birthday and with his eyesight sadly failing, AW was forced to put down his pen. His prolific output of seventy volumes, which had achieved sales of over one million copies, had come to an end. In the first month of 1991 he was admitted into Westmorland General Hospital where he died two weeks later. After cremation his ashes, as he requested, were scattered near the Innominate Tarn on Haystacks; a spot many feel should be renamed Wainwright's Tarn.

Shortly after his death the uplifting introduction to his last book, *Wainwright in the Valleys of Lakeland*, was found still in his typewriter. Filled with humour, tinged a little with sadness, AW's last message to his readers is 'to stop griping and to count your blessings every night at the close of every day'.

4

From Buttermere I took the road northwards which hugs the shore of lovely Crummock Water, allowing stunning views of the brown rising fells. Some sheep were feeding on the lush grass which forms the roadside verge while others preferred the solitude of the craggy uplands of Grasmore which look menacingly down on the valley. The lake ends in a wide sweep of green where Lorton Vale provides a natural lowland route alongside the River Cocker into Cockermouth. But my route lay to the west, where I discovered the fells reduce quickly in height until soon they become like the gentle wooded slopes which might be found in Surrey. After skirting the waters of lovely Loweswater, which was bathed in morning sunshine, these hills melted completely away to reveal a landscape of soft meadowland. This stretches unbroken to the coastal towns of Whitehaven, Workington and Maryport, then continues northwards to form the banks of the Solway Firth. It seemed quite incredible looking on this flat pastoral scene, to think that Pillar, Great Gable and Scafell Pike lay less that a dozen miles away.

I stood on the beach at St Bees listening to the rhythmic murmur of the pebbles as the moving tide pushed them backwards and forwards, as it has done since prehistoric times. A handful of visitors were walking along the sea shore, watching the sunlight bounce off the waves, listening to oyster catchers screech at the gulls and breathing in the salty cool air which brought with it the pungent smell of seaweed. Below, a black and white spaniel was enjoying himself, splashing his paws on the waters edge, while his middle-aged owner looked on with amusement.

Turning to the right I could see the ascending freckled fields which form the grassy curve of St Bees Head, ending in the dark red of sandstone cliffs which tumble 300 feet down to the sea; this is northern England's most westerly point. I took the well-worn path part way up this splendid headland, then I stopped to gaze out over the inviting waves. Directly ahead, clothed in a blue mist, lay the profile of the Isle of Man, looking like an illustration from a book of fairy tales. This once formed a stepping stone for the Vikings who having settled in Ireland were then drawn to the Cumbrian mountains, for it is said it reminded them of their homeland. But this small town of St Bees, which was originally known as Kirkby Beagogh, owes its existence not to the Vikings but to a Christian saint. In the 7th century a number of nuns, together with their leader, St Bega, sailed to England from Ireland then were shipwrecked off this treacherous coast. But fortunately aid and accommodation was given to them by the caring Lady of Egremont, who soon became a close friend of the saint.

Having been received with such marvellous hospitality the nuns decided they would like to create a religious settlement in the area, but the Lord of Egremont was not too keen on the venture. However, being a diplomatic man and not wanting to upset his wife he said that the nuns could indeed stay. They would be given as much land as would be covered by snow the next morning, which just happened to be Midsummer's Day! But his clever ploy failed miserably, for on awakening the following day he was astonished to find that snow had indeed fallen over a three mile portion of his land close to the coast. So accepting this event as divine intervention, he gave the nuns land on which to build their sanctuary around which grew the present town.

Returning down the hillside to where an emerald lawn meets the sea wall, I stopped to read a notice which announced: *Start of Wainwright's Coast to Coast Walk*. In recent years this increasingly popular route, has transformed St Bees from a little-known coastal town into one which has become familiar to thousands of dedicated walkers.

When Alfred Wainwright had completed his book, *Pennine Way Companion*, which charts the route of the famous Pennine Way long distance footpath, he was spurred on to create another similar walk. He decided that a route that linked the Irish Sea to the North Sea would be ideal, for it would cross terrain than was less bleak than the Pennine Way and importantly, could be completed in the normal two weeks holiday period. So, in 1972, putting his ruler on the map he drew a line from St Bees to Robin Hood's Bay, on the Yorkshire Coast, and the blueprint of the 192 mile walk was established. He also decided that to walk from west to east seemed to be the right approach, although this had 'no foundation in logic' and some walkers prefer to make the journey in the opposite direction.

It took him a year to complete, using rights of way and wherever possible keeping to the high land. The walk passes through only two towns, Kirkby Stephen and Richmond, but embraces three National Parks: The Lake District, the Yorkshire Dales and the North Yorks Moors. Its route through Lakeland continues from St Bees, through Cleator and into Ennerdale then over Red Pike and Haystacks before descending into Borrowdale. Another ascent is made over Greenup Edge and Helm Crag before the serenity of Grasmere is met. The path is then followed past Grisedale Tarn into Patterdale, then over

Kidsty Pike to Haweswater and on to Shap. Lakeland is now left behind as the walk continues into the northern edge of the Yorkshire Dales.

Since its creation AW's walk has proved so popular that the Ordnance Survey have produced special maps of the path, an accommodation list has been written and a video of the walk has been marketed. At Kirkby Stephen, there is even a Coast-to-Coast Chip Shop in which AW once feasted on his favourite meal! Following a series of TV programmes about the walk that he made with presenter Eric Robson over 10,000 people rushed out to buy copies of his guidebook. But one ritual which AW insisted ought to be carried out by those who attempt the walk, is to begin by dipping their boots in the waters of the Irish Sea and end by a similar dowsing in the North Sea.

After enjoying a cup of tea and a cheese sandwich in a splendid, old fashioned café that looks out towards the headland, I drove half a mile to the little town whose streets were almost deserted. The Priory Church was sleeping in the sunshine, a cat was curled up outside a cottage and the only sound was the laughter of two scholars from St Bees School who somehow had managed to escape from their lessons.

The religious house which St Bega had founded here in 650 managed to survive for two centuries. Then the Vikings, who according to a local legend were led by a warrior giant named Rottin, finally destroyed it. But half a century, after the Conquest, King Henry I allowed a Priory to be built on the sacred site. Although it was occasionally raided by the Scots, this existed for over 400 years and around it grew the small settlement which is today St Bees. After King Henry VIII brought an end to all such religious houses the building became a partial ruin, but the local people still used the site as a place of Christian worship. In the early 17th century, after the turmoil of the Reformation was beginning to settle, restoration of the building began and today it has become the local Parish Church; its pride, I discovered, is a magnificent Norman doorway which has survived on the west side. Strangely, it was in the chancel of this church that the first Theological College in England was established in 1817 by the Bishop of Chester, but was closed towards the end of the last century..

I peeped through the impressive gateway of St Bees School. Surrounded by neatly manicured playing fields and framed by a cloudless sky, I could see the handsome sandstone buildings. Here, pupils were probably wrestling with the horrors of Differentiation, Integration and French Verbs, while catching a tantalising glance of the inviting sand and sea. This famous Public School which has now opened its doors to both boys and girls, owes its existence to a local man. Edmund Grindal, who was born in a house on Cross Hill, found great success in the time of the first Elizabeth. He rose to become the Archbishop of York and then went on to even greater office as the Archbishop of Canterbury, but he never forgot St Bees. In 1583 he founded a Grammar School here for local boys, which continued in the manner he had set down for almost three centuries. Then in 1879 it expanded its educational horizons, since which time it has grown to become Cumbria's most famous Public School.

As I walked back to my car I began to remember an incident from the 1980s which illustrates the remarkable history of this corner of Cumbria. Workmen who were excavating outside the library, which lies close to the Priory Church, unearthed a lead coffin. When this was opened it was found to contain the mummified body of a 13th century knight. Pathologists at the West Cumberland Hospital who later examined the remains were astonished to find that after 700 years the knight's blood was still viscous! The remains were later re-buried, but the shroud can been seen at the museum in Whitehaven.

5

As I sauntered along a sun-lit street in Gosforth I noticed a sun-tanned, middle-aged woman who was hard at work on hands and knees. Surrounded by bunches of cut-flowers and ferns, she was busily pulling up weeds and scrubbing the moss off the side of the war memorial. Dodging the cars which now speed through this former Viking village I managed to cross the road to join her and we began to chat.

"It's my turn this month to look after the memorial, but for some reason the flowers in my garden are late this year so I've had to buy some. These will only last a week, but at least they brighten things up."

I then asked her if she had known any of the local men who are remembered on the memorial. As she stood up I could see that my words had brought back painful memories, for the smile had fallen from her face.

"My brother. He was the pilot of a Lancaster Bomber that was shot down in 1944. He was just twenty years old and I was only sixteen at the time. And he had only just qualified as a pilot officer; the family had been so proud.

The terrible thing was that the plane almost made it back home after a raid over Germany, but a fighter which had followed brought it down. It had a mixed crew from Britain, Canada, USA and South Africa – they all died."

She then told me how the village postman, knowing that the telegram he had to deliver contained such bad news, had waited until her father returned home from work. Her mother had been distraught at losing her only son, then there followed the horror of receiving his personal belongings which included his dress uniform which had hardly been used.

"That's why I help to look after the memorial. But understandably the young people of the village have little interest, unlike my generation who lived through the war and experienced such personal suffering. To them it seems almost ancient history."

We then spoke of the changes that had occurred in Gosforth during her lifetime. She told me that most of the residents are now newcomers, many of them being employed at the controversial British Nuclear Fuels site at Sellafield.

"Of course you only read bad news about the site in the newspapers. There are many hundreds of people, including my husband, who have retired fit and healthy after working a lifetime among the radio active material."

I continued my stroll through the village that is known as the 'Gateway to Wasdale and Ennerdale', for here the roads to these remote valleys meet. It was once the first changing place for the horses that sped passengers south from Whitehaven and it still retains an atmosphere of bustle. But many of today's visitors come to this part of Cumbria for one reason, to see the tallest and most beautiful Viking cross in England. In the quiet churchyard of St Mary-the-Virgin I found this unique sandstone column towering up into the turquoise sky. Here I ran my fingers over the ornate carvings made by Norse hands a thousand years ago, behind which lay a confusion of mind. For in these marvellous symbols mingle both the myths of their Nordic gods and the truth of Christianity which was still being accepted. Yggdrasil, the sacred ash tree which was said to support the universe, is represented by the round tree-like lower part. But the upper portion, which is square, has on it the symbols of the Trinity.

Two other unique features of this churchyard I discovered in the shade of the east end. Here grows a cork tree which was planted in 1833 and is claimed to be the northernmost of its type in the whole of Europe. Nearby is what must surely be the only tool shed which is a listed building! It was constructed from medieval stone taken from the old church.

The great tragedy of this holy spot is that the vigour of the 18th century was outmatched by its ignorance. The church was extensively reconstructed using poor quality material, leading to the destruction of many of its treasures. This included another of its four Viking crosses which was cut down to provide the base for a sundial!

In the quietness of the church interior I gazed at the famous Fishing Stone on which is carved a Viking ship together with the god, Thor. I saw two hogback tombstones that once covered the grave of warriors, and which are said to have been carved by the most talented Viking sculptor in Britain. Then I stood in silence beside the bronze plaque that remembers a more recent warrior; Pilot Officer John Birnie, who gave his young life in the cockpit of a blazing Lancaster.

6

Gosforth to Sawrey

I enter Wasdale, gaze across England's deepest lake, see England's highest mountain, and I learn how walking and climbing really began. I am startled by Ratty in Eskdale, then I follow the Romans over notorious Hard Knott Pass to reach lovely Hawkshead village. I drink some real tea and think about the young Wordsworth before joining Japanese visitors in the home of Tom Kitten and Jemima Puddle-duck.

1

The sun continued to shine, the Cumbrian sky remained cloudless and there was hardly a car to be seen as I drove east from Gosforth. Suddenly in dramatic fashion, as I reached a highpoint on the narrow lane, came the view which never fails to quicken the heart. Before me, in breathtaking splendour lay Wasdale, the valley which many regard as being the most beautiful in the whole of Lakeland. I paused to take in the wild serenity of this captivating scene; the sweep of green in the valley, the dancing silver of the lake and the savage grandeur of the towering mountains which rise up to form the roof of England.

Slowly I drove down the bare, boulder strewn hillside, then after parking my car on a patch of flat turf I walked down to the shoreline of Wastwater. In silence I gazed out over England's deepest lake watching a black-headed gull glide across to the southern bank from which ascends the famous scree slopes. These piles of tumbled stones which stretch for almost two miles, when seen from this point appear to rise vertically from the water. They hang in huge triangles of grey and cobalt, tinged with streaks of red from iron, diminishing in size until they finally end at a ridge of jagged crags and narrow gullies. Their summits are the little known Illgill Head and Whin Rigg, which descend more gently to the south into the serenity of hidden Miterdale.

As I looked across Wastwater, memories came flooding back of a splendid days walk which I once had many years ago, when I took the screeside path

Wastwater, England's deepest lake, lies close to Scafell Pike, England's highest mountain.

which meanders precariously above this wild lake. I remember making an early start from the village of Strands which lies a mile from the western edge. I soon discovered that walking along the screes is slow but fascinating, the rounded rocks moved a little at times under my weight, but proved to be quite safe with just the occasional scramble. They actually slope upwards at an angle of about forty-five degrees, then continue down to the bottom of the lake which has a depth of 258 feet (77m). A local man once told me that during the last war commandos did some of their training here prior to D-day, by first swimming across the icy water then by climbing up to the summit ridge! In more recent times divers, while searching for a missing French student, found by chance the body of a woman which had been dumped in the water. An inscribed wedding ring found on the body led to the arrest and conviction of her husband, who had killed her.

From the screes my walk continued up to the hamlet of Wasdale Head, then over famous Black Sail Pass beneath Pillar Mountain, to reach the remote head of Ennerdale. Another ascent over Scarth Gap then I dropped down once more to the eastern end of lovely Buttermere Lake. Here I followed a marvellous shoreline path which links up Buttermere, Crummock Water and Loweswater to end a splendid excursion in the village of Mockerkin.

After spending half an hour remembering this classic walk from my past and feasting on the rugged beauty of the lake I returned to my car to continue my journey up the valley to Wasdale Head. Through my windscreen I could see a sweeping panorama of summits whose crags, paths and ridges stood out in amazing detail in the bright light. Yewbarrow, Kirkfell, the conical form of Great Gable, Lingmell and the unrivalled bulk of England's highest mountain, Scafell Pike, are the names which made this remote valley the cradle of rock climbing in the Lake District.

Although there were about twenty cars parked at the point where the road ends at Wasdale Head, I saw only four people wandering around this quiet, evocative hamlet. They smiled then whispered "Hello", for there is a feeling here which is akin to being in church; it is the quietest place in Lakeland and silence must be maintained. Fortunately, cars can penetrate no further up this glacier formed valley; the two passes which forge a tenuous link to other parts of Lakeland are strictly for the walker. Sty Head Pass climbs up the valley between Lingmell and Great Gable, leading to Borrowdale or alternatively, to the Langdale Valley, and Black Sail Pass curves northwards alongside Kirk Fell to reach Ennerdale.

The history of Wasdale is fascinating for it is closely tied up with the Norsemen, who having arrived here twelve centuries ago from the Isle of Man, made it their own. It remained one of the most isolated communities in England until recent times when visitors discovered its unique character and then new residents, known as off-comers, arrived. Under fifty people from five ancient farming families remain, making their living in the traditional way from the sheep. The hardiest breed is the Herdwick, who are said to have been originally brought here by the invaders. These white-faced, small animals, with their coarse wool are ideally suited for Lakeland, for they have an amazing ability to survive among the mountains in appalling winter conditions. But many Cumbrian farmers now cross Herdwicks with Swaledale sheep, as their wool brings a higher price.

The toughness and stamina of these Wasdale farmers is legendary. Nearly every day sees them effortlessly climbing with their Border Collie dogs to the very tops of the fells, watching over their flock of a thousand sheep or more and endlessly carrying out repairs to their dry stone walls. Then at different times of the year, which is part of their unchanging calendar, the animals are brought down from the mountains for dipping and marking and clipping, and the most hectic time of all, lambing. It is no surprise that it was a Wasdale man, Jos Naylor, who rewrote the record book for fell-running. One of his many astonishing feats was to run a distance of 91 miles, ascending 34,000 feet, within 24 hours!

With the hot sunshine on my back, which is a rare event at Wasdale Head, I strolled along a green track fringed by walls made from rounded beck stones, to reach the tiny church of St Olav. It was once boasted that this was the smallest church in England, which is not quite true for there are at least two others which are smaller. However, it could well be judged by some to have the saddest churchyard in England, for beneath its green turf lie the bodies of adventurous men who died while rock climbing on these mountains.

Appropriately lying in the shadow of Great Gable, their moss laden grave stones tell how tragedy struck so quickly in the midst of triumph. I bent beneath the overhanging branches of yew trees to read some of the poignant inscriptions:

> Max Philipp Gunter Franz, died 1953, Central Buttress, Scafell.
> Claud Deane Frankland, killed on Great Gable, 1927.
> Rolland Ernest Sargent of Hull, died on Green Gable, 1944.
> Frank Roberts, killed on Pillar Rock, 1935.
> Gustave Robert Speaker, died on Great Gable, 1942.

I then stepped into the interior of this lovely church building which is said to

The graves of climbers killed in Lakeland stand appropriately in the shadow of Great Gable at Wasdale Head

have been erected before the Reformation, some experts even believe its wooden beams came from Norse longships. In the early days it was a chapelry belonging to St Bees Priory, which until last century remained little more that a simple shelter to keep out the gales which so often sweep down from the fells. Its floor was made from earth, its windows had no glass, there were no seats and instead of a door it had a hurdle to keep out the sheep. Restoration finally came in 1892 followed by the consecration of the churchyard in 1901, for prior to this Wasdale's dead were buried in Eskdale. Surprisingly, it was only in 1977 that it was named, being appropriately dedicated to King Olaf of Norway, a warring Norseman who changed his ways and became a Christian.

2

"It's a warm one today – too hot for walking far I can tell you. And I've arrived too late!"

A tall young man had eagerly descended down Sty Head Pass with the thoughts of an ice cold shandy in his mind. Then like me he had been bitterly disappointed for the bar of the famous Wasdale Head Hotel had closed twenty minutes earlier.

I strolled along a path which led me behind the building to Mosedale Beck, where I had to be contented with a drink of the cool, rushing water. I then sat in a sheltered spot on the green bank. Surrounded by the towering mountains which form the very soul of Lakeland, I began to think of the past generations who have been drawn to this remote valley seeking both peace and adventure. For the British, more than any other race, seem to have been born with a burning desire to walk and climb and explore.

Although both the Greeks and the Romans were in the habit of taking short, leisurely strolls during which they would enjoy polite conversation, none seem to have been tempted to take longer walks. In later times men did walk long distances to visit the shrines of saints, but these pilgrimages were journeys of penance rather than pleasure. At this time walking was generally looked on as being the only option for those who could not afford a horse on which to ride; only slowly did this attitude begin to change. As early as the 12th century the British had gained something of a reputation for enjoying travel for its own sake and by the time Elizabeth I came to the throne they were beginning to record their walking excursions. These early "ramblers' included Thomas Coryate, who walked from Odcombe in Somerset, to Venice and back in 1608, and became known as the Odcombian Legge-Stretcher; William Lithgow, a Scotsman, whose broken love affair led him to journey on foot for nineteen years, reaching as far as Egypt and Syria; and the great Elizabethan writer, Ben Jonson, who in spite of weighing almost 20 stones walked from London up the Great North Road to tour Scotland.

By the early 18th century the walking tour had become an accepted, if eccentric activity for the few. These were often wealthy men who could afford to ride, but now chose to walk. Also around this time another form of walking was becoming popular, spurred on by the fashion for gambling, this was related to speed rather than pleasure. Race walking events, using the heel and toe technique, now became commonplace along the rough highways of England. This bred a new generation of walkers known as 'peds', who often covered very long distances. One of the great pioneers of race walking was Yorkshireman Foster Powell, 'The Astonishing Pedestrian'. He began his record breaking career in 1764 at the age of thirty, walking at a pace that many regarded as being dangerous. In 1773 his reputation was made when he walked from London to York and back, a distance of 402 miles, in under six days. But the greatest ever ped was Captain Robert Barclay, a man of amazing stamina and endurance who walked '20 or 30 miles before breakfast'. In 1809 he gained national fame when he became the first man to walk 1000 miles in 1000 hours.

But walking over the mountains of Lakeland owes more to the Romantic Movement, which began in the mid 18th century and continued for almost a century. This was a revolution of thought which embraced art, philosophy and poetry, having as its basis a 'back to nature' movement. Its followers set out to travel, explore and above all, appreciate the joy of landscape. The poet, Thomas Gray, became the first real tourist to write about his travels here in 1769, recorded in his *Journal of the Lakes*. Others quickly followed, leading first to a handful, then a steady flow of wealthy tourists intent on discovering the splendour of Lakeland. This was further influenced by the hazards of the French Revolution, which stopped the Grand Tour, forcing many to seek enlightenment nearer to home.

While at Cambridge University in 1790, William Wordsworth started out with his friend, Robert Jones, on his first real walking tour. This journey through France, Italy and Switzerland, was the beginning of what was to be a lifetime of long distance walking, often accompanied by his sister, Dorothy. In later years, having settled back in his native Lakeland, his immense stature as a poet attracted other great minds to visit him and even live here. Walking became a source of constant inspiration for many in this ever growing literary set, which of course included Coleridge, De Quincey, and Southey. Coleridge, who it is said had a strange habit of walking from side to side, also became a friend of William Hazlitt who later wrote the first classic essay on the joys of walking. But De Quincey's walking was more a form of therapy, for after taking opium at Oxford to relieve toothache he became addicted to the drug. He found that only by walking a distance of at least fourteen miles each day could he find any relief.

3

With the exception of Pillar Rock, the large summits of the Lakeland mountains are accessible by walking. Some routes occasionally require a little scrambling, which means using the hands, but rock-climbing, involving the use of ropes and other equipment, generally takes place on the sheer crags which lie on the sides of the mountains. In 1786 when rock climbing as we now know it was unknown, Mont Blanc was first conquered. This event seemed to particularly appeal to the English, who were soon attempting to stand on every major Alpine peak. But in Lakeland it was Coleridge, who by chance, became the first person to record his success on what is now classified as a rock climb. In 1802, while on a nine-day walking tour he ascended to the summit of Scafell, then with trepidation he took a short cut down a rocky cliff which is now known as Broad Stand.

But for the next twenty years the crags of Lakeland had little appeal, only the unconquered summit of Pillar Rock seem to have lured the adventurous. This was eventually climbed for the first time in 1826 by John Atkinson, who worked as a shepherd in Ennerdale, followed in 1869 by the first woman to reach the summit, Miss A. Baker who lived at Gosforth. This led others to attempt the feat, including the eccentric retired clergyman, James Jackson. While working as the vicar at Rivington Church in Lancashire he had climbed up the steeple to repair the weathercock, which gained him the nickname of Steeple Jackson. In 1875 at the age of 79, with the help of a younger

The Reverend James 'Steeple' Jackson, who fell to his death from Pillar Rock at the age of 82

man, he reached the summit of Pillar Rock, which again he repeated the next year. Sadly, two years later he failed to return to the hotel here at Wasdale Head and a search party found he had fallen to his death.

The utter peacefulness of Wasdale Head, together with its closeness to many of the finest mountains made it popular with Victorian walkers and cragsmen, as the early rock climbers became known. In 1856 a local man, Will Ritson decided to provide simple accommodation at his farmhouse which became renamed the Huntsman Inn, from which the Wasdale Head Hotel has grown. Ritson was a larger than life character who was a keen huntsman and wrestler. He had a sparkling wit which made him the friend to many of Lakeland's literary giants, particularly the enigmatic Professor Wilson of Windermere, who shared a taste for all types of sports.

Here, increasingly came the mountain enthusiasts who are now recognised as the pioneers of rock climbing, many being founders of the Alpine Club which was created in 1856. Most were middle class professional people who started to climb while still at university, then continued throughout their lives. The Visitor's Book at the hotel, which was started in 1860, became a Climber's Book in 1890 in which was recorded the details of many first ascents. This is now regarded as an important historical document.

Among the many legendary names from this period are Haskett-Smith who first climbed Napes Needle, the Abraham brothers from Keswick who became renowned for their mountain photography, and dare-devil Owen Glynne Jones. These early climbers would be amazed to see the way the sport has developed over the last century. It now boasts a mass of equipment whose technical jargon is a puzzle to the outsider. Most climbers of today dress in highly coloured designer fashions and jangle up the rockface with such items as snap-link karabiners, pitons, webbing harnesses, nylon slings and belays. Having, of course, first carefully studied their climbing guide book which grades each climb from Easy to Extremely Severe, of which there are over 1500 in the Lake District. However, one thing that has not changed is the courage and sense of adventure which rock climbers still possess, attempting athletic feats over dizzy heights which, to the onlooker, seem quite astonishing.

Perhaps the best known of the present generation of British climbers is Chris Bonington, who for many years has lived with his wife Wendy and two sons, Daniel and Rupert, in Hesket Newmarket here in Lakeland. He was born in London on the 6th August 1934 and following the break up of his parents marriage when he was just a baby, he was brought up by both his mother and grandmother. His education at University College School followed, when he first began to display the characteristics which he was destined to put to good use in later years. His nature was that of a determined loner whose first boyhood adventures began with him taking solitary cycling tours. But it was during the winter of 1951, after admiring the skill of rock-climbers who were scaling the crags of Snowdonia, that he was first struck with a desire to climb. After being introduced by a family friend to the rudiments of the sport on the slopes of Harrison's Rocks in Kent, climbing quickly became his passion. For he found that his temperament was ideally suited to the unique demands of the sport: athletic ability, no fear of heights, and the sheer nerve and determination needed to overcome the many challenges of the rock face. Instinctively he knew that this was where his future would lie.

After completing his National Service he decided to make the army his career. He attended Sandhurst and was Commissioned in 1956, then he spent five years in the forces, becoming a Mountaineering Instructor in the Army Outward Bound School. But even before this time his climbing ability had already come to prominence, for in 1953 he had made the first winter ascent of Raven's Gully on Buachaille Etive Mor in Scotland with Hamish MacInnes. During the late fifties he went on to pioneer several first ascents in the Avon

Chris Bonington, one of the world's leading climbers, on a route called Prana on Black Crag in Borrowdale *(Photo: Alan Hinkes, Chris Bonington Picture Library)*

Gorge, then came his first Alpine season in 1957 when he made an unsuccessful attempt on the Eigerwand. Now having reached a peak of fitness and
rapidly becoming more experienced he began to climb at ever heightening
standards which led to a string of successes. These included the first British
ascent of the South-west Pillar of the Drus (1958), the Cima Grande Direct
(1959) and the Central Pillar of Freney (1961). In 1960 he undertook his first
Himalayan expedition, reaching the summit of Annapurna II with Dick Grant,
then with Ian Clough in 1962 he enhanced his reputation even further when
they made the first British ascent of the formidable North Wall of the Eiger.

He had become a management trainee with Unilever in 1961, but the lure
of the mountains had quickly become too strong. The following year he
abandoned all thoughts of a business career, hoping that he would be able to
earn his future living from the precarious world of freelance writing and
photography. Recently married to Wendy Marchant, she accompanied him in
November 1962 together with a team of six climbers, including Don Whillans
and Ian Clough, for further adventures in South America. This remarkable
expedition, highlighted in his book *The Next Horizon*, ended with the first
successful ascent of the Central Tower of Paine in Patagonia.

In the early sixties he had made his home here in Lakeland, enabling him
to explore and climb the mountains which now lay on his doorstep. This led
to several first Lakeland ascents including The Medlar and Totalitarian above
Thirlmere and The Last Laugh on Castle Rock. The fascinating story of his
chance ascent of the Holy Ghost on Scafell, he later related in a TV series and
book, *Lakeland Rock*.

The opportunity to establish himself as a mountain photographer, which
was an essential part of his future financial plans, also came to fruition at this
time. The *Daily Telegraph*, who had bought the exclusive story rights for a
forthcoming attempt on the Eiger Direct, asked him to take photographs of the
climb for their magazine. His exciting images of the team fighting their way
up this most challenging of mountains under winter conditions, captured the
publics imagination. But the event was marred by tragedy, for climber John
Harlin had plunged 5,000 feet to his death.

Just six weeks after facing the hazards of frost-bite on the Eiger he flew out
to Ecuador, again on a photographic assignment from the Daily Telegraph. An
exciting jungle trek from the Amazon Basin with Sebastian Snow ended with
an ascent of the world's highest active volcano, Sangay. But when an Indian
came running into their camp with an important message he suspected something dreadful had happened. It was the very worst news any parent could ever
hear, for his two-and-a-half year old son, Conrad, had been drowned when he
tumbled into a swollen stream. Grief stricken he returned quickly home to
Wendy, who for a week had had to bear her suffering alone. Now together

they were able to share the terrible burden of sorrow and heartache that the accident had brought.

Still recovering from this horrific episode he was asked if he would like to join a team who were about to attempt the first ascent of The Old Man of Hoy. This impressive rock pinnacle which soars 300 feet from the sea off the Orkney Islands, is completely sheer on every face. Three days later the successful climb ended with a cairn being built on the flat summit together with a bonfire! The following year he returned with a BBC television team who recorded for armchair adventurers three different spectacular ascents. Viewers watched with awe as the climbers scaled the slender face, which included among the team the legendary Joe Brown and Dougal Haston.

By the early seventies he had become recognised not only as one of the world's leading climbers, but also as a gifted writer and photographer who was able to capture in his books the spirit of mountain adventure. Over the last two decades he has ventured from the Antarctic to the Nile, from his native crags in Lakeland to the highest peaks of the Himalayas. In 1970 he led the highly successful expedition which climbed the South Face of Annarpurna, then in 1985 at the age of fifty, he at last stood triumphantly on the summit of Everest. However, in contrast to his many successes, he has also suffered the anguish of seeing some of his closest friends die on the unforgiving mountains. Avalanches swept Ian Clough to his death on Annarpurna and Nick Estcourt on K2, and Everest had claimed the lives of Tighe, Burke, Tasker, and Boardman.

Now in his early sixties with a beard that has turned from black to grey, and a host of awards to his credit, Chris Bonington defies the passing of time. Still filled with the urge for adventure which he first discovered in his youth, he continues to plan expeditions to remote places, climb up hair-raising rock faces and in the great tradition of Steeple Jackson, he will probably still be doing so two decades from now!

4

As rock climbing began its infancy, fell walking in Lakeland was also changing, for it was no longer the exclusive pursuit of the middle class intellectual or the literary pedestrian. The building of the railways led to Lakeland becoming accessible to the office worker and the factory hand, who could escape at weekends from the monotony of the city. Walking also began to be more organised with the creation of walking clubs. These were often attached to churches or were founded by followers of the newly created Labour Party. Youth too was further encouraged to join the great escape to the countryside when the Boys Scout Movement was founded by Baden-Powell after the Boer War. 'Hiking' which was the new term for walking, became increasingly popular in the twenties and its many followers often became the butt of jokes. The sight of large groups of over-weight walkers wearing brief shorts, hob-nailed boots and bent over with huge rucksacks was ideal material for the cartoonist.

However, this ridicule was taken in good part by walking devotees who continued to increase in numbers. Special trains, packed to the brim with hikers, made early departures each Sunday morning from northern towns, heading to the Lakes, the Dales or the Peak District. The philosophy of many of these walkers is summed up by the lines from the *Manchester Rambler*:

I may be a wage slave on Monday.
But I'm a free man on Sunday.

In 1935 the sport became even more organised with the setting up of the Ramblers' Association, which is particularly active in ensuring that walkers have freedom to roam over the countryside. The association's first full time Secretary in 1952 was Tom Stephenson, who became the founder of Britain's first long distance footpath, The Pennine Way, and who influenced the creation of our National Parks. It was also in the thirties that the Youth Hostel Association first became active in this country, having been founded in 1907 in Germany. It was sponsored in the early years by Dr G.M. Trevelyan to encourage young people to walk in the countryside by providing cheap, simple accommodation and is now firmly established as part of Lakeland's culture.

If Wordsworth and Coleridge were to return to Lakeland today they would no doubt be both encouraged and dismayed by the number of walkers and climbers that take to the hills. For the real threat to Lakeland now seems to have resulted from the success of past generations in 'selling' to so many the unique beauty of this corner of England.

5

From Santon Bridge I drove along a winding lane which meandered by the wooded entrance to lonely Miterdale, a spot said to be haunted by the Beckside Boggle. The tale began when a farmer's wife, whose husband was away on business in Whitehaven, remained at home with her baby, busily making tallow candles. An odd looking gypsy-woman knocked at the farmhouse door asking for lodgings, and much against her better judgement, the kindly mother invited the stranger inside. While seated in the warmth of the fireside the visitor drifted into sleep and her shawl fell away from her face. The farmer's wife was appalled to see she was entertaining not a woman, but a man, whose hand was clutching a wicked looking knife. Fearing for both herself and her child, in panic she poured a boiling pan of fat over his head, on which he horribly choked to death. When the farmer returned home he was shocked to find his terrified wife staring at the grotesque corpse. The body was secretly buried by the couple, but its spirit is said to still haunt what is now a ruined farm.

I had arrived in Eskdale Green but it was more like Toytown, for suddenly a piercing hoot echoed down the valley. From beneath a tunnel of green foliage appeared a shining, miniature steam locomotive painted in red and black, with its beaming driver looking like a giant as he dwarfed the small cab. Behind him were four blue carriages full of smiling passengers, who were delighted by the shock they had brought to us curious travellers.

Known affectionately as the Ratty, the Ravenglass and Eskdale Railway is England's oldest narrow gauge steam railway. It links the coastal town of Ravenglass with the hamlet of Dalegarth; seven miles of some of Lakeland's most splendid countryside. But this much-loved railway began life not as a service to enchant visitors, but as a means to transport iron ore from the mines of Eskdale. It was first opened in 1875, having a gauge of three feet, then when the mines proved to be uneconomical, it was used to carry stone from the quarries and passengers were now also allowed.

During the First World War the gauge was reduced to sixteen inches, but the following half a century brought financial problems which were to cast doubt over its survival. However, the many railway enthusiasts for which the north is renowned, were determined that Ratty would never close. An appeal was launched in the early sixties, which thankfully raised the necessary finance to purchase the line and ensure its success. One of its devotees was Alfred Wainwright who compiled a small booklet, *Walks from Ratty*, which encouraged walkers to use the little train to explore the valley.

With cloudless skies above and the towering hills on each side, I continued my journey up Eskdale, passing The King, which is the valley's famous inn. Up to the Great War this was called The King of Prussia, but with patriotic fury it was quickly renamed The King George. At times the road came close to the clear waters of the little River Esk, then parted from then to reveal fields full of wild flowers overlooked by the splendid profile of Harter Fell. Skirting the village of Boot, and the churchyard in which rests the celebrated huntsman, Tommy Dobson, I drove with trepidation up the steep 1 in 3 gradients and hairpin bends of Hard Knott Pass.

Lying adjacent to this high twisting road, perched on an island of windswept grass, I stopped to look at the ruins of what must surely be England's most impressive Roman Fort. Although only the outline of the tumbled buildings remain, there is a unique feeling of utter timelessness about this place. Alone, in the shadow of the high summits of Scafell, I was constantly looking over my shoulder. For here in this rugged terrain, it is easy to imagine that the Legions might return any minute to claim back Mediobogdvm, which they abandoned sixteen centuries ago.

Where the gradient levels, in a brown bowl of wild mountains, I came to the upper reaches of the River Duddon. On my right, near enchanting Cockly Beck, I could see the descending road dropping into the narrow Duddon Valley which lies between Harter Fell and Grey Friar. But my route lay ahead, over the majestic Path of the Stallion, known now as Wrynose Pass. As a Lancastrian I halted in reverence near the high-point where the Three Shires Stone stands erect in redundant splendour. For prior to March 1974 this was the ancient point where the counties of Lancashire, Westmorland and Cumberland met. But at the sweep of a pen Lancashire lost its Lakeland heritage, and Westmorland and Cumberland were swept away to form the new county of Cumbria; an event which many regret.

With the lofty bulk of Crinkle Crags and Pike o' Blisco hiding from me the full expanse of the Langdale Valley, I quickly descended from the wild uplands into the gentleness of Hawkshead Village.

"The coach will be coming at three thirty, so make sure you are back here on time. Have you got that clear?"

A young woman teacher, dressed in brief shorts which revealed, what John Betjeman might well have described as 'thumping big legs', was addressing a group of school children.

"Yes miss," they answered in unison. Then like young puppies who have unexpectedly been released from their leads, they dashed in the direction of the main street. Here, in the souvenir shops and cafés which hide in every corner of this lovely village, they proceeded to happily spend their money.

I joined them and the many other visitors who flock here to follow in the footsteps of the young William Wordsworth and the more mature Beatrix Potter. Now thankfully free from the hazards of most of the traffic this charming cluster of old inns, flower-bedecked cottages and two-storey shops, which hide under narrow arched alleyways, is a joy to explore. For an hour I sauntered backwards and forwards, admiring the 17th century Town Hall which was once a meat market; looking in small, low-roofed gift shops which sell jars of home-made jam, views of Tarn Hows and Wainwright books and videos; while all the time I was trying to resist the delicious aroma of roast lamb which was drifting out of the kitchen of the Red Lion.

For a few moments my attention was directed away from food as I gazed into what was once a solicitor's office in which Beatrix Potter's husband, William Heelis, worked. I suspect that the sober world of yesterday's lawyers would be shocked if they could see what lies in this building today. For gone

A quiet alleyway in lovely Hawkshead Village.

are the dusty shelves of wills, leases and land deeds, replaced by ...... Mrs Tiggy-Winkle! Now known as The Beatrix Potter Gallery, which is owned by the National Trust, it houses an annually changing exhibition of her original drawings.

But my need for refreshment was pressing, it could no longer be ignored. I dashed from the main street up a cobbled alleyway, passing Anne Tyson's little cottage where Wordsworth once lodged, and into the Grandy Nook Teashop. In the nick of time I was saved from unconsciousness by a plate of freshly baked scones and a pot of tea, thankfully made with real tea leaves and not those terrible tea bags. In comfort, I spent half an hour gazing out of the teashop window, watching both the residents and visitors go about their business, and daydreaming about the village's history.

It is hard to believe, but Hawkshead, which is everyone's idea of an enchanting English village, once echoed with the cries of ferocious Norsemen. Like those who invaded Wasdale, they probably arrived here from the Isle of Man, then like visitors still do, fell under its spell and decided to make it their new home. By the 13th century they had forgotten their former blood-thirsty ways and their original stockaded settlement, now a hamlet, had become the property of the Monks of Furness Abbey. It was administered from Hawkshead Hall which lies about a mile from the present village. This arrangement came to an end at the Dissolution, when the Hall came into the possession of the Kendall family, then later the Nicholsons.

Although mining and timber provided local men with employment, it was wool which became the main source of livelihood and created Hawkshead's present face. It became a centre for this lucrative trade, markets sprang up, drawing in merchants from Kendal who needed it for their Kendal Green Cloth. This led to the establishment of the many coaching inns and small shops which are now such a delightful feature of life here, but the roads remained notoriously narrow and unmade. By the late 18th century, when cotton goods had begun to rob the wool-merchants of much of their revenue, the first trickle of tourists were beginning to arrive here. Today, although sheep still play an important role in the local economy, this trickle of curious travellers has grown to a mighty rush, which keeps many of the local people employed throughout the year.

With my energy now fully restored I climbed up a narrow pathway which leads from the village to the edge of a gentle, rounded hill, to be quickly rewarded with a stunning view. Below me, on the site where a Norseman named Hankr probably built his first camp, rose the light grey walls of the Parish Church. It lay in a sea of emerald grass, which was broken here and there by the yellow of buttercups and the dark fingers of slanting tombstones; the final idyllic resting place of farmers and cobblers, wheelwrights and

William Worsworth was a pupil at Hawkshead Grammar School, founded in 1585 by Archbishop Sandys

charcoal burners. Beyond, stood the tiny rooftops and the colour-washed walls of the village which ended suddenly in a sweep of meadowland. My eyes were then led on to the darker green of rising woodland which spread up low hills, then onwards to the distant horizon which was encompassed by the pale blue of the high fells.

When Wordsworth saw this church of St Michael and All Angels, on his return from Cambridge in 1788, he knew he had reached his homeland. He wrote:

"I saw the snow-white church upon the hill
Sit like a throned lady sending out
A gracious look all over her domain"

A notice at the church door told me that the Helm Wind Ensemble would be performing at 8.0 pm and there would be no charge. In the quiet of the interior I wandered down the aisle alongside huge columns, admiring the marble monuments and murals, and reading Burial in Woollen certificates. These testify that the people of Hawkshead were once put to rest in shrouds made from only wool and from nothing else! To ensure the survival of the woollen industry a law was passed in 1679 stating that all burials should be in woollen or a fine of £5 would be imposed. Of course the people of Hawkshead had a vested interest ensuring that this was obeyed.

Before leaving the church I read some of the requests for prayers; a poignant reminder of the sufferings of so many people and from which none of us ever completely escapes:

Please pray for my son to regain his health.
Please pray for my wife who is having a triple by-pass operation.
Please pray for the missing newly born baby.
Thankyou for prayers answered.

Once more in the bright sunshine I strolled down the hillside passing Hawkshead Grammar School which was founded by local man, Archbishop Sandys, in 1585. Unknown to him, two centuries later a young pupil named William Wordsworth would carve his initials on a desk here, then go on to carve his name forever on England's Wall of Fame.

6

Estwaite Water was like a silver mirror trapped in a circle of morning mist. This created a marvellous atmosphere of mystery in which almost anything seemed possible. If the solitary fisherman, who was poised like a black statue in his little rowing boat, had hooked Excalibur instead of a trout, neither of us would have been surprised. For of course I was no longer in Lakeland but in Fairyland; over the hill lay the homes of Peter Rabbit, Tom Kitten, Ginger and Pickles, Jemima Puddle-duck, and Mrs Tiggy-Winkle. A place where us humans step with nervous apprehension, knowing that beneath every hedgerow and down every rabbit-hole pairs of small eyes are watching our every move.

I turned into the car park which lies adjacent to the Tower Bank Arms in Near Sawrey, to find it was almost full. My modest family saloon seemed out of place here, for nearly every gleaming vehicle was a BMW or an up-market Rover. These had been hired by wealthy Japanese visitors in London, to speed them up-north to the village of their childhood dreams. I joined them as they wandered in bewildered reverence through the sunlit streets of this lovely village of white washed farms and cottage gardens. Occasionally their excited chatter would break the silence. Although I could not understand the language I could guess that they had identified yet another landmark from one of their much loved volumes. For when Beatrix Potter wrote her remarkable tales, unwittingly she had created a world which is truly international. This has quickly been seized upon by the enterprising owner of a village tea-garden, who advertises his refreshments in both English and Japanese.

Joining in with a group of smiling Beatrix Potter admirers who had just arrived by motor-coach, I walked up the narrow garden pathway to Hill Top, the home which she adored. Suddenly I had an odd feeling of familiarity; perhaps I had been here before? But then I realised that in this garden I had stepped out of reality and into a fascinating world of fiction. This very pathway had once been trod by a policeman who was searching for Pigling Bland, I was staring at the old front door on which Cousin Ribby had knocked, and this was not really Hill Top at all, for it was the home of Tom Kitten or was it Jemima Puddle-duck's farm? Confused, I entered the cosy rooms of this small farmhouse to look at the furniture, pictures, and the scores of intimate objects which once surrounded our most famous children's author.

Helen Beatrix Potter was born in July 1866 at No 2, Bolton Gardens, a rather sombre, four storey high, terraced house which overlooked a wooded square in South Kensington, London. The house has now sadly been demolished, for it was hit by a land-mine which was dropped during the Second World War. Both her parents, Rupert and Helen, were wealthy, being members of pros-perous Lancashire cotton families. But Rupert had decided not to join the family business, instead he had pursued a career in law, which had brought him south to work in Lincoln's Inn.

So it was in this atmosphere of middle-class affluence that Beatrix spent her formative years. The household employed a cook and housekeeper, a coachman, a groom, and later a Scottish nurse to look after the children, for when she was six years old her brother, Bertram, was born. At this period she saw little of her parents, her life being under the sole control of Nurse McKenzie. Her father who had fostered a love for the arts, spent much of his time socializing with many of the famous names of the time. These included his close friend the renowned artist, John Everett Millais, who was married to the former wife of John Ruskin. He was also fascinated by photography, later becoming one of the pioneers in the new art.

Beatrix's in-born love of the countryside became apparent during her childhood when she spent idyllic holidays away from the bustle of Victorian London. Edmund Potter, her retired grandfather had bought a large house and estate named Camfield Place in Hertfordshire, which is now the home of novelist Barbara Cartland. It was here that she first became aware of the beauty of meadows and hedgerows, the sound of the wind and the subtle changes brought to the landscape as autumn slipped into winter. The children also discovered the more rugged splendour of the north, for the Potters rented out a country mansion named Dalguise which lies near Dunkeld in Perthshire: this became their summer home for eleven years.

But Beatrix was sixteen years old before she was first introduced to Lakeland, the region that was later destined to bring her such fame. For in 1882 her parents found that Dalguise was no longer available, so they rented

This picturesque cottage at Near Sawrey, which is now a tea-room, featured in several of Beatrix Potter's famous tales, including 'Tom Kitten'.

Wray Castle, the well known Victorian mansion whose castellated profile looks out over Lake Windermere. Here they entertained many imminent guests including the Quaker reformer, John Bright, and Canon Rawnsley, who in 1895 was to become one of the founders of the National Trust. His views on the need to preserve the natural beauty of Lakeland had a lasting influence on the young Beatrix, who had fallen in love with the unspoilt splendour which surrounded her holiday home.

From early childhood Beatrix had discovered she had a natural talent for sketching and painting, which was encouraged by her parents who both had artistic leanings. In the loneliness of Bolton Gardens, then later in the more inviting atmosphere of Dalguise and a number of rented Lakeland homes, she meticulously recorded in sketch-books details of buildings and landscape and animals. This became her welcomed escape from a cloistered Victorian world which allowed her no friends, apart from Bertram, and little personal freedom. This lonely frustrating existence led her increasingly to create a world of fantasy which slowly began to come alive in her sketches. Drawing the small wild animals which she had seen while on holiday, she clothed them like humans and showed them acting out adventures which indulged her creative mind. Ever secretive, she also began to write a journal of her innermost thoughts which started when she was fifteen and continued in to her early thirties. To avoid prying eyes she wrote this in an elaborate code which was only deciphered after her death.

Her first step in to the commercial world came in 1890 when she was 24 years old. She had bought a pet rabbit in London, which she named Benjamin Bouncer, and he became her inspiration for a series of designs which were used as illustrations on greeting cards and in a booklet. But this initial success was short lived, for the following year she received a rejection of sketches she sent to publishers Frederick Warne, although they were 'pleased with the designs'. In spite of this set-back she now had confidence in her own ability, and it had become apparent to all who knew her that she was quickly developing into an accomplished artist.

It was during this period that, probably for her own amusement, she sent a series of illustrated letters to the children of her former governess, Annie Moore. One of these, written in 1893, concerned the antics of four rabbits named Hopsy, Mopsy, Cottontail and Peter. This became the basis for her first children's book, *The Tale of Peter Rabbit*, which was rejected by six different publishers. Unperturbed, she decided to have 250 copies of the book printed herself, giving most away as gifts and selling the rest.

But Canon Rawnsley, acting on her behalf, was still continuing to try to get a publisher interested and at last he found success with Frederick Warne. A contract was signed in June 1902 for both paper and cloth backed editions using Beatrix's text and her coloured illustrations. It was published three months later with an initial print run of 8,000 copies which were immediately sold.

This, her first commercial book publication, required her to make frequent visits to the London offices of Frederick Warne. Here she dealt with Norman Warne, who was the youngest son of the late founder of the company, and a close friendship was quickly established. At the same time she had written another two books, *The Tailor of Gloucester* and *The Tale of Squirrel Nutkin*, which were being considered. For by 1903 it was apparent that the public had begun to love her meticulous work; 50,000 copies of *The Tale of Peter Rabbit* had already been sold.

Another important milestone in her life came in 1904, for her friendship with Norman Warne had blossomed into love, leading to a proposal of marriage. But although she was now 38 years old, she remained dominated by her parents who opposed the match, because they felt he was not from her class. However, in spite of the opposition she accepted his proposal, but news of her engagement was confined at first to her immediate family. Sadly, their marriage was never to be; the following year Norman was taken ill with pernicious anaemia and he died at the early age of 37.

Overcome with grief, Beatrix now had only her happy memories of their brief love affair to comfort her. Slowly she made the gigantic effort of picking up the threads of her life. She continued working on her ever-successful books, which would always be associated with Norman, and decided to look around for an independent home in the Lake District.

In 1905, using money saved from her royalties together with a legacy from an aunt, she came here to Near Sawrey and purchased Hill Top. But this was both a home and a business venture, for Hill Top was a working farm. The building was extended so that her farm manager and his wife could live in one part, while Beatrix lived in the main portion of the house. This village, which has now appropriately become a place of pilgrimage for her world-wide family of fans, is the place in which she found lasting happiness. It also became the setting for six of her famous tales, which she continued to produce at the rate of one a year.

After purchasing Hill Top, each time money from her royalties became available, she began to expand her ownership of land and buildings in the area. The necessary legal transactions which this required, brought her into close contact with William Heelis, who worked as a solicitor in Hawkshead. Their association flourished into a close friendship, which eventually led to this tall, handsome man who was in his early forties, asking her to marry him. Despite the opposition of her ageing parents she accepted his offer and the couple were married in October 1913, in London. Their home became Castle Cottage, which also lies in Near Sawrey, but she continued to spend much of her day in her beloved Hill Top.

Beatrix Potter and her husband grew to become familiar figures in the life of rural Lakeland, taking part in many different social, agricultural and charity events for the next three decades. In 1930 the knowledge she had acquired on her farm led to her becoming the first woman president of the Herdwick Sheepbreeders' Association; regarded as a great honour in Lakeland circles.

Her books continued to sell in large numbers, and new titles continued to be added to her list, captivating each new generation. But health problems began to trouble her in the late thirties which led to her having a serious operation in a Liverpool hospital, for the removal of her womb. From this she fully recovered, but in September 1943 she was again ill, this time with bronchitis. Her condition slowly worsened, aggravating a heart problem which resulted in her death a few days before Christmas. Her body was cremated and her ashes spread on the hills which overlook her adopted village which had brought her such happiness. William Heelis, grief stricken by his loss, died less than two years later.

Among her many bequeaths was a magnificent gift to the National Trust, of 4,000 acres of land in Cumbria, together with fifteen farms. Her beloved Hill Top, she instructed, should remain unchanged with the rooms containing her original furnishings. Since her death over half a century ago a huge Beatrix Potter industry has grown in a way which the author, who shunned personal publicity, would find hard to believe. Her marvellous animal characters adorn products as diverse as postage stamps and drinking mugs, from porcelain figures to children's clothes. The lovable antics of Tom Kitten, Jemima Puddle-duck, Mrs Tiggy-Winkle and the Tailor of Gloucester continue to enchant children. And a Beatrix Potter Society now promotes the study and appreciation of her life.

7

Sawrey to Walney Island

I reach the Rusland Valley, see the grave of Arthur Ransome, and think about the Swallows and Amazons. I join walkers and cyclists in Coniston, remembering the tragic death of Donald Campbell and the genius of John Ruskin. In the lovely Vale of Deadly Nightshade I explore Furness Abbey, I see George Romney's hometown, look where Trident Submarines are built, then end up on windswept Walney Island.

1

I paused on the brow of a hill to look down on the sweep of the Rusland Valley. By Lakeland standards this is gentle terrain, an inviting landscape of lush pastures on which healthy cows contentedly feed. Here and there I could see the half hidden rooftops of cottages and ancient farms, which my map revealed were served by a maze of narrow roads. To the north, through Satterthwaite, lay the dark-green arms of the Grizedale Forest which stretch outwards to link Coniston Water to Windermere. A series of clear becks pour off these low wooded hills to form the river known as the Rusland Pool, which meanders to the south reaching the River Leven near Haverthwaite.

I suppose in the normal course of events few visitors would ever venture to this serene corner. For lovely as this valley surely is, it cannot compete with the savage grandeur of England's best mountain scenery which lie just a few miles away. Yet come they do, from America, Japan, Australia, Canada, France, Germany and dozens of other countries. What all these visitors have in common, whether they are eight or eighty, is that they have been enchanted. Some may give the outward appearance of declining years, but do not be fooled by grey hair or wrinkled faces. For at sometime in their lives they began to read a book whose hypnotic pages endows its readers with perpetual childhood. These bewitched people now travel thousands of miles on a literary pilgrimage to visit the grave of the book's author, Arthur Ransome, and to gaze in awe on the blue waters which saw the adventures of the Swallows and Amazons.

On a splendid green knoll, overlooking a watery meadow I found St Paul's Church. Although less than 250 years old, and largely rebuilt last century, it emits an atmosphere of timeless tranquillity. It was in 1956 that Arthur Ransome first discovered the peacefulness of this holy place. Having extensively travelled to many beautiful countries it was this churchyard, in the centre of the land he loved most, that he chose for his final resting place. He told the vicar at the time, the Reverend Boulter, that he had a particular liking for a spot beneath a pine tree. So here, with only the cry of the wind and the sound of the birds, his ashes were buried in 1967, to be joined by those of his second wife, Evgenia, in 1975.

The ashes of Swallows and Amazons author, Author Ransome, lies buried with his wife Evgenia in the Rusland Valley. She had once been Trotsky's personal secretary.

Like so many who have come to love Lakeland, Arthur Mitchell Ransome was an adopted Cumbrian, having been born at Leeds on the 18th January 1884. He was the eldest child of Edith and Cyril Ransome, his father being the Professor of History at what was later to become the University of Leeds. His parents gave him an early introduction to the splendour of the mountains, for he was carried as a baby to the summit of Coniston Old Man. He claimed in his autobiography to be the youngest human being to have made the ascent. Here too at High Nibthwaite, where Coniston Water pours into the River Crake, he spent enchanting summer holidays with his family. Idyllic days in which, with his brother and sisters, he discovered the joy of nature, explored the lake and talked with many fascinating local characters; a period which had a profound effect on the rest of his life.

In 1892 he was sent as a boarder to a Lakeland prep school, Windermere Old College, where much of his life was made a misery by bullying. This in part resulted from his dislike of 'character building' games which were forced on him by a headmaster who was a devoted sportsman. He also had the disability of being extremely short sighted; this affected his class work but went unnoticed for some years. However, one happy episode he remembered from this period was the Great Frost of 1895 which resulted in the lake freezing over; an event which happens only about three times each century. This memory of skating on the ice, the brisk cold air and the loveliness of the snow covered fells remained with him into manhood, giving him the inspiration for his book, *Winter Holiday*.

Sadly, following an accident which had led to the amputation of his leg, Cyril Ransome died prematurely in 1897. His good-looking widow, Edith, who was a devoted mother, then tried to influence her eldest son into taking up a safe, respectable profession. But after further education at Rugby, followed by a course in science at his father's former college in Leeds, it was Arthur's love of books which was to draw him into a literary career. This began in the early years of this century when he found a job in the offices of publishers Grant Richards in London, starting as an errand-boy. After six months he left to join the Unicorn Press, using his spare time to write freelance articles for various magazines. After a year he decided he wanted to write full-time. So he left the publishing world to pen book-reviews and small features, earning little money but being stimulated by the company of both struggling would-be writers and those who had met success in the colourful world of Bohemian Chelsea. These included G.K. Chesterton, his brother Cecil, Hilaire Belloc and Edward Thomas.

It was while spending a holiday near Coniston in 1903 that he had a chance meeting with the artist and writer, W.G. Collingwood, who had been the devoted friend of Ruskin. At this time Collingwood who was fifty years old, and his wife Edith, made their living selling landscape paintings of the Lakes. Ransome was received with genuine affection into their home, Lanehead, beginning what was to become a lifelong friendship with all the family. He later fell in love with one of their daughters, Barbara, which almost led to marriage. For many years they remained his second family and it was the Collingwood's grandchildren who became the inspiration for the Walkers, known as the Swallows, in his classic tales.

Ransome's first book, *The Souls of the Streets*, was published in 1904 when he was twenty one years old. It was poorly received, as was his second collection of essays, *The Stone Lady (1905)*, for he was still learning the rudiments of his craft. But quickly his style and characterisation improved, which became apparent when *Bohemia In London* appeared in 1907. His life was also quickly changing for in 1908 he fell under the spell of Ivy Constance Walker, a slim, attractive twenty-six-year-old woman. They were married the next year and settled near Petersfield in Hampshire, but in spite of the birth of a daughter, Tabitha, it soon became apparent that they were completely unsuited to each other.

By this time Ransome's literary career had become firmly established, he was writing articles and reviews for magazines, reading manuscripts for publishers, and his books, mainly anthologies and biographies, were well received. But in 1912, his book on the works of Oscar Wilde which was published by Martin Secker, was said by Lord Alfred Douglas to contain untrue statements concerning their relationship. This disagreement eventually developed into a highly publicised libel case; a nightmare period of intense worry for the sensitive author. The case of Lord Alfred Douglas versus Ransome and Others came to trial in April 1913, it lasted for four days, happily ending with a resounding victory for Ransome who was awarded costs. He had at last escaped from the uncertainty that had cast a shadow over his life for over a year.

In June 1913, elated by his success in court but becoming ever more aware of the friction in his marriage with Ivy, he left England for a tour of Russia. This journey, which was undertaken to collect material for *Old Peter's Russian Tales*, a study in folklore, became a turning point in his life. He enjoyed exploring the country and eventually he mastered the language. He returned to England, but at the outbreak of the First World War he found himself unsuitable for military service due to being short sighted. However, he seized an opportunity which arose for him to become the Russian Correspondent for the Daily News.

Also working in Russia for the *Daily Mail* at this time was Hugh Walpole. Strangely, this New Zealand born writer, was the same age as Ransome, suffered from poor eyesight, and was also destined to become forever associated with Lakeland. The two men who were already acquainted, became deeply involved in gathering news of the momentous events which were to shake the world. At the suggestion of Ransome an Anglo-Russian Bureau was set up to co-ordinate their activities, which had Walpole as its Director. Later the pair became embroiled in a disagreement concerning the effectiveness of the agency, this led to a break in their friendship which lasted for 16 years.

Ransome lived in Russia throughout the period of the Revolution, meeting many of the leading Bolsheviks and seeing and recording the suffering of the people. He is said to have even defeated Lenin at chess, but it was Trotsky's personal secretary, Evgenia Petrovna Shelepina, who was to change his life. The couple fell deeply in love, his marriage to the hysterical Ivy having now completely broken down. He continued his work as both a journalist and unofficial diplomat in Russia until 1919, then he moved with Evgenia to Reval in Estonia, acting as a correspondent for The Manchester Guardian. His book, *The Crisis in Russia*, which was published in 1921 was his personal defence of the Russian Revolution.

After undertaking an adventurous 500 mile sail in the Baltic, which he recorded in *Racundra's First Cruise (1923)*, he and Evgenia were married the following year in Reval. Then it was back to his beloved Lakeland that he brought his Russian wife in 1925, having bought a cottage called Low Lubberburn in the Winster Valley. His assignments for the Manchester Guardian continued, taking him to Egypt and to China, but he then decided to end his career as a full-time journalist to concentrate on what he now really wanted to do, write children's stories.

When *Swallows and Amazons* was first published in 1930 it only met moderate success, as did his second book in the series, *Swallowdale*. But in 1932, with the publication of *Peter Duck*, he at last caught the imagination of young readers which resulted in a best seller. And the adventures of the Swallows: Susan, John, Roger and Titty Walker; and the Amazons: Nancy and Peggy Blackett, still continue to enthral both the young and the young at heart, sixty years after they first appeared. Over a fifteen year period he wrote twelve books in the series, five of which have a Lakeland setting. Wildcat Island, which features prominently in *Swallows and Amazons*, is based largely on Peel Island in Coniston Water. The actual boat, *Amazon*, which was owned by a friend of Ransome's, has now been restored and is regularly sailed by members of the Arthur Ransome Society.

When asked what made him write *Swallows and Amazons* he said that its inspiration came entirely from his own childhood adventures around Coniston. 'I could not help writing it. It almost wrote itself.'

I walked away from Arthur Ransome's grave thinking that this man who has brought pleasure to so many must indeed be resting in peace, lying here in the heart of the countryside which he loved so much.

2

Never will I forget my first glimpse of Coniston Water, peeping out beneath an umbrella of green leaves and bathed in the glow of morning sunshine. I had ascended from Hawkshead up a narrow lane, bounded by sturdy dry stone walls and banks of wild roses. Then quite suddenly the lake came into view, a shimmering bowl of silver lying far below, guarded by the towering Coniston Fells. Then just as suddenly, it disappeared; it was grasped from my view by the overhanging trees as I descended into Coniston village.

"Fifteen miles to go lads and we can't cut any corners."

A group of red faced cyclists, whose bikes were heavily laden down with panniers, had stopped in Yewdale Road to consult a map. Reluctantly accepting the word of their leader they rode away in the direction of Torver.

The village streets were already overflowing with visitors and the delicious smell of morning coffee filled the air. Groups of laughing girls in heavy boots and coloured shorts mingled with sedate elderly people, who had come on coaches from Nottingham, Durham and York. Healthily tanned Americans were sauntering along the pavements, talking about their visit to the Ruskin Museum and wondering what souvenirs to take back to California. Would it be that cute clock with a face made from Westmorland Stone, or maybe that watercolour of Tarn Hows, or perhaps even a real Shepherd's Crook with a handle made from a deers antler? Now that would be a real talking point, but would it fit in the car?

Coniston is at heart a working village whose destiny has been shaped by its spectacular setting, which inevitably draws in visitors. It was once a part of Lancashire and it still retains that friendly no-nonsense approach which is typical of the Lancastrian. The Co-op built their first shop here in 1800 and here they remain, one of the few independent Co-ops to survive and it still pay dividends to its members.

Built on Saxon roots the village grew from a few scattered cottages which centred around the estate of Coniston Hall, to its present size in about sixty years. This expansion began in 1859 when its famous copper-mines, which were first worked in Roman times, and its slate quarries came into prominence. Men with new skills were needed, and many of these came with their families from Ireland and Cornwall. This resulted in a larger, more cosmopolitan community, who worshipped in new Catholic, Baptist and Methodist churches. The days of mining have long since ended, the former home of the mine manager was made into a youth hostel in 1931 and it is now the oldest in Lakeland. Generations of walkers and cyclists still remember with affection the basic accommodation offered in the early days of Coppermines Hostel. Lying in an isolated valley, just a mile from the village, it lives with the ghosts of the past. Overlooked by the splendour of the rising fells, ravens hunt for food among the forlorn scars of rusting trucks, abandoned tunnels and piles of green slate.

Dominating the scene on the western side is Coniston Old Man, a mountain which is regarded as almost an extension of the village itself. Rising to 2633 feet (803 metres), it forms part of an impressive group of much-loved summits which include Swirl How, Wetherlam, Grey Friar and the formidable Dow Crag. I remember over thirty years ago, setting out one cold November day to climb up the Old Man, as many visitors do. Patches of half-melted snow lay in the gullies and a thick, penetrating mist completely enveloped everything above the 1000 feet contour. Holding out little hope of obtaining any views I continued to within a few feet of the summit, then it happened: as if by magic I stepped out of the mist into what seemed to be a mystical world of bright light. The sky was a vivid blue, the sun was a globe of glowing yellow, and the only land which I could see was a few square yards around the summit cairn. Below me, in all directions lay a sea of fluffy white clouds which stretched to the far horizon, completely obscuring all the other peaks. Then I noticed the rare phenomenon which is known as the Brocken Spectre; the sun was casting my huge shadow on to the clouds like a rainbow, giving me a fascinating multi-coloured halo. What had at first seemed to be a dull day had turned out to be one of the most memorable.

There is a belief, which has become part of recent folklore, that everyone can remember the exact moment when they first heard the terrible news that President Kennedy had been assassinated. In the Sun Hotel at Coniston I was reminded of another great tragedy, which I suspect is similarly engrained in the minds of many British people. Preserved on the wall is the front page of the Daily Mirror for January 5th 1967, which contains the poignant headline, "I'm Going!", together with a hazy photograph of a speeding boat tumbling over in the water. This was the last moment in the life of that courageous adventurer, Donald Campbell, who died on Lake Coniston while attempting to raise his own world water speed record in his famous boat, Bluebird. This hotel was his base here in Coniston, and in the centre of the village both him and his chief mechanic, Leo Villa, are remembered by a simple memorial stone.

Donald Campbell and his chief mechanic, Leo Villa, at Coniston
(Photo: Westmorland Gazette)

"It was before my time, of course," the barman told me, "But I wish I had been here then. Those other photos on the wall are of Anthony Hopkins who came to Coniston when he was playing the part of Campbell for a TV film."

I walked from the bar with my half pint of bitter,

thinking of the intense drama which was acted out here twenty seven years ago.

Donald Campbell was born on the 23rd March 1921, into an adventurous family, for his father was Sir Malcolm Campbell, a man filled with a love for speed. He achieved nine world records on land and three more on water, then in 1936, became the first person to travel at 300 mph. After being educated at Uppingham School, Donald, completed an engineering apprenticeship then went on to become a director of an engineering company. Born with rugged good looks, a natural gift for speaking and a sense of adventure, many women found him irresistible. This was to lead him into many love affairs and at the time of his death when he was just 45, he had been married three times.

Although he had always taken a keen interest in the achievements of his father, at the time of Sir Malcolm's death in 1948, he had never driven anything faster than a family car. But filled with a sincere patriotism, he saw it as being his duty to carry on with the quest for speed which had become almost a family tradition. Just nine months later he came here to Coniston with Bluebird, making his first attempt to better his father's water speed record of 141 mph. Due to problems with both the engine and the weather, he was unsuccessful, but the following year he came within a fraction of achieving his goal.

By 1951 he had proved both to himself and his team, that he had the necessary ability to successfully follow in his father's footsteps. This was borne out when he won the prestigious Oltranza Cup in Italy, which was dedicated to the memory of Sir Henry Segrave who had died while attempting the water speed record on Lake Windermere. But more problems followed later in the year when Bluebird II sank here on Coniston Water after hitting a half-submerged obstacle. Both Campbell and Villa, had to be rescued from the water by a motor launch.

It was apparent that a new boat was now needed and it would require jet-propulsion to have any hope of taking the record, which was at this time held by America. Devoting himself full-time to raising the necessary funds and creating the best design, it was four years before his new Bluebird was launched on Ullswater. After completing trials he made his attempt on the world record in July 1955, and newspaper headlines recorded his triumph: Campbell had reached an astonishing 202.32 mph, regaining the title for Britain. Elated by his success, the next few years saw him improving this record several times. By November 1958 he had passed the 400 kilometre per hour milestone, then in May 1959 at Coniston, he pushed it further upwards to 260.35 mph.

It was during this period that he decided to also become involved, like his father had been, in breaking the land speed record which was held by John Cobb. An all-British Bluebird car, using a Bristol-Siddeley engine, was designed by Norris Brothers Engineers. However, disaster came on its inaugural run at Bonneville Salt Flats in the USA. A strong wind resulted in the car veering from the course at around 365 mph and crashing; Campbell escaped serious injury but Bluebird was a write-off. However, refusing to accept defeat he insisted that a replacement car should be quickly built and in July 1964 his confidence was rewarded; a new world land speed record of 403.1 mph was his. In the same year he also improved on his world water speed record, bringing it up to 276.33 mph.

When he came here to Coniston in the late autumn of 1966 he was returning to the Lakeland village which had been at the heart of his success. His confident and courageous personality, in the great tradition of British folk heroes, brought welcome colour to the scene. But inwardly, as preparations for his record attempt got underway, he is said to have been apprehensive. Being of a highly superstitious nature, when he drew the ace of spades during a card game he regarded this as a bad omen.

His worst fears were sadly realised on January 4th 1967, when he attempted to push Bluebird above the 300 mph barrier. A devoted public learned in horror and disbelief that the famous hydroplane, driven by a highly powerful Orpheus engine, had turned over as it skimmed across Coniston Water and Donald Campbell had been killed. It was a moment of tragic grief which will forever be remembered by the people of Coniston, the village which had become synonymous with Campbell's quest for speed.

Campbell's famous *Bluebird* skimming across Coniston Water.

Laughing walkers were seated in the hot sunshine outside of The Sun, their bulging rucksacks piled high on the floor. They were happily quenching their thirst before perhaps, making an afternoon assault on the Old Man. I strolled down the lane back to the village centre and in to the quietness of Saint Andrew's Church. Here I sat for a few minutes, reading the Parish Newsletter which told how we have 'got out of the habit of Bible-reading' which is the 'most straightforward way of hearing God'. It also mentioned social events which included the annual Char Fishing Competition, a rummage sale in the Coniston Institute, and fundraising at Torver by the sale of a book with the intriguing title of *Edward Dickinson's Secret Diary of a Lakeland Farmer*.

Although typical in many ways of the scores of lovely Lakeland churches which stand in nearly every village, St Andrew's had a unique honour bestowed on it in 1900. For John Ruskin, regarded as one of the greatest intellects of the Victorian age, declined the chance of being laid to rest in Westminster Abbey, but instead chose Coniston churchyard. I found the elaborately carved cross that marks his tomb, shrouded by overhanging foliage close to the perimeter wall. This was designed by his friend and biographer W.G. Collingwood and has become a place of pilgrimage for admirers of Ruskin who come here from all parts of the world. His other memorial, which I had seen earlier, lies on Friar's Crag near Keswick. Which appropriately, for Ruskin was deeply concerned with conservation, was the first National Trust property acquired in Lakeland.

John Ruskin was born in Brunswick Square, London on the 8th February 1819, the son of John James Ruskin, a successful wine merchant, and Margaret Cock. From an early age he accompanied both his parents on business trips throughout the country, which led to him becoming familiar with the pattern of the English landscape, together with the art and architecture of the country mansions in which they stayed. He also showed an unusually early literary leaning, for encouraged by his father, he began to write verse from the age of six. His first poem, *Iteriad*, which concerned a visit to the Lake District, was published in the *Spiritual Times* in 1830 when he was just eleven. At the same time he was showing a striking artistic talent, making highly detailed sketches of features which took his eye.

What was to become a life-long association with Italy, and the works of the painter J.M.W. Turner, began in 1833. He was given a travel book about the country which had been illustrated by Turner, and this led him to emulate the style. Then two years later he was taken on a continental tour by his family, which allowed him to both see and sketch much of what he had previously read about. So that when he entered Christ Church, Oxford in 1837 he had already a sound appreciation of the arts nurtured by devoted parents. At this time he wrote the first of fourteen features for the *Architectural Magazine*, entitled *The Poetry of Architecture*.

Having gained BA and MA degrees by 1843, Ruskin's brilliant first volume of *Modern Painters* was published. In it he defended the work of Turner, which had come under criticism, but at the same time he had set his future career path as a writer about art. The work was to continue in four other volumes over the next seventeen years, revealing Ruskin to be not a mere art historian, but a free thinker and philosopher. During this period he also wrote his celebrated *Seven Lamps of Architecture* and the three volumes of *Stones of Venice*.

In 1848 Ruskin met and married a good-looking Scottish girl named Elfie Gray, but sadly the match was doomed to failure. Perhaps due to his over-close relationship with his parents that continued into manhood, he was unable to cope with the physical side of marriage. His frustration led at times to him being cruel and even violent towards his wife, resulting in a complete breakdown of their relationship. It ended in 1854 with an annulment on the grounds that it had never been consummated, and later Elfie became the wife of the painter, John Everett Millais, with whom she had fallen deeply in love.

The next decades saw Ruskin's reputation as England's leading art authority and critic consolidated, when in 1869 he was appointed as Oxford University's first Professor of Fine Art. But he was also gaining notoriety for his radical political views, becoming a thorn in the side of many influential capitalists. His outspoken words on the politics of economics were published in the newly established *Cornhill Magazine*, in a series of articles under the title *Unto this Last*. These were later published in a book, which he regarded as his most important work, outlining the philosophy behind many of his socialist ideas.

Following the death of his father in 1864 he inherited a large fortune, which allowed him to put some of his theories into practice. He acquired nine houses in Marylebone in London, which he let to tenants at a low rent. He was aided in the scheme, aimed at improving the terrible housing conditions of the time, by Octavia Hill who was sympathetic with his views. She later became one of the founders of the National Trust.

Ruskin's love of Lakeland led him to purchase, in 1871, a damp and decaying cottage named Brantwood, which looks out over Coniston Lake towards the high fells. It had been the home of wood-engraver and poet W.J. Linton, who was about to divorce his wife, novelist and guide book writer E. Lynn Linton. Ruskin saw it as possessing the 'finest views I know in Cumberland or Lancashire' and he proceeded to spend thousands of pounds in restoring it as his new home.

So Brantwood was destined to become one of the great centres for political and cultural thought in Europe for the next thirty years. Ruskin's philosophy, in spite of deteriorating health, continued to influence many other great minds including, Proust, Mahatma Gandi and Tolstoy, who wrote: 'Ruskin was one of the most remarkable of men, not only of England and our time but of all countries and all times....'

Ruskin chose Coniston churchyard instead of Westminster Abbey as his final resting place. The ornate cross which marks his grave was designed by his friend and biographer, W.G. Collingwood.

3

Early one morning, a rather travel-weary car, speckled with the mud of a dozen different Lakeland valleys, departed from Coniston village. With the blue of Coniston Water visible on its left, and the mist laden mountain summits on its right, it headed in determined fashion through lovely Torver village. Soon the mountains had become a mere backcloth to a historic landscape of rich meadowland, woodland glades and sleepy villages whose ancient church towers protrude from green folds. It was entering the delights of a corner of Cumbria which juts independently out into the Irish Sea; its identity boastfully acclaimed by each major town who have proudly added 'in-Furness' to the end of their names.

I drove through Broughton-in-Furness, Kirkby-in-Furness and Askam-in-Furness, till I arrived at my destination of Dalton-in-Furness. But to say that 'I had arrived' perhaps gives the wrong impression, for my arrival was anything but smooth. The problem was that an army of industrious workmen had begun to tear up the main roads of the town with grim enthusiasm. Just at the moment that I thought I had arrived, I found my way barred by a 'No Entry' sign. At first unperturbed, I drove up another road, made a large detour, then ended up at another 'No Entry' sign! After this had recurred for the sixth time my confidence began to falter, so I stopped to ask a local woman if she could direct me to the churchyard in which George Romney was buried.

"That will be St. Mary's, I think. But it's a bit difficult to drive to from here."

Nevertheless, her dubious instructions proved to be a success. Five minutes later, red faced and perspiring, I was thankfully parking in a quiet backwater outside the lovely sandstone building. Not a soul stirred in this former capital of Furness, it was as if the pied-piper had lured the entire population away. Looking down towards Market Street I could see the sturdy walls of the Pele Tower, which has become known as Dalton Castle. It was built in the 13th century, so after 700 years of stalwart service, it deserves its present retirement. During its long history it has been hit by the arrows of the army of Robert-the-Bruce, it has held prisoners of Cromwell's model army, and until 1925, it was here that the ancient Court Leet proclaimed local justice.

Walking into the sunlit churchyard I discovered the solitary grave of George Romney, surrounded by an emerald lawn whitened by patches of daisies. It is surprising that this spot has not become a more popular place of pilgrimage, for not only was Romney one of our greatest artists, but his astonishing life story has the fascination of an 18th century soap opera.

It was in a small farmhouse at Beckside, close to Dalton, that George Romney was born on the 26th December 1734. He was the third son of John

Romney, a mild mannered farmer and cabinet maker who, although formally uneducated, displayed a wide range of talents, and Anne Simpson, who is said to have been a practical wife and mother. George received only a brief education at Dendron village school, which lies two miles south of Dalton. He is said to have spent most of his time sketching, which his parents thought was a waste of money, so after a year he left school to begin work in the same trade as his father. But his natural leaning towards art continued to be stimulated by three different sources. At home he was fascinated by a copy of Leonardo da Vinci's *Treatise on Painting*, which he read passionately; his chance friendship with a local watch-maker named John Williamson, which led to many lively discussions on both art and science; and the influence of a friend of the Romneys, Mrs Gardner, who recognised his outstanding natural artistic ability, which was becoming ever more apparent.

Motivated by the advice of Mrs Gardner, John Romney decided to allow his 21-year-old son to take up a late apprenticeship with a portrait painter named Christopher Steele. Based in Kendal, he at first was engaged in the mundane tasks of the profession, but as his talent became recognised he was allowed more demanding drawing work.

It was while in lodgings in Kendal that Romney fell sick and was nursed by Mary Abbott, who was the daughter of the widowed owner of the house. Their closeness blossomed into love, but was threatened by a separation, for Steele told his pupil that he was needed for new work in York. In desperation the couple quickly married on October 14th 1756; an event which Romney was later to regret, because the responsibility of marriage hindered his ambition to become an artist of repute..

However, after almost a year in York, during which time he was sent money by Mary who was working in service, he returned to Kendal where they set up home. Now released by Steele from his indentured apprenticeship, for which he paid ten pounds, he began to make his own living as a portrait painter. Some of his first commissions came from the powerful Strickland family of Sizergh Castle, whose example led to more local patronage. But as the gentry of Kendal would only pay low rates for his work, to make a living he needed to paint very fast. This led to a rate of production greater than any other artist of the period.

By 1762, Mary had given birth to both a son and a daughter, and as a result of working extremely hard, George Romney had managed to save up one hundred guineas. However, he was still burning with ambition, and now decided that his only chance of national recognition was if he could show his talents in London. So with Mary's approval, he divided their savings in half, and set off on horseback for the capital with the intention that the family would join him as soon he became established.

After spending two weeks at the Castle Inn he moved into lodgings near the Mansion House, then began the uphill task of seeking commissions in a city that seemed to be full of portrait painters. He knew no one of influence, so he had to rely entirely on the quality of his work to forge his reputation. But it was an exciting period of enlightenment in which to live, for many imminent men had begun to realise that Britain lacked any real school of painting, which they were determined to change. The Royal Academy and the National Gallery were not yet in existence, and there was only one single art school in all of London. Our great paintings lay in private collections, owned by Royalty and the nobility, and were out of bounds for lowly artists such as Romney to view and study.

But slowly Romney managed to gain a tenuous foothold in the city's art world, painting the portraits of wealthy men and their families for a mere three guineas. His ability was brought further to public notice, leading to more work, when his *Death of Wolfe* gained him a merit award of twenty five guineas in a competition organised by the Society of Arts. However, his great rivals at this time, which included Joshua Reynolds and Benjamin West, could boast one important advantage over him which allowed them to charge high prices for their paintings: they had toured through Italy, studying the works of the great masters at first hand, which was now regarded as an essential part of any artists training.

In his burning quest for recognition, Romney selfishly ignored the needs of his wife and family, who were struggling back in Lakeland. His daughter had died, then Mary and his son, had been forced to go to live with her father-in-law at Dalton. Her position had become even worse when he sent for twenty guineas out of the original fifty guineas he had given her to live on! This he needed for the foreign travel which he felt was essential to further his career.

Romney journeyed to Paris in 1764, with Thomas Greene, a lawyer who was a friend from his school days. Here, for a few months, he studied the works of the French Masters, which he saw as a useful part of his education. He returned to London, his status now improved, and he began a heavy workload which lasted for almost a decade. His intention was to save enough money to finance an Italian tour, which he eventually achieved in 1773 when he was thirty eight years old. Studying the great works of such artists as Titian, Tintoret, and Michelangelo, he spent over two years living in this artist's Mecca, before returning once more to London. But, although he was now a fully educated painter, he found himself almost penniless and almost forgotten.

With a little apprehension, for he was timid by nature, he took the advice of fellow artists and rented a large house in Cavendish Square. This was seen as a suitable place in which members of Society, his potential customers, would feel comfortable. Spurred on by his friends, writers Richard Cumberland and William Hayley, he was soon to become recognised as one of the most gifted artists of the period. His position was further strengthened by the patronage of the Duke of Richmond, which led to an avalanche of work.

Now earning enough money to easily support his family in London, he still remained reluctant to bring them south to live with him. Most of his patrons did not even know that he was married, and he was enjoying well-earned fame and a carefree, bachelor way of life. He also probably suspected that an uneducated wife who had a country accent, would not easily be accepted by the company he now kept and she may even hinder his future prospects. But inside he was troubled by his conscience, for he knew that he had shabbily treated a devoted woman who had accepted his absence with a minimum of complaint.

By 1781 Romney was able to charge twenty guineas for his three-quarter lengths studies, which due to his fast painting, resulted in a large annual income. John Wesley said that Romney 'struck off an exact likeness at once, and did more in one hour than Sir Joshua did in ten'.

The following year saw another important milestone in his career when he was introduced to Emma Lyon, the seventeen-year-old daughter of a black-smith from Neston in Cheshire. Her outstanding beauty had made her the talk of London society, and she was destined to find her place in history as the notorious Lady Hamilton, mistress of Horatio Nelson. She became Romney's most famous model, who he called his 'divine lady'. He painted her in a large variety of character poses over the following nine years, including *Sensibility*, *Joan of Arc*, *Lady Macbeth*, *Cassandra* and *Calypso*. She became immortalised by his genius, while at the same time her presence led to a late flowering of his talent, but whether or not they ever became lovers is open to speculation.

Sir Joshua Reynolds, who had been the most famous British painter of his day and Romney's main rival, died in 1792. This no doubt made Romney dwell on his own mortality, leading him on to plan a new studio near the Edgware Road where he could teach young painters in his declining years. But the ill-conceived scheme caused him much worry, and he was persuaded to abandon it in favour of a more modest house in Hampstead. He moved into this new residence in 1798, but although he was only aged 64, his health had begun to deteriorate due to years of exhausting work.

Since his first arrival in London, Romney had made only a few brief visits back home, though as his fortunes improved he had seen that Mary had been well taken care of and he often met his son, who had taken holy orders. However, now declining in both mind and body, without a word to any of his friends, he returned back to Kendal. After an absence of 37 years he was once more living with the woman who had nursed him in youth, and who now nursed him during his final three years.

From his sick bed he read of the triumphant return from Naples of his friend and model, Lady Hamilton with her lover, Nelson, and also perhaps heard of their secret scandal. For on the January 25th 1801 she had given birth to the admiral's child, Horatia, who was passed off as the illegitimate daughter of one of his ship's company. The child was later baptised as Horatia Nelson Thompson, being put in the care of a Mrs Gibson in London. After Nelson's death at Trafalgar, the child joined her mother in France where she stayed until Emma Hamilton died in 1815. She then returned to live in England, later marrying the Reverend Phillip Ward and having a large family of nine children. She lived until 1881, but although she knew Nelson was her father, it is said that she did not believe that Romney's famous model was really her mother.

George Romney died on the 15th November 1802 and was laid to rest here in Dalton. It was intended that a monument to commemorate his achievements would be erected in the church but the lay rector refused permission, so this was placed in Kendal Parish Church. His friend Hayley, was the first to write his biography in 1809, but this was not well received. Later his son John, who had taken up residence in the family home of Whitestock near Kendal, wrote his own version of the life of his father. Several poems were also written about him, included the famous *Romney's Remorse* by Tennyson. Today his portraits remain ever popular, being represented in many galleries in both Britain and America, where he is judged to be just behind Gainsborough and Reynolds in his artistic merit.

I took a final look at Romney's grave, then I strolled inside of the church where I admired the spaciousness of its cool interior. Here I read a leaflet which told me that its parishioners 'believe that all our work for God and His Kingdom in Dalton and St Mary's must be undergirded by PRAYER'. Then in the Visitor's Book I saw the name of an Australian woman who had come to see the building where her great-grandmother had been married, and I read the comments of a Buddhist who wrote 'we should unite in prayer for peace'.

4

In the hush of morning, with the bright sunlight slanting over the hedgerows, I drove down a narrow lane that passed under a broken archway, then into the leafy Vale of Deadly Nightshade. Here, I walked alongside the red sandstone walls and the carved Norman arches of one of England's most dramatic ruins: Furness Abbey. On lush green lawns, once trod by Cistercian monks, I watched blackbirds and magpies forage for food. Over the high roofless shell, which once echoed with the chants of these holy men, the only sound which I heard was the whistle of the wind.

The story of Furness Abbey, began not here in Cumbria, but in Tulketh, which lies near Preston in Lancashire. Land had been given in 1123, by Stephen, who was the nephew of King Henry I, to an order of monks who came from Savigny in France. But Tulketh proved to be an unsuitable site, so in 1127 they moved further north to what was at the time, a remote valley, and began to build their magnificent Abbey of St Mary. Twenty years later the Savignac Order was merged with the powerful Cistercian Order, which ensured a prosperous future.

In common with most of the towns and villages of Cumbria during the 13th and 14th centuries, the Abbey and its holdings suffered by the raids of the Scots. But in spite of these it continued to expand, receiving gifts of land and forest and farms. It grew in wealth to become second only to the great Fountains Abbey in Yorkshire, owning most of the land in the Furness peninsula. It also established daughter houses in Lincolnshire, Ireland and the Isle of Man, which acted as bases for its missionary work.

The serene ruins of Furness Abbey, which date from the 12th century, lie in the green Vale of Deadly Nightshade.

For four centuries it brought both religious guidance and employment to this corner of Lakeland, then came the terrible period during the reign of Henry VIII, when the suppression of the monasteries began. At first some of the monks, aided by local people from Furness, rebelled against the closure, but they were no match for the King's forces. The inevitable end came in 1537, when Furness Abbey followed the path of so many great religious houses. Its treasures were taken, lead was torn from its roof and its tumbled stones carted away. Much of its land was given to notorious Thomas Cromwell, who sold it through agents to wealthy unscrupulous men. The site of the Abbey eventually came into the possession of the Cavendish family, who in 1923 placed it under the care of the Office of Works, which is now English Heritage.

For an hour I wandered among these peaceful stones, gazing up at empty windows which once glistened with the colours of stained glass; admiring arches which have been fashioned by Norman hands; and absorbing the spirituality of this holy place, which was created by four hundred years of prayer. When Wordsworth came here in 1845 he discovered, like most visitors do, this same feeling of utter serenity. He later wrote: 'They sit, they walk Among the Ruins, but no idle talk is heard'.

Reluctantly, I departed from the Vale of Deadly Nightshade.

5

"You're either born chubby or not. Luckily I'm not," was part of the conversation which I overheard as I walked from the car park in Crellin Street in Barrow-in-Furness. It came from two young girls who were sitting on a bench in the sunshine, their lips the colour of rubies and their faces liberally tanned by make-up. They seemed to be trying to justify their actions, for on each of their laps rested a huge carton of fish, chips and peas!

For many visitors to Lakeland, Barrow is a puzzle, for in this land of mountain and lakes it seems strangely out of place. Here men talk not of Herdwicks and crop yields, but of steel and of computers, for it is a place where the shepherd's crook has been replaced by the micrometer. As I walked past the modern shops of Dalton Street, which was bustling with young people, I could hear the sounds which are characteristic of this friendly working town. The melodious chime of the town hall clock, the distant sound of a ship's hooter, and the startling cry of a gull as it soared over the chimney pots.

I stood in a shop doorway at the end of Duke Street, sheltering from the brisk coastal breeze and admiring the statue of Ironmaster, Henry William Schneider. For this man, together with James Ramsden who has a similar statue just half a mile away, are the fathers of this modern town. Up to 1850 Barrow was a hamlet of sandstone cottages, with a cobbled street, a pub named the Ship Inn and a wooden jetty. It had remained about this size for a century

The imposing profile of the Town Hall dominates the skyline of Barrow-in-Furness

or more, but all was to change. Any young man living here at this time would have seen the most astonishing transformation of any town in England by the time he reached old age.

It was haematite, a rich iron ore much sought after by the iron-masters of the Industrial Revolution, which was the key to the growth of Barrow. When it was discovered around Furness something like a gold-rush followed, for there were fortunes to be made. Schneider, a thrustful Victorian financier who was willing to take risks, struck it lucky. His speculation on a mine near Dalton began to pay dividends, for the ore proved to be particularly suitable for the production of steel. In 1859 he joined forces with Robert Hannay; instead of just selling the ore they built a furnace to turn it into iron, then later using the Bessemer process, they began to produce that lifeblood of engineering, steel. Men flocked in from all parts of Britain seeking work in both the mines and in the Iron Works and a new town began to take shape.

But transport was the missing link yet needed to complete the new found prosperity, and this was provided by James Ramsden. He was the enterprising general manager of the Furness Railway who also became involved in both steelmaking and in shipbuilding. Also paramount in this industrial expansion was the sombre and shy, seventh Duke of Devonshire, who owned most of the land around Barrow. His aristocratic presence became a powerful symbol of the confidence of the town. By the turn of the century the iron mining industry had become uneconomic, with many miners being forced to emigrate with their families to Australia and America. But by this time the engineering industry had mushroomed with shipbuilding, which had begun here in 1871, now employing thousands of workers.

I continued my stroll along the spacious streets, occasionally stopping to look at distant views of giant cranes highlighted by the sun. I then remembered a link that my hometown of Horwich, in Lancashire, has with Barrow. For Horwich was once a railway town where coppersmiths, boilermakers, blacksmiths and dozens of other talented craftsmen merged their skills to build giant steam locomotives. Many of these trades were also in demand here in Barrow, so there was often an ebb and flow of workers between the two towns, with many Horwichites finding a new life here in Furness.

Opposite to the impressive red-stoned town hall, with its ornate clock tower, I discovered one of Cumbria's newest Tourist Information Centres. Its cost has now been fully justified for the town has recently been voted the Holiday Destination of the Year, which is the tourist industry's most prestigious award. Here, in sparkling opulence, visitors can decide whether to soak up the history of Holker Hall, walk the thirty-three mile route of the Cistercian Way, or perhaps take a balloon flight over the Lakeland mountains. I decided I would like to visit Walney Island, so I bought a local map to point me in the right direction.

Strangers like myself can easily be confused by the geography of Barrow, for its huge expanse of docks and shipyards shroud the town's coastline, which in turn is sheltered by a series of islands. I took the road from Schneider Square which led me to a bridge which spans the choppy water of what appears to be a river, but is really the docks. Here, in massive cream-coloured buildings, which have become landmarks visible for miles around, VSEL known as Vickers, build Trident Submarines. Behind forlorn Victorian gateways, guarded by security-men, hide high-tech designs that are the envy of the world. This is Barrow Island, which from the map appears not to be an island at all, but a small peninsula which is linked by a narrow piece of land to the town centre. However, this is man-made, for the docks were created by partially. filling in the channel which separated the island from the mainland. It was prime minister, William Gladstone, who came here in 1867 to open the first of these impressive enterprises.

Soon I was crossing over another bridge which was built in 1908 to replace a steam ferry, joining Barrow Island to Walney Island over the narrow Walney Channel. This brought me to Vickerstown, which was built like Leverhulme's Port Sunlight, on the model village principle. A place where craftsmen, foremen and managers live in comfort, within site of the liners, tankers, warships and submarines which are their life-work. Among the many well-known vessels which have been built in these yards, are *HMS Resolution*, a 7,000-ton nuclear submarine launched in 1966 which was armed with Polaris missiles and the aircraft carrier *HMS Invincible*, which in 1977 was our largest and most expensive warship. Barrow's maritime and engineering heritage can now be experienced in a marvellous new Dock Museum, which charts its rise from a small village.

The transition from the suburbia of Vickerstown to the remoteness of Walney Island is quite astonishing; in the blink of an eye I had left all feelings of industry far behind. I was now looking on a flat green landscape, which was windswept and unspoilt, where the grey waters of the Irish Sea turned white as they smacked the sandy beach. It reminded me of that lovely Norfolk coastline near Wells-next-the-sea. A glance at the map reveals that the island is flat, narrow and long, stretching for eleven miles from the Duddon Sands in the north, down to the edge of Morecambe Bay in the south. At its widest it is only about a mile, which is reduced to less than a quarter of a mile in other places. But it is an essential part of Barrow's success story, for it shelters the town from the might of the sea, making it the ideal place in which to build ships.

I drove slowly south down the winding coastal road, breathing the bracing salt air which rushed in through the open window. On my right lay the sunlit sea, while on my left lay treeless, fertile meadowland on which sheep and cattle were feeding. The only person I saw on the inviting beach was an elderly man and his black dog who seemed to have the world to themselves.

The road then led me across the island to Biggar, a small village which was one of Walney's earliest settlements. Here I sat for half an hour in the cosy Queen's Arms, drinking half a pint of Bitter and listening to the voice of Tom Jones singing *The Green Green Grass of Home*. Some locals believe that the ancient oak beams, which support the roof of this pub, came off a Spanish ship from the Armada which was wrecked off this coast.

I then strolled through the deserted cobbled streets of this windswept cluster of houses which rest on a highpoint on the edge of the sea. Originally none of the lighted windows of these homes ever pointed seawards, in case they might be used as a guide by invaders. Until 1945 the village's chief citizen, following an ancient tradition, was known as a Grave and his two assistants were called

Lookers. I was joined by an old friendly sheep dog who seemed delighted to have found a companion. Together we wandered past an inscribed stone which boasts that Biggar has been occupied for nine centuries, then on to a gap between the cottages where I could see the rooftops and cranes of Barrow glinting in the sunlight across the water.

South of Biggar the island exudes a feeling of intense remoteness; it is a flat windswept place where the land is overshadowed by wide skies and choppy seas. Notices warn of quicksand, sheep nibble guardedly on sea-washed turf, while sea birds screech overhead, angry at any

A friendly collie guards the entrance to Biggar village, the oldest settlement on windswept Walney Island.

human intrusion. For this is their territory by right, a nature reserve which is the largest mixed nesting ground of Herring and Lesser Black-Backed Gulls in Europe. In winter bird-watchers come here to see Red-Throated Divers, Bar-tailed Godwit and Cormorants, with occasional sightings of very rare species such as the Paddy-field Warbler and the White-Throated Sparrow. The island's southern tip is Haws Point on which stands the Walney Lighthouse, which was built in 1790 to guide ships into the Lune. At this time Barrow was a mere hamlet, the birth of its shipyards lay almost a century into the future. Standing 75 feet high with 91 steps, its first light was provided by oil, then came acetylene in 1909 and finally electricity in 1953. Its powerful 450,000 candle-power which beams out across the water for over 20 miles, has meant a welcome sign of home for generations of sailors.

In 1994, when Peggy Braithwaite retired from here, it was the end of an era, for she had been the only principal woman Lighthouse Keeper in England. She arrived in Walney from Piel Island as a child, when her father, Fred Swarbrick, took over as the Keeper. She joined the lighthouse staff in 1948, then following the death of her father in 1952 became an auxiliary keeper, working with her sister. She took full control in 1975, being awarded a much deserved British Empire Medal for her dedication in keeping the light burning in this remote, gale swept corner of Cumbria.

8

Walney Island to Kirkstone Pass

I look at Piel Island where Lambert Simnel landed, see Stan Laurel's birthplace at Ulverston, then make a pilgrimage to Swarthmoor Hall, the Cradle of Quakerism. I explore the splendour of Cartmel, find Grange unchanged, then ponder over the Finsthwaite Princess. I take the ferry across Windermere, pass through Troutbeck, then I end by drinking mulled wine in the Kirkstone Pass Inn, thinking about Cumbria's early aviators.

1

I wonder if you enjoy, like I do, those unspoilt stretches of England's coastline where rolling green countryside sweeps down to the very edge of the sea? If so, then I can recommend a splendid road which hugs the north-eastern coast of the Furness Peninsula, allowing breathtaking views across the glistening waters of Morecambe Bay.

With the sun high in the sky I left the remoteness of Walney Island and the busy streets of Barrow-in-Furness behind. I joined this quiet road at Rampside, a small seaside village which was originally a Saxon settlement then was later occupied by the Vikings; today it is a place where Barrovians come on summer days to paddle in rocky pools. Its 16th century hall has a romantic tale to tell, for it was built by a young man to win the hand of the girl he loved. Her father, for reasons unknown, insisted that his daughter could only marry if she had a house to live in which had twelve chimneys! The young man, not in the slightest perturbed by this odd request, built Rampside Hall with twelve chimneys in line along the rooftop, and won the girl of his dreams. On every wedding anniversary, to commemorate his success, twelve fires were lit and twelve columns of smoke rose high into the Cumbrian sky. In modern times this was repeated on Christmas Day, with the chimneys becoming known as the Twelve Apostles.

I drove through the peaceful village, passing the inviting Concle Inn, to reach the early Victorian causeway which links Rampside to tiny Roa Island.

The Lifeboat Station on Roa Island looks out towards Piel Castle,
where Lambert Simnel landed in the fifteenth century.

The tide was out, small fishing boats lay marooned in channels of sand on both sides of the road, and the only person in sight was an out-of-breath cyclist who was battling with the stiff breeze. On my left I could see the low outline of Foulney Island, a haven for terns and other sea-birds, which is also linked to Rampside by a spur of shingle.

Roa Island was once the landing place for ships from Ireland whose cargoes were loaded into railway trucks. But this early section of the Furness Railway which steamed across the causeway has long since been dismantled. Today the island remains a windswept cluster of houses and a hotel which serves as a weekend rendezvous for sailors and bird-watchers. I parked near to the impressive lifeboat station, which has been here since 1864, overlooking the choppy grey water. Nearby a middle-aged man was struggling to extricate himself from a multi-coloured wet-suit, watched by hungry gulls who screeched overhead. A nearby sign announced: Piel Castle. Ferries generally available, Easter to September from this Jetty.

I stood alone on the shingle beach, the cool breeze blowing across the half mile of water which separates Roa from one of Cumbria's most fascinating spots, Piel Island. Framed in a sky of pale blue I could see a small boat bobbing in the water, a row of white buildings, and the craggy profile of a castle, which is reputed to be haunted. It is strange to think that in this unlikely setting, five centuries ago, a bizarre event occurred which might easily have changed the course of English history.

Piel's claim to fame arose during that remarkable period towards the end of the 15th century, which many historians regard as one of England's great milestones. In August 1485 Henry Tudor's Lancastrian army met the forces of King Richard III at the epic Battle of Bosworth Field. Richard, labelled by contemporary sources as a 'cruel monster', was killed and his army defeated. It is said that his crown, which was found lying in a thorn bush, was retrieved and placed on the victor's head. Two months later King Henry VII was crowned in Westminster Abbey, creating the powerful House of Tudor and bringing to a close the Middle Ages.

Although King Henry VII's reign was destined to be extremely successful, bringing relative peace and financial stability to the country, he was haunted in the early years by the fear of rebellion. There were powerful men who still had sympathy with Richard's cause, and who wished to place another successor on the throne. A number of half-hearted uprisings occurred in the north, including one in the spring of 1486 which resulted in some rebels hiding in the Lakeland mountains. But in September, when Henry was celebrating the birth of his son Arthur, at Winchester, news came of a more alarming event. An impostor, said to be the eleven-year-old Earl of Warwick who had escaped from the Tower, was claiming he was the rightful heir to the throne and was gaining support.

The young impostor was Lambert Simnel, the son of an Oxford organ-maker. He had been carefully selected for the role as he was of the same age and height as the Earl, and dressed in fine clothes gave a good impersonation. The real Earl, who had been in prison for over a year, was not widely known so Simnel was readily accepted by many of Richard's former followers. Only a selected few knew his real identity, including the man who thought up the scheme, a priest named William Seymour who had ambitions to become an Archbishop.

Although Henry showed the real Earl of Warwick to his Councillors and convinced them of the boy's authenticity, the Yorkists still held out hope of staging a rebellion centred around Simnel. Under the guidance of the Earl of Lincoln and with the aid of Richard III's sister, Margaret of Burgandy, two thousand German mercenaries were recruited. This army, under their leader Martin Schwartz, landed in Ireland where they joined forces with other armed sympathisers. On Whitsun Day 1487, Lambert Simnel was crowned King Edward VI in Dublin Cathedral, in front of an admiring crowd. The new 'King' and his invading army then set sail for England, landing here on Piel island on June 4th. The island at this time was in the ownership of Furness Abbey, having been part of the land which had been granted to them in 1127 by King Stephen. Also known as Foudrey, it had originally been used as a landing stage, then in the 14th century a small castle had been built which was used as a fortified warehouse.

From Piel the invading army landed on the Furness Peninsula, then began their march eastwards into Yorkshire. But the Irish supporters were poorly armed and their hope of gaining recruits from rebellious Englishmen never materialised. They then turned southwards, passing through Sherwood Forest to reach Newark. Meanwhile King Henry's forces, who had been waiting at Kenilworth, learned of Lincoln's position and began their advance. A fierce and bloody battle followed on June 16th near to the village of Stoke. Over two thousand of Henry's men and four thousand of the rebels died, including both Lincoln and Schwartz. The House of Tudor had survived its first great threat and Henry VII had consolidated his position, but at no small price.

Lambert Simnel, the pawn in this plot which could have so easily overthrown the King, managed to survive the battle and was taken prisoner. But Henry, in a bout of confidence and with a touch of humour which belied his stern profile, gave the young lad a job! He started as a low servant-boy working in the Royal Kitchen, then later became a falconer, living a peaceful and uneventful life. But in old age, no doubt, he was bought many a free pint of ale at his local inn for relating how he was once crowned as King of England!

Piel continued to be used by the monks up to the Dissolution, when it became crown property. The castle was then of little importance as a fortification, but the island itself gained a reputation for being a haven for smugglers. This was recognised by the customs men, who built a Customs House here in the 18th century, to curtail illicit trade. As the Furness iron industry grew hundreds of ships were anchored off the island, and the Ship Inn together with Pilot's houses were built near the castle.

Following the example set by Lambert Simnel, the landlord of the Ship Inn is regarded as the King of Piel, and he has the power to create Knights of Piel. Any person selected for this honour, is seated in a special Abbot's chair wearing the ceremonial dress of oilskins and a Viking helmet, while holding a Viking sword. The King reads from his ancient charter, then pours a gallon of beer over the new knight's head. Always the first duty of the new knight is to buy everyone in the pub a drink, but if he is ever shipwrecked on Piel, he is entitled to free lodgings!

It is not surprising, in view of its colourful history, that this patch of Cumbrian coastline is reputed to have started another legend. It is said that one day a barnacle shell was seen on the beach from which the legs and feathers of a bird were seen protruding. It was then assumed that the bird was hatching from the shell, so it was named a Barnacle Goose!

From Rampside I continued my journey up this marvellous coastal road, its twists and turns separating tranquil lush meadowland from the murmuring shingle and the silver sea. I passed cottages which advertised 'Fresh Oysters' and 'Shrimps' for sale, I watched grey sea-birds probing their long bills into sandy pools, and I looked at Aldingham's ancient church which is almost lapped by the waves; some believe that St Cuthbert's body once rested here, but that was before much of the parish was lost to the pounding sea.

From a high point beyond the limestone cottages of Baycliff village, I paused to gaze over the narrowing bay whose shallows are cut deep by the Ulverston Channel. Across the water lay the pale blue shoreline that stretches up from Flookburgh to the 160 feet high cliffs of Humphrey Head. It was here that England's last wolf was killed by a member of the Harrington family; a brave act which won him the hand of the beautiful Adela. Here too once lived a hermit, alongside the Holy Well of St Agnes. The mineral water from this well was once in great demand, for it was reputed to cure rheumatic ailments.

I parked my car close to the sea shore at Bardsea, then strolled up the hill to the elevated village church of the Holy Trinity. The view from this churchyard is quite stunning, a sweeping panorama that embraces the Pennine hills, the Lakeland mountains and the splendour of sand and sea. For half an hour I sat looking out over this ancient landscape, trying to identify landmarks and enjoying the ever changing colours of the bay as the sun began to set.

Before leaving this lovely churchyard I read two grave inscriptions which poignantly illustrate the passing of time. John Clegg who died in old age in 1892, has his final resting place a few paces from that of Maria Alberdina Francess Brown who died in 1992, aged 100. So here lie two people whose lives span the period from the Battle of Waterloo to our age of technology which has put a man on the moon and brought a computer into nearly every home.

2

"Can you direct me to Argyle Street please?" I asked the old man who was returning to his Ulverston home loaded with a heavy shopping bag.

"It's only a stone's throw away. Turn left over the hill, then sharp left again and you'll be there."

He was quite right for within two minutes I was entering the little quiet street of two-up and two-down neat terraced houses. At last I had reached the end of my unlikely pilgrimage, for a small plaque that was fixed to the wall of number three stated: Stan Laurel Was Born In This House 16th June 1890.

When a man is born in a castle or a stately home, then in manhood attains greatness, it is not completely unexpected. But there is something infinitely more satisfying in seeing the once modest home of a great man. For it is a forceful reminder that privilege and wealth are not the sole means to achieve success and it gives us all hope.

I stood for a few minutes in silence, gazing at the grey limestone walls and the red sandstone doorway which stands on the edge of a clean flagged pavement. Little has changed here since the time, now a century ago, that young Stan Laurel stepped over this doorstep to perhaps play hopscotch, or top and whip, or to go bird nesting. He would have been just one of the local kids, most of whose future was highly predictable. Some would find employment in the shipyards at Barrow, others perhaps would find a more healthy outdoor life on the land, while many would taste the horrors of trench warfare in France. But for him life would be so different, for his path lay far from Argyle Street and the struggles of factory life. Wealth and world wide fame awaited him under the blue skies of Hollywood.

The key to the success of Stan Laurel was the example set by his father who came from a theatrical family. He was a local playwright connected with the music hall circuit, which was the most popular form of entertainment towards the end of the last century. At one time he owned a number of run-down theatres in the north, but later he invested all his money in a large theatre in Blythe which proved disastrous, for he lost everything. Stan, having inherited his father's taste for show-business, followed in the family tradition from an early age, taking a comedy role in touring companies whenever he could find the work. But his real name of Arthur Stanley Jefferson was too formal for a comedian, and when shortened to Stan Jefferson contained thirteen letters which were considered unlucky. So the name that was to become part of a Hollywood legend was created when he was told to look to his 'laurels', which is exactly what he did.

In 1910 at the age of only 20, his big break came when he was offered a job in a large vaudeville troupe. This group of very talented young artistes, which included Charlie Chaplin, started a lucrative tour throughout America which was the show-business land of opportunity. The tour proved to be highly successful, then when it ended Stan decided to remain in the USA and by 1917 he had been drawn, inevitably, to the splendour of Hollywood. There he secured a position with the famous Hal Roach Studio, working first as a writer and director, then later having proved himself, he starred in his own comedy film series.

His partner-to-be, Oliver Nowell Hardy, was born on the 18th January 1892 in Atlanta, Georgia. He studied law at the University of Georgia, but soon decided he preferred the stage to any academic career. After making his first film in 1913 he too became a director of comedy films, then he moved to Hollywood in 1918. But it was 1926 before Hal Roach starred the two actors together, beginning what was to be one of the greatest comedy teams of all time. Their first classic film was *Putting the Pants on Philip*, which concerned the hilarious adventures of a kilted scotsman in America.

Pathetically thin Laurel contrasted marvellously with the overweight Hardy right from the start of their partnership, and the form of their successful routines fell naturally into place. For the next six years they created a short film nearly every month, relying mainly on their natural ability for spontaneity, rather than working from a script. In 1931 they made their first full length film, *Pardon Us*, and in the following year made both feature and short films. *The Music Box*, made in 1932, gained them an Academy Award and they were now the most popular comedy duo in the world, having survived the transition from silent films to talkies which had ended many other careers. People world-wide escaped from the despair of recession by clamouring to the cinema where they could laugh at Laurel and Hardy's outrageous antics. These often ended in Ollie's frown followed by his famous lines "another fine mess you've got me in to", leading to Stan bursting into tears.

Sadly, in the late thirties, they had a dispute with their creator, Hal Roach. This eventually led to a final break in 1940 when they moved to the larger, more powerful Hollywood studios. Their success continued through the war years, producing such classics as *A Chump at Oxford (1940)*, which also boasted the young Peter Cushing among the cast, and *The Bull Fighters (1945)*. But after more than two decades at the very top of their profession, they then began to experience a decline. By the end of the forties their films were no longer in fashion, only in the music halls of Britain and America could they still draw in the crowds. It was during one of these tours in 1947 that Stan brought his pal Ollie back to his hometown, and they were photographed outside his birthplace here in Argyle Street.

Oliver Hardy died of a heart attack in 1957, but his partner from Lancashire was more fortunate, for he lived to see the beginning of a revival of their popularity which happily still continues today. He also received a much deserved Special Comedy Award in 1960, five years before his death.

Of all the great comedians who have been talented enough to make the world laugh at itself, Laurel and Hardy rank supreme. Their unique combination of slap-stick humour and pathos has proved itself to have that timeless quality that is the test of genius. Today's generation watch on videos the same routines that their grand-parents saw on the silent screen and are enthralled by the comic antics which have brought smiles to the faces of millions of people. The skinny, solemn faced Laurel ever puzzled by the wonders of life and always doing the wrong thing and the rotund Hardy in his tight jacket and air of ragged dignity, have gained themselves a special place in the show-business hall of fame.

I rang the bell at Stan Laurel's childhood home and the door was answered by its present owner, Mabel Radcliffe, a lively, bright eyed woman who sadly has been recently widowed. Although the star's birthplace is a private residence, after explaining my interest she kindly invited me inside her immaculate terraced home for a short chat.

"I bought the house because it was just the right size for me," she explained, "and not because of Stan Laurel."

She then went on to tell me that the creation of a Laurel and Hardy Museum in the town, together with the recognition given to Laurel's old home, is due to the devotion of local man, Bill Cubin. For over thirty years he has been a Town Councillor, being twice the Mayor of Ulverston, and since childhood he has been a Laurel and Hardy fan.

"I now have a Visitor's Book," Mabel explained, "which was first signed by comedy actress Bella Emburg when she came to Ulverston to open an extension to the Museum in 1992."

Mabel then explained how Laurel and Hardy fans from all over the world have arrived here to photograph his birthplace. One of the most colourful of these visitors was an Italian Count who still writes to find out the latest news about the town.

"Since my husband died so tragically from Muscular Dystrophy I now ask anyone who takes a photo if they would kindly make a donation to the charity which carries out research into the disease. Its just a small way of trying to help."

Before I departed from Argyle Street I signed the Visitor's Book, then asked Mabel if she would pose for my photo outside her unique home. As I walked back to my car I noticed that the terraced house opposite has found an appropriate name, Laurel View!

Stan Laurel has been given Ulverston's greatest honour – he now has a pub named after him!

I parked my car close to the centre of Ulverston, overlooked by Hartleys Brewery which produces the most popular beverage in these parts. I soon discovered that the town is an interesting place to explore for it has changed little over the past century. It has narrow cobbled streets down which hide solid stone cottages, overlooked here and there, by larger Victorian houses and even grander Georgian homes. Local people were buying food, not in huge supermarkets or even in branches of too familiar chain stores, but in small shops that I suspect have been family businesses for generations. As I stood in the sunshine at the corner of the Market Square looking across to the war memorial, visitors with the accents of America, Australia and France wandered past me. They were purchasing that tube of toothpaste which always runs out on holiday, from J. Hewitt's pharmacy which was first established here in 1750, then perhaps a Lakeland guide book from nearby James Atkinsons, which is the oldest bookshop in Cumbria.

One of the popular events which continued in the town until the 1920s, and is still remembered by older residents, was the Hiring Fair. This open air employment exchange was held here twice a year, at Whitsuntide and Martinmas. In a festive atmosphere, created by a fair-ground with musicians and side shows, large crowds from all over Lakeland would converge on the town. Farm-workers, who had no Trade Union and few statutory rights, made individual deals in the street with farmers and landowners. After much light-hearted bantering they would eventually settle their rates of pay and hours of work for the next year, sealing their bond with a handshake.

The stone houses of this fascinating town are surrounded by a wide sweep of gentle green hills, the most prominent being Hoad Hill. On its summit stands an impressive monument whose design is similar to the Eddystone Lighthouse, towering 100 feet up to the lantern. Far below can be seen the grey line of the short Ulverston Canal which was cut by Rennie to link the town with the sea. Across the brown expanse of Ulverston Sands, where the tide meets the waters of the River Leven, can be seen the outline of Flookburgh and the cliffs of Humphrey Head.

The monument on Hoad Hill remembers Sir John Barrow who was born in a small cottage at Dragley Beck in 1764, which lies on the outskirts of the town. He came from farming stock, but his talent for hard work with an aptitude for mathematics and a sense of adventure, became apparent when he attended Town Bank Grammar School. This led him as a young man on an expedition to China, of which he wrote an outstanding book which brought him immediate fame. In 1804 he was given the prestigious position of Secretary to the Admiralty, a post he held for forty years, during one of the most exciting periods in naval history. He was one of the founders of the Royal Geographical Society, and was particularly interested in encouraging the exploration of the polar regions. This led to him being immortalised on the world map, for Cape Barrow, the Barrow Straits and Point Barrow all remember his name.

There was no way I could leave Ulverston without visiting Bill Cubin's Laurel and Hardy Museum, for it is the only one in the world. For two hours I browsed at press cuttings, posters, letters, furniture from Laurel's birthplace and hundreds of other pieces of memorabilia of the great comedy team. Then, I laughed with other visitors at the clips from some of their marvellous films. This immediately brought back to me half-forgotten memories of when I last saw these timeless comic antics, which was at a sixpenny children's matinee in the fifties in my home town.

As I left the museum, I began to ponder on a snippet that I had read from an old newspaper. This suggested that the film star Clint Eastwood was really the secret son of Stan Laurel. And I must admit that there is quite a striking resemblance between the two men.

3

"Have you come to have a look round Swarthmoor?" shouted a young, bearded man who was hurrying up the garden-path towards the entrance to the Elizabethan Hall.

"Yes, I was hoping to," I answered, "but I'm not a Quaker–merely a curious visitor."

He smiled. "That's fine, we welcome visitors. Please will you wait in this room. I'm afraid it's a bit crowded."

I opened the large oak door of the Great Hall to which he was pointing, and was surprised to be greeted by a sea of faces. A few were seated, but most, looking uncomfortable due to the hot day, were sat on the floor. I later learned that this group of mainly teenage American Quakers had come here to Swarthmoor Hall on a pilgrimage. For this house is regarded by many to be the historical centre of their world-wide religion.

A few minutes later the bearded man, who as resident warden lives in part of the house with his young family, came into the magnificently panelled room. He then gave us a lively and entertaining chat about Swarthmoor's history, explaining its connections with George Fox, Judge Fell and his wife Margaret. He ended his talk by saying, "Now please explore the house at your own pace. Sit on the chairs, lift any lids, open any drawers that you wish. This freedom is part of our policy here at Swarthmoor."

This comment would have astonished those guardians of National Trust properties who forbid the slightest interference with any of their furnishings!

Elizabethan Swarthmoor Hall at Ulverston is known as the cradle of Quakerism.

Swarthmoor Hall lies up a narrow country lane in the midst of green fields, less than a mile from the centre of Ulverston. It was built about 1586 by George Fell, who was a wealthy lawyer and landowner. His son, Thomas, who was born in 1598, followed the same profession as his father, becoming a Justice of the Peace and later an MP, and a supporter of Cromwell's parliament. In 1632 he brought his new bride, seventeen-year-old Margaret Askew, to the Hall where they lived happily together for twenty-six years. Here Margaret, who was sixteen years younger than her husband, became the mistress of a large estate and the mother of nine children.

At this time, although it had been a century since King Henry VIII had broken with Rome, the country was still full of religious uncertainty. In the early years conflict had mainly been between those who adhered to the Roman Catholic faith and those who wished to be Protestants. But the creation of the Church of England had brought disappointment to many who wanted different religious change. Some did not accept the teachings of a new prayer book, while others wanted more far-reaching reforms. These different groups, known as Dissenters, met unlawfully in secret to worship God in their own way. They were often hounded by the authorities, sometimes imprisoned and occasionally they died for their religious beliefs. Many left England for more tolerant lands such as Holland, then they journeyed on to become the founding fathers of a new country which is now the USA.

It was in this climate of religious upheaval that George Fox, who was to become associated with Swarthmoor, was born in 1624 at Fenny Drayton in Leicestershire; just four years after the voyage of the Mayflower. His father, Christopher Fox, was a weaver and his mother, Mary Lago, came from a family of gentlefolk. Leicestershire, at this time, had a reputation for being a centre for radical religious activity, which no doubt influenced his early life. As a youth he became a shoemaker's apprentice, but from being a young child his mind had been absorbed with spiritual matters. Questioning both Protestant and Puritan teachings he began to strive to find his own religious fulfilment. This led him to leave home in 1643, beginning what was to become a life of wandering, at first seeking 'the pure knowledge of God and Christ alone', then later as a preacher passing his message on to others.

Personal enlightenment came to him in 1647, when he was twenty-three years old. Dismissing much of what was preached by learned theologians, he now believed that 'to be bred at Oxford or Cambridge was not sufficient to fit a man to be a minister of Christ'. He also felt that going to church was not important, and that the spirit of God lay in the hearts of all men and women. Filled now with an irresistible desire to tell others about his new-found convictions, he travelled through the Midlands and into Yorkshire, spreading his word of God. This on several occasions led to a clash with local religious leaders, resulting in him being imprisoned for months for breaking the law of blasphemy. But like-minded people began to join his ranks, some having reached similar religious beliefs as Fox by their own independent paths, including James Nayler and Richard Farnsworth. Known in these early days as the Children of Light, they were first called 'Quakers' by Justice Bennet at Derby, who bid them to 'tremble at the Word of the Lord'. This was originally regarded as a term of abuse, but gradually came into common use to describe followers of their new religion, who saw themselves as 'Seekers' of God and whose official name is now the Religious Society of Friends.

In the early days Quakers became noted for their plainness of dress, peaceful manners and principles, and their silent religious meetings. But charismatic George Fox, who was of a 'striking appearance' with penetrating eyes, wore a leather doublet and breeches for his many preaching journeys through Britain. This he saw as the right clothing to protect him from the weather, but at times it led to him being criticised by others.

One of the far-reaching events on his travels came in 1652 in Lancashire when he saw a vision of the thousands of people who were seeking religious truth. He recorded in his famous journal:

'As we went I spied a great high hill called Pendle Hill and I went on the top of it with much ado, it was so steep; but I was moved of the Lord to go atop of it; and when I came atop of it I saw Lancashire sea; and there atop of the hill I was moved to sound the day of the Lord; and the Lord let me see a-top of the hill in what places he had a great people to be gathered'.

It was later the same year that he first came here to Swarthmoor Hall where he met Margaret Fell and her children, together with the Rector of Ulverston, William Lampitt. Immediately and much to the anger of the Rector, Margaret seemed to be agreeing with the religious words spoken by Fox. He was given hospitality in the house and later met Judge Fell, who had been away on circuit. It is said that Fox walked in to the Judge's parlour unannounced, did not remove his hat which was the customary courtesy, and began to speak using terms which did not take into account the powerful position of the Judge. However, Thomas Fell was an unusually tolerant man, perhaps recognising that Fox's words had already convinced his own wife and most of his household. His kindliness extended even further, for he was soon to allow his home to be used for the Meeting of Friends each Sunday.

Judge Fell's recognition of the movement, although he was never to become a Quaker himself, was another important milestone in its history. Many new followers from the villages of Furness joined the ranks of Margaret Fell and her children, coming here to Swarthmoor Hall, which has become known as the known as the Cradle of Quakerism. By 1654 Quaker communities had sprung up in many parts of the north, the Kendal area being a particularly important base. During the next decade its successful ministry spread into southern England, producing around 40,000 members, in spite of persecution and imprisonment

In 1658 Judge Fell, described by Fox as 'mighty serviceable to Truth', died at the age of sixty. But Swarthmoor Hall continued to be used as the organis-ational base for Quakerism, which led to Margaret Fell being imprisoned in Lancaster Castle for four and a half years. On her release she toured the gaols of England, giving consolation to others who were also suffering religious persecution. By 1669 her friendship with George Fox had grown into love, and the couple were married.

Quakers continued to be imprisoned for their beliefs during the reign of King Charles II, leading many to seek asylum in the American colonies. Among these was William Penn a prominent member and a frequent visitor to Swarthmoor Hall, who became the founder of Pennsylvania. But the passing of the Toleration Act of 1689 at last allowed Quakers to worship freely; George Fox had lived to see what he desired most. Now weak and infirm after suffering in so many prisons he lived just two more years, dying on the 13th January 1691. Margaret, a woman of astonishing spiritual vigour, lived on till she was eighty-eight years old, dying on the 23rd April 1702. She lies buried in an unmarked grave at the Sunbreck burial ground, just three miles from her beloved Swarthmoor Hall.

From this seed sown by George Fox, Margaret Fell and their Friends during the 17th century, has grown a world-wide Quaker membership of 240,000. They differ from other religious groups in that their emphasis is 'on daily life and experience, rather than on particular religious occasions'. They gather for silent worship in simple Meeting Houses in which there are no religious ornaments and no appointed ministers. Any person at the meeting can speak when inspired to do so, which is called a Vocal Ministry. They are ardent peace campaigners, opposing all forms of violence and they refuse to take up arms in any wars.

I continued my exploration of the lovely rooms that echo with so many memories of these devout people. I saw the study where Judge Fell and George Fox had their first historic meeting, the four poster bed in which Margaret Fell gave birth to her nine children, and the chest which Fox brought out of Worcester Prison in 1675.

"Say, just try this chair. Although it looks hard it's really comfortable," said a middle-aged Quaker who had travelled 3000 miles to visit Cumbria.

Like two schoolboys we took it in turn to sit down on the 17th century chair, then we opened desk lids and dusty oak drawers, and ran our fingers over roof beams which had once been part of the Armada fleet. For this was a unique opportunity not to be wasted!

4

I escaped from the busyness of the A590 road at Haverthwaite, taking a splendid meandering lane, overhung with tunnels of foliage. Occasionally I would catch a glimpse of the flat marshy fields on my right, which sweep down to the isolation of Cartmel Sands and the silver glint of the sea. Hidden in a corner of this headland is Holker Hall, the Elizabethan stately home of Lord and Lady Cavendish. Surrounded by acres of parkland and gardens, it was here that the famous Holker Shorthorn Cattle were first bred by a former Duke of Devonshire during the last century.

Cartmel, that most perfect of Lakeland villages, lay before me like Avalon, rising upwards from the morning mist. As I strolled through its awakening streets I thought how appropriate is its name, which is said to mean 'a camp among the hills'. But these hills are not menacing and craggy, but gentle, green and inviting. The most popular walk, so I'm told, is up to the top of Hampfell, which has the "Best view in the Lakes," according to a local man I met.

I stood in the Market Square, alongside the village's ancient stone fish-slabs and the water-pump, watching the stream of visitors that pour into Cartmel each day. They were browsing in book-shops, buying postcards of the Priory, walking beneath the 14th century gateway and being tempted by plates of scones and cream. But it is on Bank Holidays that the crowds really come here, for the bustle and colour of Cartmel Races has become one of Lakeland's most cherished events. This marvellous steeplechase takes place on a course just a stones throw from the village centre, and like most things in Cartmel, has an ecclesiastical origin. For it is said that the races were first run by the monks as part of their leisure activities at Whitsun. This is still remembered by a unique Steeplechase Service, which is appropriately held in the Priory Church each August.

After strolling down inviting alleyways, admiring tiny cottages bedecked with flowers, and watching a pied-wagtail hop from stone to stone in the crystal waters of the little river, I went to see the Priory. It was King Ecfreth of Northumbria who first forged Cartmel's holy links when he gave this green valley to Saint Cuthbert, but it was supernatural intervention that decided the site of this cathedral in miniature. It was founded in 1188 by the powerful William Marshal, who as Regent of England after the death of King John, found fame by expelling the French. But the Augustian Canons intended to build their church on a high hilltop, until they were guided by a mysterious voice. It told them that their site must be 'in a valley between two rivers, where one runs north and one runs south'.

This lovely church looked breathtaking in the soft morning sunshine, its mellow limestone walls towering upwards into a cloudless sky. It remains one of the few in England which survived the Dissolution in its entirety, finding a new role in 1534 as the local parish church. For an hour I wandered among its Norman arches, gazed upwards to its lofty chancel, read epitaphs on ancient tombs and looked for the bullet holes made by Cromwell's soldiers. Then I had to dash, lunch awaited me at Grange-over-Sands.

There was a time, when steam-trains sped through little country stations and passengers sat in waiting rooms heated by roaring coal-fires. Here they read brightly coloured posters on which smiling girls in modest swim-suits said invitingly, 'Come to Bournemouth or Hastings or Grange-over-Sands'. Well I'm happy to report that Grange-over-Sands has survived the competition from a hundred foreign holiday destinations, and still retains its quiet Edwardian elegance. In its ornamental gardens there are immaculate flower beds and manicured green lawns in which there is not a daisy or a weed to be seen. On benches sit smiling groups of visitors who feed crusts to pintail and pochard ducks, watch black-headed gulls soar overhead and intently read their newspapers. The headlines may say 'Peace in Ireland' or 'John Major in USA', but if it read 'Lily Langtry leaves London' or 'King Edward opens Parliament', you get the feeling no one would raise an eyebrow. For Grange is timeless, it bathes in an atmosphere of confident perpetuity; no one who lives here is in any doubt it will remain unchanged a century from now.

A sign warns of the hidden dangers of quicksand at Grange-over-Sands

From the gardens I wandered up Main Street looking into shop-windows; many of these family businesses I suspect began when the Furness Line first came here in 1887. Young couples with children and retired men with white hair, who have come to live here 'because its much warmer than Arnside', were avidly reading advertisements outside the Tourist Information Office. They were wondering whether to book a coach trip to see 'The Langdale Pikes', or perhaps 'Keswick and Eight Lakes'. Some were even contemplating that unique adventure of being guided over the sands, the route from which Grange-over-Sands takes its name.

A narrow alleyway fringed with ivy clad limestone walls, led me across the railway line and on to the quiet promenade. Here I looked out over the glistening sandy shoreline to the Kent Channel and the full splendour of Morecambe Bay. Beyond the murmuring waves lay the grey outline of Arnside rising gently upwards to its wooded heights. Then turning inland I could see the sweep of green meadowland, ending at the horizon with the prominent shape of Yorkshire's Ingleborough. Here, with the breeze on my face and the smell of seaweed in the air, I sat for half an hour trying to identify a dozen such landmarks. Then reluctantly I left the Cumbrian coast.

5

It was a perfect summer morning and Lakeland looked magical. The hot rising sun had melted away the dew and was now bringing alive a dozen shades of green. As I drove slowly towards Finsthwaite I glanced over lichen covered walls to hidden dells which were carpeted with the yellow of buttercups. Beyond rose darkened woodland glades, coloured here and there with the vivid purple of foxgloves; the secluded home of badgers, stoats and red-deer. My eyes were led ever upwards from this umbrella of foliage to the lonely summit of Great Green Howes, one of a series of low hills which separate Windermere from Coniston.

When I arrived at the village it was barely awake. Collie dogs were still stretching near cottage doors, a farmer was about to drive his tractor away to begin the days work and a bread-man was making his first delivery. I parked my car close to St Peter's church and was immediately greeted by a marmalade cat who seemed determined to accompany me into the churchyard. She was an affectionate female who demanded a stroke, then together we began to search for a special grave.

It was not until 1676 that Finsthwaite gained its independence, for prior to this it lay in the parish of Hawkshead. Half a century later its first church was built, but this was replaced in 1874 by this present impressive building with its attractive central tower. Its benefactor was Mr Newby Wilson and its configuration is based on the Norman Transitional style, which won a competition organised by the Diocesan Church Extension Society. The architects, Paley and Austin of Lancaster, were judged to have created a design which was especially suitable for a 'mountain chapel'.

Walking around the churchyard with my feline companion I began to read the poignant inscriptions which are carved on half-hidden grave-stones. These tragedies from the past included: 'John Harrison Burns, killed in an air raid whilst on duty, 23 December 1940' and 'Elizabeth Mari Lewthwaite who fell while walking in Wasdale, 6 July 1969, aged 18.'

After half an hour of searching in the hot sunshine I at last found what had really drawn me to this hidden village: the final resting place of the woman who has become known as the Finsthwaite Princess. She lies beneath a simple marble cross on the far side of the churchyard. The inscription, which gives no clue to her identity, reads:

In Memoriam
Clementina Johannes Sobiesky Douglass
of Waterside
Buried 16th day of May 1771
Behold Thy King Cometh

This weathered cross marks the grave of the mysterious Finsthwaite Princess.

It may well be that the strange truth of her life story will forever be shrouded in mystery, for some romantics believe she was the daughter of Bonnie Prince Charlie and that her secret is bound up with the tragic rebellion of '45.

Prince Charles Edward Stuart, widely known as the Young Pretender or Bonnie Prince Charlie, was born in Rome in 1720. He was the eldest son of Prince James Francis Edward, the Old Pretender, and Princess Maria Clementina Sobieska, who was the grand-daughter of the King of Poland. The family lived in exile in Europe while the Jacobite cause smouldered on in Scotland, where Bonnie Prince Charlie was considered by many to be the rightful Prince of Wales and his father, as the only surviving son of King James II, the heir to the throne.

The Prince, who had inherited the attractive fair features of his mother, was given extensive military training with a view to the task which might await him. In 1743 he gratefully accepted help from the French Government in his quest to regain the throne of Britain for his father. He headed a French fleet which left Dunkirk with seven thousand soldiers, but they hit terrible storms which drove them back and the operation had to be abandoned.

Two years later he resumed his struggle by secretly returning to his ancestral homeland where he managed to muster a large fighting force from the Highland Clans. They took Edinburgh, won the battle of Prestonpans and continued southwards, capturing Carlisle. But their progress was halted at Derby, for they found little Jacobite support in England, superior forces were facing them and unrest had begun to fester in their own ranks. The Prince wanted to proceed to London, which in view of the events which followed many feel would have been the right move to make, but he was over ruled. A retreat to Scotland followed, with a minor success at Falkirk, followed by a regrouping near Inverness.

In April 1746 the terrible Battle at Culloden took place which resulted in the total defeat of Bonnie Prince Charlie's forces by the infamous Duke of Cumberland. A callous and cruel order was made by the Duke to give no quarter, which resulted in both prisoners and the wounded being put to the sword. The Prince made his escape to the Western Isles, an episode which is forever remembered by the haunting words of the *Skye Boat Song*. After a period in hiding a French man-o'-war sped him to the continent where he remained in exile for the rest of his life.

At the age of 52, in 1772, he married the pretty nineteen-year-old Princess Louisa of Stolberg, but no children resulted from the union. However, earlier, while he had been leading the Jacobite uprising in Scotland in 1745, he had taken a mistress, Clementina Walkinshaw, who was the daughter of one of his active supporters. She had devotedly nursed him during an illness he had contracted following the Battle of Falkirk. The couple later lived together in exile for a number of years, often using false names and having at times a stormy relationship, but one which resulted in 1753 in the birth of a child, Charlotte.

The liaison inevitably came to an end, with Clementina taking her young daughter to live with her in Paris. Bonnie Prince Charlie, a man who had received so much devotion from his followers and whose future once looked so full of promise, quickly began to degenerate. He was unable to face the reality of his situation for the Jacobite cause was lost forever; his life now became one of debauchery and drunkenness. However, one small happiness came to him in 1784, just four years before his death. Charlotte, with love and devotion, began to look after him in these, his declining years. He gave her the title Duchess of Albany, but sadly she too was destined to die prematurely, less than two years after the death of her father. This was as a result of injuries received after she fell from her horse.

The last of the Stuart claimants to the throne was Prince Henry, who was the surviving brother of Bonnie Prince Charlie. In his youth he was known by the Jacobites as the Duke of York, then following the death of his brother as Henry IX. He took holy orders in the Roman Catholic Church, was made the Bishop of Ostia, Vellerro and Frascari in 1745, then two years later was created Cardinal. His self proclaimed title of Henry IX of England was never recognised by the church who knew him as His Serene Highness, Henry Benedict Mary Clement, Cardinal Duke of York. Following his death in 1807 his body was placed close to his father and brother, in the crypt of St Peter's in Rome, while the heart of his mother, Clementina, lies in a marble urn in the Church of the Apostles.

Charlotte, Duchess of Albany, had been the mistress of Archbishop Ferdinand de Rohan, to whom she had three children. Their son, who went under the self-styled title of Count Rochenstar was a frequent visitor to Scotland where he died in 1850. His tomb can be seen in Dunkeld Cathedral.

Staring at this intriguing grave at Finsthwaite I began to ponder about the mysterious woman who lies buried here. Who was she? Where did she come from? Why did she settle here in Lakeland and where does she fit in to one of the most romantic tales in British history?

Local tradition gives us few clues. It relates that she first arrived here in 1745 as the resident of Waterside House. She was accompanied by two servants, had 'wondrously fair hair', and remained here until her death in 1771, living a hermit like existence. Although she made no attempt to conceal her name, she requested that no tombstone or inscription should mark her last resting place. This seems to have at first been complied with, but her grave had to be moved when the old church was demolished in 1873. Then in 1913 the vicar of Staveley, Canon C.G. Townley, decided that a cross ought to be erected, perhaps because many visitors wanted to see her grave.

Although her age is not known, if her arrival in Finsthwaite was really 1745 and she was an adult which has been implied, it is unlikely that she was a daughter of Bonnie Prince Charlie, who himself was only 25 years old at the time. Also, there does not seem to be any evidence that he was the father of any children, other than Charlotte. Sir Compton Mackenzie, who researched the possibility for his book, *Prince Charlie and His Ladies*, decided it was improbable she was the Prince's child.

Another, more likely possibility, is that she was a Polish Princess, perhaps a close relative of the Prince's mother who had a similar name. She may well have accompanied the Prince on his ill-fated journey to Britain, helping to boost the morale of wavering Jacobites. The name Douglas, which appears on her grave inscription, is also an alias that the Prince is known to have used. But why she chose to settle here at Finsthwaite is also a mystery, although it is possible that Jacobite sympathizers lived in the district. It was said that a Scottish thistle was planted on her grave shortly after her burial.

It has also been suggested that the Finsthwaite Princess may not have been a princess at all, but merely a wealthy eccentric woman who lived in a fantasy world. Her obsession being triggered by the turmoil of the Jacobite rebellion, she assumed the identity of one of the exiled royal family. This theory may have resulted from the true tale of another local eccentric named Kitty Dawson. When she was a young girl her lover was killed by a bolt of lightening, a tragedy which turned her mind. The rest of her life was spent as a recluse in a cabin in Graythwaite woods near Finsthwaite, her food being supplied by the local people.

I stroked the head of the marmalade cat then walked from the serenity of this tranquil churchyard towards the lychgate, which is guarded by two splendid yew trees. Glancing backwards I was still uncertain whether Clementina Johannes Sobiesky Douglas is a princess or a crank, but what is certain is that her final resting place is one of the loveliest in England.

6

I passed the sign which announced 'Ferry Queue Approximate Wait 20 Minutes', before my car was halted by the line of other vehicles waiting to cross over Windermere. At last my time came, I was guided within a hairsbreadth of a gleaming Mercedes whose owner looked on with apprehension. I could now enjoy the ten minute crossing of England's longest lake. There has been a ferry-crossing here at the lake's narrowest point for at least five centuries, linking Ferry House Point on the west bank, to Ferry Nab at Bowness; these are separated by only 500 yards of water. Wordsworth came this way as a young undergraduate from Cambridge, but in his day the ferry was a simple rowing boat with an oil lamp to show the way after darkness.

However placid and safe the lake may seem in summertime, when winter comes it is another story. For with a gale blowing and the mist down to the waters edge it takes on a more sinister face. This has given rise to the legend of the Crier of Claife, an event which took place here during the 16th century. It began when a party of revellers were enjoying an evening of drinking at an old inn which stood at Ferry House Point. A call for the ferry was heard from the Nab, so the ferry-man, who was completely sober, rowed his boat across the stormy lake to pick up the passenger. But when he returned the revellers were surprised to see that he was alone, and were even more shocked by his appearance for he was 'ghastly and dumb with horror'. The following morning he was still speechless, but he now had a raging fever and he soon died without revealing what horror he had seen. For the next few weeks blood-curdling shrieks and howling were heard coming from the nab, as if some tormented spirit had taken up residence. The boatmen became too afraid to venture out on to the lake after dark, so a priest was called to exorcise the haunted spot. This did not rid the area completely of the curse, but had the effect of moving the spirit to a disused slate quarry on Latterbarrow, beyond Claife Heights. It is said that the terrible howls are still occasionally heard echoing from the lonely hilltop.

Once more I thankfully left most of the holiday traffic behind me when I began the ascent up the Patterdale Road. Passing through the lovely straggling village of Troutbeck, with its popular Mortal Man Inn and associations with Beatrix Potter, I continued ever upwards until I reached a high point on the road. Here I paused to catch a final look at a corner of Windermere which was visible as a distant patch of blue, far below in the valley. The twisting course of the Trout Beck was marked by a line of trees, and the rising fellside was highlighted by a dark web of drystone walls.

"Yes we're often cut off by the snow in wintertime. It lasted for almost three weeks last year."

I had arrived at Lakeland's highest pub, the Kirkstone Pass Inn, and the landlord was speaking as he poured me a glass of hot mulled wine, which is a local speciality. I returned to my seat beside the flickering open fire, in a corner of the large single room which echoes with memories of past travellers. Here stags heads and old photos from the last century line the walls, bearded men and tanned face girls talk of Striding Edge and High Street, while others listen for the 'Poor Old Lad' which is the pubs resident ghost.

It is said that there has been a building here at the Top O' Kirkston since 1461, but this was little more than a shepherd's hut. During the late 18th century stables were added, then in 1840, under the direction of Parson Sewell of Troutbeck, it was developed into an inn. Sitting just below the 1500 feet contour it became a popular hostelry known to generation of tourists. Often bathed in low clouds and encompassed by the mountains, it exudes a feeling of remoteness that epitomises the best of Lakeland. Having no mains supplies its water come fresh from the fells, its electricity is produced from a diesel generator and its sewerage goes into a septic tank, making it completely self sufficient.

Consumed by the heady atmosphere of mulled wine and a warm fire it took a big effort for me to rouse myself. I was almost tempted to book a night in one of the four poster beds at the inn, but I knew that the splendour of Ullswater lay just round the corner.

7

Lakeland visitors who escape to these fell tops which overlook Kirkstone Pass often congratulate themselves on having thrown off the trappings of our noisy age. Then it happens! First a quiet whistle fills the air, followed rapidly by an ear bursting roar as 'another' Tornado Jet zooms over the mountains. The curses of the walker are unheard by the RAF pilot, who absorbed by his low-level flying practice, disappears in seconds over the Solway Firth to frighten the sheep of Scotland.

But surprisingly, aeronautical displays are nothing new in Lakeland, for Wordsworth and Coleridge may well have had their peace disturbed in this way. It all started in 1783 when Frenchmen Pilatre de Rozier and the Marquis d'Arlandes began the first ever aerial voyage in a hot-air balloon from a garden in Paris. This craze to float through the air reached Cumbria in 1825 when Charles and William Green made a balloon ascent from Kendal, using coal-gas produced at a new gas works, as a lifting agent. Their adventurous flight lasted for under half an hour, ending in a field just two miles from where they started. But a few weeks later, Charles Green accompanied by the teenage daughter of a local draper, achieved a more successful flight. They ascended to 5300 feet before landing over 23 miles from Kendal, at a farm near Appleby. Ballooning continued to draw in the crowds at many venues in Lakeland over the next half century, to which was added the spice of parachute jumping. The first recorded parachute jump in the area was made by a publican name Higgins. It took place at a Sports Gala at Cleator, near Whitehaven in 1889.

In 1903 American bicycle makers, Wilbur and Orville Wright, wrote another important chapter in aviation history when they made the world's first powered and controlled flight in an aeroplane. Foremost among the aviation pioneers in England was another American who later became a British subject, S.F. Cody. He was a larger than life character who adopted the title 'Colonel', which often led to him being mistaken for Colonel W.F. 'Buffalo Bill' Cody. After initially inventing a man-lifting kite, in 1908 he built British Army Aeroplane No. 1 which he used the same year to achieve the first powered and sustained flight in Great Britain. The first British born men to successfully fly an aeroplane were A.V. Roe, who had received his engineering training at Horwich Locomotive Works in Lancashire, and J.T.C. Moore-Brabazon, who later became Lord Brabazon.

In an atmosphere of frenzied excitement these early aviators continually battled against each other, always intent on designing more powerful machines which would enable them to achieve the many 'firsts' which were now up for the taking. The Daily Mail encouraged them by offering a £1000 prize for the first man to fly across the English Channel and £10,000 for the first flight from London to Manchester. After Frenchman, Louis Bleriot, took the first prize in July 1909, there was widespread hope that an Englishman would achieve the second.

Among the many would-be aviators who could not resist the challenge, was the Reverend Sidney Swann, who in 1905 had become the vicar at Crosby Ravensworth, near Shap. Earlier, while at Cambridge he had become a renowned oarsman, then after spending time in Japan as a missionary, he returned to England where he took up long distance cycling. He then became acquainted with S.F. Cody, who included among his many activities, organising cycle and horse racing.

Swann's hidden talent for engineering came to light at this time in his own Cumbrian parish. When not seeing to the spiritual needs of his flock he became involved in building a stone cutting machine for a local stone mason and a footbridge which he designed to span the River Eden. In 1909 his thoughts began to turn to aviation which led to him designing a monoplane. This he had constructed in a week by the Austin Motor Company in Birmingham, for he was hoping to snatch one of the cash prizes which was on offer. But the test flight at Aintree Race-course proved largely disappointing. It was underpowered and unstable, which led to it eventually tipping over and almost crushing Swann, but fortunately he managed to escape.

In 1910 he doggedly continued with his aviation experiments at Crosby Ravensworth where he built a new flying machine. This he tested in a flat meadow near Meaburn Hall, but it too seemed prone to a number of problems. Meanwhile he heard that the much sought after Daily Mail prize had been given to Lois Paulhan. This French test pilot had successfully flown from Hendon to Manchester in twelve hours, spending three and three quarter hours in the air.

Swann persevered for several more weeks with his biplane, at last getting it off the ground but only for about 30 yards. Lack of both finance and enthusiasm, eventually led to Lakeland's first aeroplane builder abandoning his aviation experiments. However, the exploits of this fascinating character still continued to make the newspaper headlines. In 1911 he broke the record for rowing across the English Channel, then after being left a widower he married Lady Bagot of Levens Hall. The First World War saw him being awarded a medal for ambulance driving at the front, then in 1917 he broke the record for cycling, running, canoeing, rowing and swimming half miles!

But as an avalanche of flying achievements continued to be recorded world-wide, including the first non-stop flight from London to Paris in 1911, other pioneers were at work in Lakeland. Notable among these were Oscar Gnosspelius who experimented with his flying-boats on the waters of Windermere and the construction by Vickers at Barrow of the first naval airship.

Since these first exciting days in the history of aviation the remarkable advances made have changed the pattern of all our lives. This is particularly highlighted by the speeds at which we can now travel. When the forerunner of the RAF, the Royal Flying Corps, was formed in 1912 it chose for its first flying machine a design by S.F. Cody which became known as Cody's Cathedral. The average speed of these RFC aircraft was around 75 mph. The RAF Tornado Jets, built by British Aerospace, which now zig-zag over the valleys of Lakeland, are capable of reaching 1300mph and cost a staggering £20 million!

I wonder what the Reverend Sidney Swann would think of this?

9

Kirkstone Pass to Shap

I dip down Kirkstone Pass to reach St Patrick's Dale, I gaze up at Helvellyn and Striding Edge, then go to see Aira Force. I think of 'Daffodils' near Ullswater, a drowned village at Mardale, then almost see an English Golden Eagle. I attend the Gipsy Horse Fair at Appleby, explore the holy ruins of Shap Abbey, then reluctantly end my Lakeland journey on England's most notorious highway.

1

I believe that added to the painkilling drugs and tranquillisers available on prescription from our National Health Service should be one named 'Ullswater'. It should be given at least once a year to patients in London, Birmingham and Bristol who feel they can no longer endure their endless suburban commuting. They should be driven north, then after refreshment at the Kirkstone Pass Inn, they should be taken to a small car-park that lies over the brow of the hill to be given a taste of the delights which await them. Quite suddenly they will see a view which is so stunning that all thoughts of despondency will fall away. However, there are side affects: they may become addicted and never want to return home again!

I stood on the edge of this same car-park, which lies close to the rock which is said to be the original Kirk Stone, looking out at the magnificent sweep of the pass. The narrow road, bounded on each side by low drystone walls, lay below me, snaking its way down the steep valley. Half hidden by patches of brown reeds, I could see a beck cascading down the hillside, guarded here and there by huge boulders which rest on its banks. But dwarfing the whole landscape were the towering fells which soar upwards from the road like huge brown pyramids, ending in a cloudless sky. Tempered into a dozen pastel shades by scree and crag and marshy mossland, they provide a dramatic frame for the distant blue of Brothers Water which lies in an island of green. Drowned in the afternoon sunlight the wild scene was completed by the call of a raven whose stark cry echoed from these Cumbrian heights.

I continued my journey northwards, slowly descending the twists and turns of this craggy highway to reach the Patterdale Valley. Brothers Water, which was mentioned by Dorothy Wordsworth in her famous *Grasmere Journal*, was shimmering in the sunlight. Shrouded by trees this delightful tarn was once known as Broad Water. Then, according to a local tale, two brothers were tragically drowned here on different occasions during the last century, so the tarn was renamed as their memorial. Overlooking the southern bank and hidden from the motorist is Hartsop Hall. Dating from the 16th century it became the home of the first Viscount Lonsdale, Sir John Lowther.

As I gazed out over the reedy shoreline of Ullswater I found it easy to understand why many people believe it to be the most enchanting of all the English lakes. For set in an amphitheatre of rising blue hills, this inspiration of poets and artists, exudes an atmosphere of romantic grandeur. Surrounded by the glimmering silver water a handful of contented visitors were standing on Glenridding Pier. This little wooded jetty, which proudly flies the Union Jack, is the place where *Raven* and *Lady of the Lake* pick up their passengers for a cruise to Howtown or Pooley Bridge. Ullswater is second only to Windermere in size, stretching over seven miles long and reaching a breadth of almost a mile at its widest point.

Patterdale was once known as Patrick's Dale, and as I strolled around this lovely straggling village I discovered two links with this much revered patron saint of Ireland. Set on the roadside is a sturdy stone structure with a sloping roof which covers St Patrick's Well, while nearby lies the local church which is also dedicated to the saint. It is believed that he stayed in the valley while on a journey home to Bewcastle, and the influence of his Christian teaching has endured.

But much of the real beauty of Patterdale is only revealed to the walker, for it lies hidden up a series of narrow valleys which penetrate deep into the heart of the mountains. I left the bustle of tourists behind to follow a lane which meanders above Glenridding Beck for a mile, leading me towards the youth hostel which rests under the shadow of Sheffield Pike. Passing whitewashed cottages with walls coloured by clematis, I was reminded that these were once the homes of lead-miners who for centuries worked these wild slopes. In 1927 a spectacular event occurred here when a dam, which was holding the waters of a elevated reservoir, suddenly bursted. The roar of the cascading torrent filled the air as it swept down the hillside. It poured through cottages and filled the basement of a hotel in which some maids were sleeping. They were only saved from drowning in their beds, which had floated almost up to the ceiling, when the windows broke and let the water escape.

In common with many thousands of walkers who come here each year, I regard the ascent of Helvellyn from Patterdale, to be one of Lakeland's finest

The craggy profile of Striding Edge which leads to the summit of Helvellyn

walks. Its great attraction is, of course, the traversing of the spectacular Striding Edge; a craggy, sharp ridge of sloping rock which never fails to thrill. Once spoken of with terror by the early travellers to the lakes, only in bad weather is it really hazardous. However, two memorials which are met along its length, may tend to make the nervous walker think about turning around!

The Dixon Memorial, which was erected in 1858, remembers Robert Dixon, who while following the Patterdale fox hounds sadly tumbled to his death from the Edge. But the most famous memorial is that to Charles Gough, for his tragic tale has been immortalised by both William Wordsworth and Sir Walter Scott. He too fell to his death while ascending Helvellyn in 1805, but it was his faithful dog who gained national fame. For the animal stayed by its master's dead body for an incredible three months, until the tragedy was finally discovered by a shepherd.

This tale reminds me of the time I once walked this famous horseshoe of Striding Edge, Helvellyn and Swirral Edge, with a party of Manchester Ramblers. Among the group was a middle-aged widower who had brought his black poodle with him as a companion. As well as completing the fifteen mile walk, the dog was constantly running backwards and forwards, so that it covered at least twice the distance. When a comment was made to this effect its owner told us, "Don't think this will be its only excursion of the day. When we return home it will bring its lead to me and demand its usual pre-bedtime walk. This always happens however many miles it has walked during the day!"

Another popular valley which radiates from Patterdale, is Grisedale, which lies between Striding Edge and St Sunday Crag. This was once used as a pack-horse route which linked Grasmere to Patterdale, reaching its high-point at lovely Grisedale Tarn. Close to the tarn is another memorial which records that this was the spot where William Wordsworth parted from his brother John. He was a sailor who later, sadly lost his life at sea.

Martindale, one of the most isolated of these eastern valleys, is situated on the far bank of Ullswater and can be reached by boat from Glenridding by alighting at Howtown. Its ancient church, which was mentioned as early as the 13th century and for many years stood roofless, lies 1000 feet above sea level. The valley has been the home of a large herd of Red Deer since Elizabethan times.

After driving for a couple of miles along the road which closely follows the shoreline of the lake, I parked my car and walked along a narrow path which led me to the spectacular waterfall of Aira Force. The cascading white water gushes beneath a single arched bridge, then it tumbles for sixty feet down a rocky chasm which is green with moss and overhung with trees. This magnificent torrent has quite rightly, attracted tourists since the days of the first Lakers. These included, of course, Dorothy and William Wordsworth who are reputed to have stayed at the 16th century Royal Hotel in nearby Dockay village. They were following in the footsteps of Mary, Queen of Scots, who is believed to have also stayed there over two centuries earlier.

Dorothy Wordsworth recorded in her journal for Thursday, April 15th 1802, the words 'When we were in the woods beyond Gowbarrow Park, we saw a few daffodils close to the waterside .... as we went along we saw that there were more and yet more,'

I walked down from Aira Force to this same spot, to look across the blue of Ullswater. It should be a place of pilgrimage for all Lakeland visitors, even though there are few daffodils to be seen today. For this is the magical landscape which inspired William Wordsworth to write what is probably our best loved poem, *Daffodils*:

I wandered lonely as a cloud
That floats on high o'er vales and hills,
When all at once I saw a crowd,
A host, of golden daffodils;
Beside the lake, beneath the trees,
Fluttering and dancing in the breeze...
The waves beside them danced; but they
Out-did the sparkling waves in glee:

The cascading water of Aira Force has been admired by visitors for three centuries.

A poet could not but be gay,
In such a jocund company;
I gazed – and gazed – but little thought
What wealth the show to me had brought:
For oft, when on my couch I lie
In vacant or in pensive mood,
They flash upon that inward eye
Which is the bliss of solitude:
And then my heart with pleasure fills,
And dances with the daffodils.

Anyone who stands on the shore of Ullswater in the bright sunshine reading the above lines, will never again need to ask, "Why is Wordsworth still spoken of in every corner of Cumbria." For it becomes immediately apparent that his simple words of genius capture the very soul of Lakeland.

2

"Heavy rain in Cumbria" was the pessimistic weather forecast which I had heard on the radio in the early morning. Any hopes that this might have been wrong were dashed as I drove through Askham for my windscreen was quickly becoming dotted with the first raindrops. A strong wind had also blown up, tossing the hawthorns which hid behind limestone walls and exposing the underside of leaves, which I am told is always a bad sign. But a large herd of magnificent black mountain ponies which were grazing close to the village seemed totally unmoved by the impending gale. As if spurred on by some invisible signal, they suddenly began an effortless gallop up the hillside, then having reached a wall, like the Grand Old Duke of York they turned around and galloped down again.

Although on the very edge of some of Lakeland's most rugged terrain this countryside, which lies to the north of Haweswater, I found to be surprisingly gentle. It is clothed in rolling green meadows, low hills and curtains of rising woodland. Secluded villages, quiet and inviting, hide in peaceful hollows overlooking the meandering path of the River Lowther. Askham, in spite of the gloomy weather, was managing to live up to its reputation for being the prettiest of them all. Its cottage gardens which lie among spacious green verges, were neat and colourful; its 14th century Hall, which is the home of the Earl of Lonsdale, seemed to be quietly sleeping; while its graceful parish church, which once boasted Robert Southey's son as its vicar, looked on with quiet dignity.

Across the valley I could see the elevated ridge which hides the sturdy ruins of Lowther Castle and its large parkland. Since the time of Edward I this site has been occupied, but the ancient house which had been largely rebuilt by Sir John Lowther in 1685, was destroyed by a terrible fire in 1726. It is said to have had the largest stables in Britain, for the family have always been great sportsmen. A new castle was built in 1802 by the second Earl of Lonsdale, and it was here that the influential fifth Earl entertained a dazzling array of society, including several foreign monarchs. In 1909, when he was the president of the National Sporting Club, he created the famous Lonsdale Belts which are awarded to British boxing champions. But following his death the building gradually fell into disuse and was eventually abandoned, today it is merely an empty shell whose stones echo with memories of departed grandeur.

With the river below me on the left, I drove slowly through the small villages of Helton and Butterwick to reach Bampton which sits astride both the River Lowther and the Haweswater Beck. I discovered that the local pub is called Saint Patrick's Well and the local church is also dedicated to the saint. Some historians believe that after Saint Patrick departed from Patterdale he came here to Bampton, which since his visit has been regarded as a holy place.

The village grammar school once had such a reputation for educating boys who went on to take holy orders that it was said that 'they drove the plough in Latin in Bampton'. I am told that the village's famous Tinklar Library, which is now housed in the vicarage, still contains many Latin volumes. It was perhaps this vigour in scholarship that motivated local man, Richard Hogarth to start up a school in Lakeland, then when it proved unsuccessful to try his luck in London. But it was his son, William Hogarth, who was to gain fame as the great 18th century painter and engraver.

In a shower of driving rain, with a trailing white mist giving the hills a ghostly look, I drove south through the gateway of Mardale. After two miles I stopped my car; gazing out over the great bulk of the Haweswater dam, I could see the choppy grey waters of the lake curving towards the far shoreline. The green of the valley, darkened by the gloom, turned to slate-blue as the land rose ever upwards till it finally disappeared into the clouds. My map told me that beyond lay the high summits of Red Crag, Raven Howe, High Raise and Kidsty Pike, but these could not be seen. Hemmed in by the gale Mardale was in dramatic mood; it was easy to see why England's only pair of breeding golden eagles have chosen to live in this place.

I continued my solitary excursion along the narrow motor road which follows the south-eastern edge of the lake, passing the Haweswater Hotel which is the only building in this isolated valley. Its boast of 'Traditional Food of the Finest Quality' seemed particularly reassuring, but I was not tempted to stop for my destination lay at the end of the road at Mardale Head. At one point, in spite of the torrents of water which swept across the road, I thought

I saw a hint of blue in the sky As if to tell me that this was foolish optimism, as I entered the small car-park, I was subjected to the full rigours of a Lakeland deluge. The water poured down with grim enthusiasm, it hammered on the roof of my car like a thousand pneumatic drills, my windscreen became a waterfall and the gale began to rock my car backwards and forwards. Had the long-departed residents of the drowned village of Mardale Green decided to seek retribution I wondered?

To a stranger like myself who has only come to know Mardale in recent years, this isolated valley, the curving silver of Haweswater and the towering fells are both striking and appealing. But there are people, sadly growing fewer each year, who remember the valley before it was transformed. They will tell you it was far more beautiful in those days, and importantly it was home to a small but proud community whose roots went back to the Norsemen. But the farmers and shepherds proved no match for the might of Manchester Corporation, whose army of workmen came with picks, shovels and mechanical diggers, to eventually tear out its very soul. But Mardale lives on in glorious defeat; a symbol of the perpetual fight to preserve Lakeland's natural countryside from the blight of the developer.

It was in 1919, when the towns and villages of England were celebrating the end of a terrible war, that the Haweswater Act was given parliamentary approval. The ever expanding population of Manchester needed more drinking water and Mardale, being one of the wettest places in the country, was an ideal catchment area. The plan was to construct a reservoir by damming the valley, which would result in the existing natural lake being doubled in length. Two smaller reservoirs, to be built in nearby Wet Sleddale and Swindale, would help to top up the water which would be sent over 70 miles along an aqueduct to Heaton Park in Manchester. However, it also meant that the ancient community of around a hundred people who lived in Mardale, would need to vacate their farms and cottages. For these, together with the 17th century Dun Bull pub, which was the great social centre of the valley, and the little church of the Holy Trinity would be covered by the water.

When the news of the impending scheme reached the isolated farmsteads of this valley which lies along an ancient pack-horse route, they were stunned. For they knew this meant the end of their homes, their fields, their living; their complete way of life would be destroyed. Many believed their community had begun in 1209 when Hugh Holme fled north to escape from a charge of treason, for he had been implicated in a conspiracy against King John. He went into hiding in what is still known as Hugh's Cave on the side of Kidsty Pike, remaining there until the hated monarch finally died in 1216. Then in romantic fashion he married a local girl, starting a Holme dynasty which became known as the Kings of Mardale. His presence attracted like-minded supporters who formed the nucleus of the valley community. Astonishingly, the direct line of the Holme family only ended in 1885 with the death of Hugh Parker Holme.

It took a decade of design and planning before the mammoth civil engineering scheme finally got underway. A new village of sixty-six bungalows was built at Burnbanks, near Bampton, to accommodate the workers and their families, of which eleven are still occupied. The huge dam, which rises to a height of 90 feet (27.5m) and is 1,150 feet (470m) long, was built using a revolutionary hollow-buttress design. A new elevated road was constructed to the head of the valley in 1931, high above what would be the new water line. In 1937, part way along this road, the new Haweswater Hotel opened for business while the landlord of the Dun Bull announced his final "last orders". Another aspect of the massive operation was the need to exhume bodies from the village churchyard which was destined to be covered by the water. This work, which was particularly distressing for relatives, got underway in 1935, with most of these being reburied in Shap cemetery, including that of Hugh Parker Holme.

Thousands of visitors, together with journalists from many newspapers came to Mardale Church on August 18th 1935 to attend the last religious service which was conducted by the Bishop of Carlisle. The following year the building was demolished and its ancient stones used in the walls of the reservoir. By this time the dalesfolk had all left their homes which lay roofless and empty in the once proud valley. By 1941 the scheme was finished, the Lakeland water having now completely covered the homes. However, in very dry summers when the water recedes, the forlorn foundations of the village can be seen in the black mud; a poignant reminder of the price paid by Mardale so that the residents of Manchester can safely drink from their taps.

3

I sat in my car in the solitude of Mardale Head for nearly two hours, staring out over Haweswater which continued to be lashed by the unrelenting storm. Occasionally clearing the downpour from my windscreen, I could see the path which follows the shoreline of the lake then ascends a small headland into the loneliness of Riggindale. Through this deep impressive valley which sweeps down from the fells of High Street, runs Riggindale Beck which empties into Haweswater. The single homestead that once lay in this splendid isolation, Riggindale Farm, was demolished when the reservoir was built leaving the landscape free from human habitation. However, during the past two decades this once little-known valley has become uniquely famous, for it is the only place in England that our King of birds, the Golden Eagle, has chosen to nest.

Remote Riggingale is home to England's only pair of nesting Golden Eagles.

Appropriately, the Royal Society for the Protection of Birds has created here their largest reserve in England. From a series of discreet huts which have been established in the valley and are manned by volunteer wardens, visitors come to view the nesting eagles. But sadly, I had chosen this atrocious day when the ceaseless rain, the high winds and the low clouds ruled out such an excursion. I was forced to make do with past memories of a journey I once made to the Scottish island of Harris which is a main breeding of the Golden Eagle. There I had been more lucky, for by chance I had come within three yards of a pair who had been too busy feeding to notice my approach. I remember vividly the wicked glare in their surprised eyes, then how they unfolded their huge wings and effortlessly soared into the sky like Harrier Jump Jets.

The Golden Eagle, *Aquila chrysaetus*, has acquired its name from the soft yellow feathers which cover its neck and head. Other parts of its body appear less striking, ranging from various shades of dark brown to patches of black. It has characteristic features common to most birds of prey, having very large eyes, a strong hooked beak and cruel sharp talons, the female being larger than the male. But the feature which is most apparent to the casual observer when it rises majestically into the air, is its huge 6.5 feet (2m) wing span ending with its wing-tip feathers spreading outwards like fingers.

It is fitting that a bird of such noble appearance as the eagle should have become associated with all manner of romantic tales over the centuries. The Saxons believed that its bone marrow could bring about miraculous cures, the American Indians used its feathers in their religious ceremonies, while others insisted that a wound caused by its claw would never heal. Always the symbol of power and might, its effigy has been used as the badge of Vikings, Norman knights, monarchs, countries, and more recently film companies. 'Eagle' has been used in the title of so many paperback novels that publishers must have found that its name guarantees a best seller! But its reputation for carrying off the occasional unsuspecting baby, remembered by many an Eagle and Child pub sign, is disputed by experts. They say it much prefers to feed on small birds, rabbits and perhaps the carcass of a dead sheep.

The distribution of the six subspecies of the Golden Eagle, which differ slightly in size and colour, is world-wide. They are found in the isolated uplands of Europe, North America and parts of Asia. Up to the 18th century, when Britain was much less populated and guns were less accurate, their habitat here extended throughout Scotland and into the hill country of northern England, Wales and Ireland. But with the spread of industrialization came persecution, the Golden Eagle began to retreat until by the early 19th century it was confined to the remote Highlands and islands of Scotland. Its numbers continued to decline throughout the last century while the only other native species, the White Tailed Eagle, was even less fortunate. For after 1916, when the last pair nested on the Isle of Skye, they disappeared completely from Britain.

Miraculously, in spite of an up-hill battle with egg collectors and some die-hard gamekeepers and landowners, by 1950 about 200 pairs of Golden Eagles had still managed to keep a tenuous foothold in Scotland. Then an age of enlightenment arrived with the passing of a bird protection act in 1954. Quickly the Golden Eagles began to expand their breeding grounds throughout Scotland, moving south as far as the Solway Firth.

In the spring of 1959 an excited Lakeland farmer reported seeing a large bird of prey, which he believed to be an eagle, soaring over a limestone crag. His report was confirmed, a path-finding Golden Eagle had made its first journey back to England for over a century. A decade later a pair began to build a nest in Lakeland, they actually laid eggs, but sadly deserted the site. However, the next year, protected by a 24-hour watch supervised by the RSPB, one of the milestones in British ornithology occurred; the first English eagle chick was successfully reared. Since that time these Kings of the mountains have made Lakeland their home and it is said that a second pair have also occasionally nested, but this site has been kept secret. A dedicated group of bird lovers, fortified by the tightening laws of the Wildlife and Countryside

Act, continue to ensure that this success story continues; now over 400 pairs of Golden Eagles nest in Britain and the once doomed White Tailed Eagle has also been re-introduced.

I stepped from my car in the driving rain then I began to scan the misty crags of Riggindale, hoping to catch a glance of Lakeland's most cherished resident. Was it just a trick of the light or was that dark image passing through the clouds an English Golden Eagle? I just could not be sure if I had seen this most elusive bird. However, when the sky is cloudless and the sun is shining I will have the perfect excuse to return here, to this most beautiful of Lakeland valleys.

4

From the brow of a green hill I stared down in wonder, for surely only a Romany charm could have created this change in the weather. When I had begun my early morning departure for Appleby the sky had been grey and dismal, the clouds growing ever darker, then rain began to grimly fall on the windscreen of my car. But now, as I looked down on the distant rooftops of the town a patch of blue was opening up directly overhead. It spread with amazing speed until in a matter of minutes the lovely green of the Eden valley was enveloped in the golden warmth of the June sun. The rolling fields, the winding lanes and the line of trees which follow the curve of the river were lit like a set from a West End play. But no stage extravaganza would ever be able to compete with the visual experience of the free show I was about to see, Appleby's Gipsy Horse Fair.

Before making my descent in to the town I stopped at the roadside to eat my packed lunch while admiring the towering backcloth of the high Pennines which rise majestically on the northern side. These brooding windswept summits, which sweep in a seemingly endless line to the distant horizon, rise to their highest point of 893m (2930 feet) at Cross Fell which is on the route of the Pennine Way. It is often subjected to the turbulent Helm Wind which blows fiercely down on to the grassy plateau adding to the difficulty of walking over the boggy terrain. I could see also the high points of Little Dun Fell and Great Dun Fell, on which rise an array of masts which form part of a weather station, and the amazing curve of the spectacular valley known as High Cup Nick.

My visual exploration of the hills was suddenly interrupted by the antics of a dark haired woman who dressed in a vivid green sweater and bright pink skirt had stepped into the road from a nearby farm house. She was furiously moving her arms up and down in an attempt to get the Fair traffic to slow down. At first I thought perhaps she was a local eccentric who despised the temporary invasion of her privacy, but soon her real intentions became apparent. Over the brow of the hill, filling the complete road, came a huge flock of lambs and sheep. Driven by the shouts of a young boy and surprisingly, without the aid of a dog he cleverly directed the healthy looking animals to a new pasture.

My progress was cut to a snails pace as I drove past the nostalgic sign which announces Appleby-in-Westmorland, for sadly Westmorland is no longer a county. I was expecting some traffic congestion but nothing as severe as this for the ancient market town had almost seized up. We crept passed the Norman Castle and the High Boundary Cross, I had time to gaze at the almshouses built for thirteen poor widows, admire the Moot Hall which lies at the bottom of Boroughgate and to wonder if the ghost of Lady Anne Clifford was looking out from her resting place in the church of St Laurence. Here laughing crowds were spilling off the pavements on each side of the road watched by young policemen in shirt sleeves who seemed completely bewildered by the town's overnight transition from rural seclusion. After half an hour in the crawling frustration of this traffic jam I made a decision to turn around, then at last, with a gasp of relief I found a single parking place.

After wiping the sweat from my brow I ventured out in to what is regarded as the most colourful gathering of Gypsies, tinkers, horse traders and those who go under the title of travelling people, in the world. This unique festival, which is loved by many but detested by the few, feels secure under the protection of a charter granted by King James II in 1685. This is of course disputed by some, who say that the charter referred only to an April Fair and not to this June Fair which originated in 1750. However, any argument is merely of academic interest, for the Horse Fair has become firmly established as one of England's most exciting events.

The River Eden, which makes a great loop around Appleby, is crossed by an impressive pack-horse bridge which is where I joined the huge crowds of both visitors and Gypsies. In frenzied excitement people were hanging over the bridge parapet and lining each green bank, watching the antics of the horses being washed and joining in with good humoured banter. About thirty snorting, wild-eyed piebalds had been ridden bare-backed into the water by both young men and girls, who seemed oblivious to their own soaking and the coldness of the Pennine water. Encouraged by the shouts of their friends and family they rode the reluctant animals to the deepest part, spurring them on with a tirade of four letter words and the occasional gentle whip.

I walked over the narrow bridge, which was overflowing with both cars and people, to the opposite bank where scores of horses were staked out awaiting their turn in the water. Here too were beautifully painted trotting carts, irresistible Shetland ponies and the splendid mosaic of humanity which only

Young Gipsies washing their horses in the River Eden at Appleby.

comes together at this place for one week each year. But who were the Gypsies and who were visitors? At first, in this age of casual dress, I found it difficult to tell. Later, after a period of Holmes-like observation I was able to spot certain clues.

Some of the Gypsy girls were the easiest to detect by their flamboyant dress, dark Romany features and their cheeky look-at-me air as they walked along the riverside. Many were indulging their love of bright colours together with a prominence of gold jewellery, which of course included golden earrings. Both the men and boys, I noticed, have a liking for tan coloured ankle boots, often carry walking sticks, with some sporting neckerchiefs and occasionally Stetson hats. But most had none of these obvious characteristics, being only identified when they began to wash, trot or sell their beloved horses.

The origins and history of the Gypsies hide under a fascinating cloak of legend and folklore. One tale tells how they originated from Adam himself after his liaison with a woman who had been created before Eve. This meant that unlike the rest of mankind they are born without original sin so need not work or suffer any punishment! Another legend, which has many variations, say that it was a Gypsy who forged the nails which were used at the Crucifixion. This resulted in them being condemned to a life of perpetual wandering.

Their country of origin has also been the subject of much speculation and debate. Atlantis is said by some to have been their home, then when it sank into the ocean they made their escape to Egypt from which they began their nomadic existence; the word *Gypsy* having been derived from *Egypt*. However, a study of the Gypsy language has revealed that it is probably from central India that their ancestors really came, first beginning their wanderings into Europe during the Middle Ages. Research carried out in 1977 suggests that there are around eight thousand travelling families in Britain but few of these have pure Romany blood flowing through their veins. Most are travelling folk, being the descendants of Irish tinkers who made a living by their skill at metalwork and by selling horses. The true Romany families are intensely proud of their origins, and although they share a common lifestyle with other travelling folk, often trading horses, they have few other links.

On the road known as The Sands, which faces the river bank, is the Grapes pub. For fifty one weeks of the year it is a typical English hostelry, but when the fair begins it takes on the role of a wild west saloon. The hot sunshine and clear skies had tempted a large colourful crowd of travellers to take their liquid nourishment from the bar to the outside pavement. Here they were shouting out the short comings of their rival's horses as they galloped to the river for washing and exchanging the latest news about their friends from every corner of Britain. Looking on, in perplexed silence stood two sombre faced policemen, perhaps hoping that the mood would remain light hearted at least until their shift ended.

I walked across the road, managing to join the crush of thirsty travellers who stood ten deep at the bar. The pain of exhaustion was visible in the faces of the bar maids as they pulled pint after pint after pint. At last I was served with my drink, but having no hope of finding a seat in the crowded room, I stood in a corner hoping to overhear snippets of conversation. But I was totally disappointed for in spite of being born in Lancashire I was completely at a loss to decipher the broad accents of the travellers. A word here and there I understood but full sentences were beyond me, so I decided to head for Fair Hill.

The ascending road remained one long traffic jam, full of visitors' cars interspersed with groups of nervous horses of every colour and shade. I walked past Appleby's famous grammar school which boasts George Washington's brothers among its former pupils, then the Gipsy encampment came into view, a large sloping field of caravans. Hundreds of horses, many with long-legged foals, were staked out on the grass verges. They appeared healthy and clean animals, but a little ill at ease with all the noise from the huge crowd. Gaily painted carts and traps were parked nearby, many labelled with that profession much loved by Gipsies, *General Dealer*, accompanied by the names of towns from Norfolk to Durham. The pungent smell of the horses filled the air, softened by the scent of wild flowers which was

A Romany fortune teller inside a traditional horse-drawn valdo.

carried by a warm breeze.

A stall-holder was busily selling saddles, harnesses and riding boots to a group of discerning horse dealers while nearby a blacksmith was shaping a red-hot horseshoe on an anvil. Suddenly the sound of a bull-whip filled the air attracting a crowd to a corner of the site. Here a bald man of about seventy, whose naked chest ended in a small beer-belly, was about to start his strong man act. He began his patter in a squeaky tone, "Excuse my voice, I've done my act twice this morning already and I've swallowed a watch and chain."

He continued his seemingly endless chatter which prompted one of his colleagues to shout, "Stop gassing and get on with it."

After taking a collection in his hat and provoking the crowd even further by taking out a penny and saying "I asked for silver. Has anyone seen brown silver before?", he at last got down to business. Taking a metal bar he began to hit it hard on the taut muscles of his forearm. The crowd gasped, a woman flinched then turned away, as he continued the blows until the bar finally bent.

I continued my stroll among the fascinating homes of what must be the most extraordinary community in Britain. Here, on the soft green turf surrounded by the blue outline of the Pennine hills which epitomises the freedom of their lifestyle, lay row upon row of caravans of every conceivable design. Some were huge mansions on wheels made from glistening chrome with immaculately clean interiors full of shimmering glass cupboards. Then there was the traditional horse drawn valdos, ornately painted with designs in yellow and green, together with a host of ordinary vans which many of us use for our holidays. Mercedes, four-wheel drives, pick-ups and piebald ponies, lay side by side, all providing their own source of power. Lurchers, a popular dog among the travellers, were tethered outside many homes with the occasional embers of last nights camp fire glowing nearby, over which hung huge black kettles.

On the main thoroughfare through the camp-site stalls had been set up to entice Gypsy and visitor alike. Hand made cushions, boots and shoes, lucky horse-shoes and expensive pieces of Royal Crown Derby porcelain, which are much treasured by Gypsies, were just a few of the many items on display. A notice board declared: *Gipsy Rosaleena, Fortune Teller will tell your Past, Present and Future. Genuine Welsh Romany. Try Your Luck*, followed by a score of similar invitations.

After two hours of feasting upon this unique visual happening I returned to the centre of Appleby, too tired to watch the Harness racing that was taking place in the evening.

5

As I drove up the ascending hillside from Appleby I took one final glance back at the green splendour of the meandering Eden Valley. The view was framed by the gold of overhanging gorse, some newly ploughed fields were revealing the rich red earth while others were ablaze with wild flowers. Larks were soaring upwards into the Cumbrian sky, small fluffy cotton-wool clouds were moving slowly over the mountain tops and I seemed to have the world to myself.

I meandered down a lane that wound its way past hedgerows, dipped and dived alongside sloping meadows, then it brought me quite suddenly into a hidden village named Maulds Meaburn. Not a soul was about, only the music of birdsong filled the air. I stopped my car hardly daring to make a sound, then began to soak up a little of the magic of the place. I could see a small river which splashed its way across a flat green meadow, it was crossed here and there by small footbridges and stepping stones. Grey stoned cottages, clad with ivy, hid in tree lined hollows on the far bank watched over by ancient Meaburn Hall. Then a jet-black jackdaw which had landed on the verge nearby, began to stare at me with a look of disdain, as if to say: "Would you mind moving on, we want to be left alone." So I quickly headed up the lane to Crosby Ravensworth and on to Shap.

I discovered a quiet, no-nonsense little café and bakers shop which faces the Bulls Head pub in Shap Village. Here, as I feasted on a splendid north-country sandwich which was brimming with cheese and chutney, I remembered a local saying which in my case rang remarkably true: "Those who have tasted Shap bread and drunk Shap water will long to do so again."

Those of us who are old enough to remember the pre-motorway days have the name 'Shap' indelibly marked in our memory from the winter weather bulletins that once came from our wirelesses. 'Overnight snow has brought chaos to the north. The road over Shap Fell is closed with dozens of lorry drivers being marooned in the cabs of their vehicles,' was a typical report that brought a sense of dread in the forties and fifties.

The A6 road was at that time the main western link between England and Scotland and it reached its high point of 872 feet near this elevated working village. Resting on the edge of superb countryside its grey houses retain a feeling of windswept remoteness which must have been felt by Bonnie Prince Charlie when he passed this way with his weary army during the uprising of 1745. They were on a twenty-seven mile foot-slog from Penrith to Kendal, with the future of the Stuart cause resting heavy on their shoulders.

"Follow the road towards Penrith then turn left down the lane towards Bampton. After a short distance you will see a sign to Shap Abbey."

I followed the waitress's instructions, which led me in the hush of early evening to one of Lakeland's truly holy places. I discovered that the imposing ruins which surround a sturdy tower, sit in blissful serenity on the tree lined banks of the River Lowther. This hidden green valley is still a perfect spot in which to worship God, for its peacefulness is contagious. I looked sky-wards to glassless windows and carved stones that both time and the evil of the Dissolution have failed to completely destroy. Though a ruin, it is a triumphant ruin, for the unknown hands which built it laboured not for personal gain, but to create a symbol of their Christian faith. Though the monks have long since gone, their Abbey largely destroyed, a feeling of spirituality seems still to cast its shadow among these Lakeland hills.

Orphaned lambs were bleating at a nearby farm, a yellow wagtail was hopping from stone to stone in the middle of the river, and I was dreaming of the year 1200 AD when the holy men first came here to construct the only Abbey in Westmorland. Their order had been founded by St Norbere at Premontre in France, officially being known as the Premonstratensians but called by the local villagers the White Canons because of the colour of the monks habits. Land had originally been given to the holy men by the rich and powerful Thomas, son of Gospatric, at Preston Patrick but it had proved to be unsuitable. So here, in the shadow of the Mardale hills rose the church dedicated to God and Saint Mary Magdalene. Only about twelve monks resided here but they brought a spark of faith that was to burn in this isolated corner for over three centuries. The cruel end, which will forever be the shame of England, finally came in 1540. The Abbot and his cannons were dispersed, the land sold, and the Abbey stones tumbled down to be used in the walls of farms and cottages around Shap.

I sat among the ancient stones which lie on manicured lawns, with a warm breeze blowing up from Haweswater on my face. I then began to wonder if that was really the sound of bird-song I could hear echoing across this valley or was it a Latin chant which I could detect?

Returning to Shap, where many of the local villagers are employed making sausages, fashioning K Shoes or extracting limestone and granite from the rising fellside, I continued my journey southwards. Here I passed Shap Spa where travellers stopped to take the waters. The twisting highway, which once bustled with a never ending line of traffic, is now quiet. This allows drivers time to admire one of the countries most impressive roads which cuts its way through towering grassy heights, interspersed with conifer plantations, with distant views of the blue Howgill Fells.

Londoners, Mancunians, Liverpudlians and Glaswegians ought to turn in reverence to the granite quarries which line this road, for many of their most cherished monuments were born on this breezy hillside. Shap granite was used to build London's Thames Embankment, Albert Memorial and the Temple Bar Memorial; Manchester's Town Hall and Royal Exchange, Liverpool's

The secluded ruins of Shap Abbey, one of Lakeland's most holy places.

imposing St. George's Hall and Glasgow's University. So those Cumbrians who have been reluctantly exiled by fate to Britain's major cities, may take a little consolation in knowing that they can still gaze on a small part of Shap Fell!

I pulled in to a layby, which lies at the high point of the road, to read the words carved on a unique memorial by the Friends of the British Commercial Vehicle Museum:

> This memorial pays tribute to the drivers and
> crews of the vehicles that made possible the
> social and commercial links between north and
> south, on this old and difficult route over Shap
> Fell, before the opening of the M6 motorway.
> Remembered too are those who built and maintained
> the road and the generations of local people who
> gave freely of food and shelter to stranded travellers
> in bad weather.

Appropriately, in this place known for centuries by northern travellers, my journey through Lakeland came to a reluctant end. Taking one last, long look at the wild landscape of sweeping hills I returned to my car. As I drove southwards my mind began to dwell on the magic of some of the unique sights which I had seen. I remembered early springtime in Kentmere, my crossing of the lovely Lyth Valley and my first misty view of Windermere. Then discovering the Roman Fort where Ambleside began, eating gingerbread at Grasmere, meeting Malaysians at Castlerigg and that unforgettable sunset over Derwentwater. Climbing Skiddaw in a gale, exploring Cockermouth, seeing where John Peel once hunted and reaching Cumbria's Transylvania. The beauty of hidden Watendlath, the descent of stunning Honister Pass and the serenity of Buttermere. Looking up to the roof of England from Wasdale, being enchanted by Hawkshead and Coniston, then finding solitude on windswept Walney Island. Drinking mulled wine in the Kirkstone Pass Inn, thinking of 'Daffodils' at Ullswater, almost seeing a Golden Eagle near Haweswater, then attending Appleby's amazing Gipsy Fair.

I then began to think of some of the many people, who over the centuries, by chance or desire, have left their mark here in Lakeland. Queen Katherine Parr at Kendal, Lambert Simnel at Piel, George Romney at Dalton and George Fox at Swarthmoor. Beatrix Potter at Sawrey, Arthur Ransome at Rusland, Hugh Walpole in Borrowdale, Stan Laurel at Ulverston and of course, Wordsworth, Coleridge, Southey and now Alfred Wainwright, almost everywhere.

With the last vestige of evening light falling from the sky I passed the county sign which announced Lancashire, making a silent vow that I would return soon to this unique corner of England.

Index